MODERN WOMEN POETS

Consorting with Angels
Essays on Modern Women Poets
DERYN REES-JONES

In this pioneering critical study, Deryn Rees-Jones discusses the work of some of the major women poets of the last hundred years, showing how they have explored what it has meant to be a woman poet writing in a male-dominated poetic tradition. Beginning with Edith Sitwell, Stevie Smith, Sylvia Plath and Anne Sexton, she shows how an older generation resisted easy categorisation by forging highly individual aesthetics and self-presentation. But despite their brilliance, their perceived eccentricity – along with the suicides of Plath and Sexton – made these major figures difficult acts to follow.

She then considers the poetry written in their wake, with essays covering poets such as Moniza Alvi, Carol Ann Duffy, Vicki Feaver, Lavinia Greenlaw, Selima Hill, Kathleen Jamie, Jackie Kay, Gwyneth Lewis, Medbh McGuckian, Alice Oswald and Jo Shapcott. Taking account of the importance to these women of the work of their male contemporaries, her incisive essays open up new perspectives on the poetry of the 20th and 21st centuries.

Eliza's Babes
Four centuries of women's poetry in English, *c*.1500-1900
edited by ROBYN BOLAM

This comprehensive anthology celebrates four centuries of women's poetry, covering over 100 poets from a wide range of social backgrounds across the English-speaking world. Familiar names – Anne Bradstreet, Aphra Behn, Elizabeth Barrett Browning, the Brontë sisters, Emily Dickinson, and Christina Rossetti – appear alongside other writers from America, Australia, Canada, India and New Zealand as well as the UK. The poets range from queens and ladies of the court to a religious martyr, a spy, a young slave, a milkmaid, labourers, servants, activists, invalids, émigrées and pioneers, a daring actor, and the daughter of a Native American chief. Whether writing out of injustice, religious or sexual passion, humour, or to celebrate their sex, their different cultures, environments, personal beliefs and relationships, these women have strong, independent spirits and voices we cannot ignore. In 1652, speaking of poems she had published as her 'babes', a woman we know only as 'Eliza' answered 'a Lady that bragged of her children': *Thine at their birth did pain thee bring,/ When mine are born, I sit and sing.*

Modern
Women Poets

edited by
DERYN REES-JONES

BLOODAXE BOOKS

ISBN: 1 85224 678 2

First published 2005 by
Bloodaxe Books Ltd,
Highgreen,
Tarset,
Northumberland NE48 1RP.

www.bloodaxebooks.com
For further information about Bloodaxe titles
please visit our website or write to
the above address for a catalogue.

Bloodaxe Books Ltd acknowledges
the financial assistance of
Arts Council England, North East.

To Alison Mark, with love

Cover printing by J. Thomson Colour Printers Ltd, Glasgow.

Printed in Great Britain by
Bell & Bain Limited, Glasgow, Scotland.

CONTENTS

INTRODUCTION

In a typically barbed letter Edith Sitwell writes to her friend, the poet Robert Nichols, in 1919, of her meeting with Charlotte Mew, the poet with whose work this anthology begins:

> I went to a depressing evening where all the guests were female poets ...so that I might meet Charlotte Mew. What a grey tragic woman – about sixty in point of age, and sucked dry of blood (though not of spirit) by poverty and an arachnoid mother. I tried to get her to come and see me, but she is a hermit, inhabited by a terrible bitterness, and though she was very nice to me, she wouldn't come. Besides her, I met an appalling woman called Madeline Caron Rock, extremely fat and exuding a glutinous hysteria from every pore. Whenever anyone mentioned living, dying, eating, sleeping, or any of the occurrences which beset us, Miss Rock would allow a gelatinous cube-like tear, still warm from her humanity, to fall upon my person and would then leave the room in a marked manner... She is rather a good poet, all the same...

As Isobel Armstrong and Joseph Bristow have remarked, 19th-century women's poetry was often seen as being limited to a 'a poetry of the heart... a consolidation of domestic virtues and a celebration of the women's sphere of home, love, duty' (*Nineteenth-Century Women Poets*, p.xxxv). It was this image of women's poetry which, as Armstrong and Bristow argue, Elizabeth Barrett Browning sought to dispel in *Aurora Leigh*, a novel-length poem about a woman poet, published in 1856. Yet even in the 20th century, the image of the woman poet as driven purely by emotion was to persist. For Sitwell, who was to become one of the most visible of 20th-century women poets, the woman poet is, in her letter, configured as either feeling too much or too little. Mew, the "real" poet, is grey, bitter; her reclusivity is contrasted with that of Rock's excessive feminine feeling which runs in parallel with her excessive physical presence. Sitwell's concession to Miss Rock – 'She is rather a good poet all the same' – speaks volumes about Sitwell's internalised misogyny and her own anxiety in placing herself as a woman in the hard, dry, impersonal poetics of Poundian modernism to which she herself was not reconciled.

Charlotte Mew's poem, 'The Farmer's Bride', was published in 1912. But her position as the most senior of the poets included in this anthology is pertinent for many, not simply chronological, reasons. 'The Farmer's Bride' is a poem written in the voice of a farmer who cannot understand why his wife (whom he admits he married 'too young'), has 'turned afraid / Of love', runs away, and eventually has to be kept under lock and key in his house, where she sleeps in the attic. The poem in other hands might have over-played the cruelties of such a marriage. But in Mew's poem the pain of the farmer, and his desire for the bride, sit painfully and ironically alongside the shock and refusal of the wife to participate in a marriage which, in its consummation, has been a physical and a mental violation. What makes the poem great is that the integrity of the farmer's passions, however cruelly executed, are upheld, and throw into acute relief the plight of the bride (whose age we never learn). In a disjunction in the poem where we are not sure whether it is the farmer's or the poem's narrative voice, Mew's bride is compared first to a leveret, then a larch, and then to wild violets; a 'wild self', she becomes a part of the untamed, untamable and unknowable natural world. At the end of the poem it is the 'down' of the bride, a soft down which recalls both the soft fur of the baby hare, the unusual softness of the larch leaf and perhaps even, the hairiness of the heart-shaped and elusively scented violet (also a well-known symbol of lesbianism) which becomes the focus of the farmer's desires. The down on the bride's arm becomes fetishised, standing in as it does not only for all that the farmer does not have, and cannot get close to, but what he himself is not. The poem, as many commentators have argued, while ostensibly being about heterosexual desire, also works as a narrative of covert lesbian sex-uality. But intimately connected with this is the way in which the monologue also produces an ironic silence, of the woman's voice (*'I've* hardly heard her speak at all' proclaims the farmer) removing the potential for dialogue between men and women in the *poem* while at the same time *demanding* a dialogue with its reader.

In placing women through a male voice, and ironising that posi-tion, we see Mew splitting and disorienting both allegiances and expectations of the poem's voice and the woman poet. This all the more so when we learn how Mew, a tiny figure only 4'11" high, with short hair and wearing a suit, would perform her poems, smoking cigarettes, at small, all-female gatherings organised by Catherine Dawson Scott. Several commentators have remarked on the brilliance of Mew's performances. Yet according to Laura Severin, when invited in 1915 to bring her poems to the more public arena of The Poetry Bookshop, run by Harold and Alida Monro (it had been Alida Monro who had engineered Sitwell's meeting with Mew), Mew declined. The Poetry Bookshop was host, Severin points out, to women poets such as Frances Cornford, Edna St Vincent Millay, Amy Lowell and Hilda Doolittle (H.D.). Yet rather than perform her poems herself, Mew instead request-ed that Alida Monro read them for her – then, and on two subsequent occasions in 1916 and 1921. Mew's choice to remain disembodied as a poet, represented through a female voice that is other than the poet, but which is often a male voice in a poem, heralds what is to become a continuing concern in 20th-century women's poetry about the relationship between gender, the body, poem and poet.

The dramatic monologue, as we have seen, offers a strategic circumvention of any direct equations between poet, poem and poetic 'I', and Mew's subtle masquerades of identity offer the reader of any history of 20th-century women's poetry an important place of departure. A continued interest by women in the dramatic poem – a genre which highlights women poets' anxieties about their self-presentation and poetic determination – can be seen variously in the poems collected here in work of Mina Loy, Ruth Pitter, Stevie Smith, U.A. Fanthorpe, Elizabeth Bartlett, Sylvia Plath, Anne Sexton, Jenny Joseph, Selima Hill, Vicki Feaver, Grace Nichols, Liz Lochhead, Jean Binta Breeze, Rita Ann Higgins, Jo Shapcott, Carol Ann Duffy, Jackie Kay and Colette Bryce. This interest, which moves across the century, suggests that as a genre the dramatic poem, most particularly the monologue, works as a place in which the unstable selfhood of the female poet can comfortably reside, providing a position which problematises and at the same time explores issues of gender, and identity, as well, potentially as "race", class, nation.

If the dramatic poem is an important feature of women's poetry, women can also be seen to be adopting other strategies for finding a place from which to write. Interestingly, both Plath and Bishop, those seemingly polar poetic opposites, are interested in surrealism – or an assimilated postmodern version of the surreal – an interest which draws together another line of connection between the poets collected here. Using surreal imagery also, I would argue, becomes part of a strategy identifiable in the work of many women, as a means, conscious or otherwise, to escape what were to become frequent later codings of women's poetry: as either minor and asexual, or minor and fuelled by political and not aesthetic concerns. The surreal cleverly manages to emphasise subjective experience while at the same time translating it into images that do not depend on a direct experiential recognition or identification. The surreal can speak publicly and often extravagantly of experiences which are usually secret, unmentionable and even unsayable. But even in the extravagance of expression it manages to retain an element of the mysterious and the covert. This sense of the surreal acting like a hinge between self and otherness, the private and the public, the blatant and the covert, the knowable and the unknowable, is of

19

particular relevance to women because, like the dramatic monologue, surreal imagery echoes as well as dramatises their own anxieties about speaking or writing in public. We see this particularly in the work of Selima Hill, Denise Riley, Penelope Shuttle, Moniza Alvi, Jo Shapcott and Carol Ann Duffy, as well as an assimilation of the dreamwork, so central to surrealism, absorbed into a writing style in the work of Medbh McGuckian, Jane Draycott or Alice Oswald.

Like the use of the dramatic monologue, an interest in myth and fairytale can also be seen as an attempt to remove an easily located self from the lyric into an embodied narrative, taking advantage of myth and fairytale's residual power to rethink the roles and representations of women. Versions by women of myths and legends and fairytales are, writes Alicia Suskin Ostriker, 'corrections...representations of what women find divine and demonic in themselves; they are retrieved images of what women have collectively and historically suffered; in some cases they are instructions for survival'. Such 'revisionary mythmaking', as Ostriker has called it, is often deeply political in its intention.We see such narratives explored variously in the work of H.D., Sitwell, Smith, Sexton, Rich, U.A. Fanthorpe, Veronica Forrest-Thomson, Liz Lochhead, Carol Ann Duffy and Vicki Feaver.

While the use of these strategies – the monologue, the surreal, the use of myth and fairytale – are one line which can be followed through the past century, other women included here eschew such masks in their politically committed poems – socialist, feminist or both. The work of Mina Loy combines feminist commitment with avant-garde practice; Anna Wickham's first-wave feminist poems foreshadow those of the second-wave feminists, although as Wickham's *Collected Poems* was not published until 1984 it is unlikely that her work was available to the younger women as model.

Lilian Mohin's anthology *One Foot on the Mountain* (1979) sought to solidify the new sense of a collective presence of women writers and to focus feminist energies at a pivotal moment in women's history and I would point the interested reader in particular to the writing of Sheila Rowbotham, Caroline Gilfillan and Stef Pixner included there. By the mid-1980s and 1990s in Britain and Ireland, feminist thinking was firmly assimilated into the mainstream of women's poetry in the work of Carol Ann Duffy, Helen Dunmore, Rita Ann Higgins, Sarah Maguire, Carol Rumens or Penelope Shuttle. Important issues of national identity and race were also being explored, sometimes hand-in-hand with feminist concerns, by writers as diverse as Una Marson, Grace Nichols, Nuala Ní Dhomhnaill, Eavan Boland, Gwyneth Lewis, Moniza Alvi, Imtiaz

Dharker, Kathleen Jamie, Carol Ann Duffy, Jackie Kay and Jo Shapcott. And while many poets have perhaps felt they had to resist writing about subjects deemed "suitable" to their sex, many have also written successfully about motherhood and the domestic, most prominently E.J. Scovell, Helen Dunmore, Kate Clanchy and Kathleen Jamie. Medbh McGuckian's poems, which are so often set in domestic interiors, frequently simultaneously explore, if covertly, both gender and national politics.

As might be expected, there is an increased development in the explicit references to body parts and specifically female biological and sexual experience as the century progresses and issues of propriety in relation to femininity and the female body become less prescriptive. Despite the dangers of commodifying extreme and difficult female experience, or of them being presented voyeuristically, traumatic subject-matter, such as rape, incest, and abuse are successfully negotiated by several women. The poems of Sharon Olds are grounded in what Vicki Feaver has described as a poetics of testimony as they bear witness in a way which transforms personal experience into political statement; Selima Hill's narrative sequences use shocking and surreal imagery to jolt and disturb received perceptions; Pascale Petit's harrowing accounts of her relationships with her parents are essentially magic realist in their aesthetic. Such explorations also go hand in hand with an interest in an interrogation of what the body means in relation to both experience and identity as it too becomes subject to the precariousness of language and the fracturing of the subject. In particular we can see women beginning to measure the body in terms of the new paradigms offered to them by science, paradigms which work to fracture and complicate the idea of the body as the site of shared female experience.

In contrast, the urge to remove the self from poetry, while undoubtedly influenced by Modernist poetics of impersonality, is particularly charged for women whose subjective experiences for so long were made invisible, silenced or distorted. While H.D.'s use of the image as a receptacle for subjective experience has clearly influenced poets such as Denise Levertov and Lousie Glück, it was another American, Elizabeth Bishop, whose adoption of an "objective" voice has proved a crucial influence in the work of some of the most prominent contemporary British poets. Bishop's *Complete Poems*, published in Britain in 1979, has had an extraordinary impact on the poetry of both men and women. She has been particularly important to Jo Shapcott and Lavinia Greenlaw; we also see her influence in younger poets such as Caitríona O'Reilly. Arising out of this movement towards the presentation of the world through an objective eye has been a move to explore the world through the lens of science; other poets who have found in science an important idiom through which to remove themselves from the still resounding stigma of "excessive femininity" include Pauline Stainer and Julia Copus. Two poets associated with the Cambridge school of poetry interrogate the confessional mode directly: Veronica Forrest-Thomson draws our attention to the process of writing itself, demanding that we 'forget the self-made self' and Denise Riley's anti-confessional lyrics ironise the many and unstable positions of the self.

Other thematic concerns recur and we see a desire for a sometimes uneasy engagement with religion and nature. The Christian poetry of Anne Ridler and Elizabeth Jennings, for example, contrasts with the more loosely "spiritual" and meditative poetry of Pauline Stainer, Gillian Allnutt and Louise Glück. Flower poems recur throughout the century, most prominently in the work of H.D., as 19th-century images of transient and fragile female beauty become rewritten. Marianne Moore's observing eye takes particular pleasure in the animal kingdom. Kathleen Raine has been the most prominent of the British nature poets; of the middle generation, Gillian Clarke and France Horovitz are prominent figures; in the work of the younger generation, Kathleen Jamie and Alice Oswald, and perhaps Katherine Pierpoint, are at the forefront of this renewed, even urgent, interest.

Many of the women poets experiment with form. Mew's early use of rhyming free verse gave her scope for modulation and development of an individual voice without sacrificing rhyme's supporting architecture. Stein's poetics of disrupted grammar and syntax looked to rethink patriarchal structures; Elizabeth Daryush's use of syllabics was, as Jane Dowson has argued, an important model for both Marianne Moore and W.H. Auden in creating a conversational tone; more recently Jenny Joseph and Anne Carson have shown a continued interest in the cross-fertilisation of poetry and prose. In contrast, the formalism of Anne Stevenson, Elizabeth Garrett and Eva Salzman hosts an often philosophical wit; in Gwyneth Lewis's English rhymes we can often hear a potentially subversive crosscurrent of Welsh cadences and alliterative patterns.

*　　*　　*

Modern Women Poets, while undoubtedly wide-ranging, does not claim to be definitive. The writing of 100 women is featured, and, had space allowed, I could have included the work of at least 50 others. My emphasis is on the British and Irish poetic traditions and those seminal poets from other countries and traditions who have helped to shape them. Such a grouping does not elide or negate difference but rather points to the rich and varied nature of cultural and aesthetic exchange. Sexton and Plath were the only women to be included in the second edition of Alvarez's influential anthology *The New Poetry*; Elizabeth Bishop, Adrienne Rich, Jorie Graham, Gwendolyn Brooks, Louise Glück, Sharon Olds, Anne Stevenson and Fleur Adcock are some of the most important and widely read poets of their generation; in 2002 the Canadian Anne Carson was the first woman to win the T.S. Eliot Prize; Imtiaz Dharker is studied as part of the National Curriculum. Similarly it is worth pointing out that in bringing together the work of these women it is certainly not my intention to isolate them from their male contemporaries, with whom many have been, or are engaged in continuing literary dialogues. Those dialogues are important, however difficult they may be at times, as Jo Shapcott wittily shows in her sequence of poems which simultaneously explore the relationships between Robert and Elizabeth Browning and Robert Lowell and Elizabeth Hardwick.

In making the many choices an anthology such as this requires, I have sometimes had to struggle with the question that many of the poets were themselves forced to address; that is how to negotiate and value women's experience in relation to poetry. My solutions have not been the same for every poet. Sometimes I felt it important to include poems which addressed issues that had an overt relationship to women's writing, or with the culture, and which negotiated women's relationships with the personal and the domestic, with children, men, their biology. To fail to feature these poems, given the number of occasions on which such poems appear, would have been a serious omission. But poems are not simply about experience, and it was also crucial not to limit any understanding of women's poetry to important but not exclusively female or feminist concerns.

The poets appear chronologically, not to show some 'evolutionary' progress, but rather to emphasise the importance of a wider social history to their genesis as writers. This has led to some interesting juxtapositions of poets who share a year of birth; Elizabeth Jennings and Elizabeth Bartlett are close contemporaries with very different publishing histories. Reading their poetry alongside each other sheds valuable light on each. With two exceptions, all the women in the anthology have produced at least two collections of poetry. In the cases of Greta Stoddart and Katherine Pierpoint, their first collections have been published long enough and created enough impact for their significance to have been fully registered. Not all the poets began publishing when they were young, and sometimes it is interesting to see how a poet who has technically come late to poetry or to publishing – figures such as Anne Ridler, Elizabeth Bartlett, Mimi Khalvati, Selima Hill – carries the dual inheritance of historical age and poetic age. Because of this, and given the long writing lives of many of the poets represented, I have felt it important to date the poems. This gives recourse to a valuable historical context, and also enables connections between poets writing at specific points in time to be made as well. Unless specific publication dates for individual poems were available, the dates given here in square brackets register the poems' inclusion in publication in full-length volumes. Where the date of writing is known, this appears in italics. A chronology of publications of all theb women poets featured is included in *Consorting with Angels*, the critical book which accompanies this anthology, so that poets' individual collections can be read in the light of their contemporaries, for easy and fuller reference.

'A woman's problem in writing poetry is different to a man's,' wrote Edith Sitwell in 1946,

> That is why I've been such a hell of a time learning to get out my poetry, there was no one [ie, no adequate female model] to point the way, and I had to learn everything – learn, among other things, not to be timid, and that was one of the most difficult things of all...[4]

Such a desire to establish a continuum of women's poetry is echoed by poets as diverse as Plath, Rich, and more recently Jo Shapcott and Colette Bryce. There are many poets and many models as this anthology proves. There are also many ways of aligning and connecting them to each other. While there is perhaps time now for consolidation and reflection on such connections as well as divergences, timidity at last seems no longer any part of the equation.

CHARLOTTE MEW

(1869-1928)

Born in London, Charlotte Mew lived for most of her life in Bloomsbury with
her mother and sister Anne, a painter. She was friendly with the novelists May
Sinclair and Olive Schreiner, as well as with Thomas Hardy, who was an early
champion of her work. Her first short story was published in *The Yellow Book*
in 1894. *The Farmer's Bride* was published in 1916, and in 1921 in the USA as
Saturday Market. Mew committed suicide in 1928, and *The Rambling Sailor*
was published posthumously in 1929.

Mew's poetry was admired by writers as diverse as H.D., Rose Macaulay,
Vita Sackville-West, Siegfried Sassoon and Edith Sitwell. She uses the dramatic
monologue to write in the voice of male and female personae, often to explore
aspects of women's passion. While her thematic concerns link her strongly with
women poets of the late 19th century, her free verse technique places her work
firmly within the auspices of Modernism. *Collected Poems*, with a memoir by
Alida Monroe, appeared in 1953, and was followed by *Collected Poems and
Prose*, edited by Val Warner in 1981, *Collected Poems and Prose* (1997) and
Charlotte Mew: Selected Poems (1999).

The Farmer's Bride

Three summers since I chose a maid,
Too young maybe – but more's to do
At harvest-time than bide and woo,
    When us was wed she turned afraid
Of love and me and all things human;
Like the shut of a winter's day.
Her smile went out, and 'twasn't a woman –
    More like a little frightened fay.
        One night, in the fall, she runned away.

'Out 'mong the sheep, her be,' they said,
'Should properly have been abed;
But sure enough she wasn't there
Lying awake with her wide brown stare.
So over seven-acre field and up-along across the down
    We chased her, flying like a hare
Before our lanterns. To Church-Town
    All in a shiver and a scare
We caught her, fetched her home at last
    And turned the key upon her, fast.

She does the work about the house
As well as most, but like a mouse:
    Happy enough to chat and play
    With birds and rabbits and such as they,
    So long as men-folk keep away.
'Not near, not near!' her eyes beseech
When one of us comes within reach.
    The women say that beasts in stall
    Look round like children at her call.
    I've hardly heard her speak at all.

Shy as a leveret, swift as he,
Straight and slight as a young larch tree,
Sweet as the first wild violets, she,
To her wild self. But what to me?

The short days shorten and the oaks are brown,
    The blue smoke rises to the low grey sky
One leaf in the still air falls slowly down,
    A magpie's spotted feathers lie
On the black earth spread white with rime,
The berries redden up to Christmas-time.
    What's Christmas-time without there be
    Some other in the house than we!

    She sleeps up in the attic there
    Alone, poor maid. 'Tis but a stair
Betwixt us. Oh! my God! the down
The soft young down of her, the brown,
The brown of her – her eyes, her hair, her hair!

[1916]

Rooms

I remember rooms that have had their part
    In the steady slowing down of the heart.
The room in Paris, the room at Geneva,
The little damp room with the seaweed smell,
And that ceaseless maddening sound of the tide –
    Rooms where for good or for ill – things died.

But there is the room where we two lie dead,
Though every morning we seem to wake and might just as well
seem to sleep again
As we shall somewhere in the other quieter, dustier bed
Out there in the sun – in the rain.

[1929]

The Trees are Down

– and he cried with a loud voice:
Hurt not the earth, neither the sea, nor the trees –
REVELATION

They are cutting down the great plane trees at the end of the gardens.
For days there has been the grate of the saw, the swish of the
branches as they fall,
The crash of trunks, the rustle of trodden leaves,
With the 'Whoops' and the 'Whoas', the loud common talk, the loud
common laughs of the men, above it all.

I remember one evening of a long past Spring
Turning in at a gate, getting out of a cart, and finding a large dead
rat in the mud of the drive.
I remember thinking: alive or dead, a rat was a god-forsaken thing,
But at least, in May, that even a rat should be alive.

The week's work here is as good as done. There is just one bough
On the roped bole, in the fine grey rain,
Green and high
And lonely against the sky.
(Down now! –)
And but for that,
If an old dead rat
Did once, for a moment, unmake the Spring, I might never have
thought of him again.

It is not for a moment the Spring is unmade today;
These were great trees, it was in them from root to stem:
When the men with the 'Whoops' and the 'Whoas' have carted the
whole of the whispering loveliness away
Half the Spring, for me, will have gone with them.

27

It is going now, and my heart has been struck with the hearts of
the planes;
Half my life it has beat with these, in the sun, in the rains,
In the March wind, the May breeze,
In the great gales that came over to them across the roofs from
the great seas.
There was only a quiet rain when they were dying;
They must have heard the sparrows flying,
And the small creeping creatures in the earth when they were lying –
But I, all day, I heard an angel crying:
'Hurt not the trees.'

[1929]

GERTRUDE STEIN

(1874-1946)

Gertrude Stein was born in Allegheny, Pennsylvania, and grew up in Vienna,
Paris and Oakland, California. She went to Radcliffe College, where she first
studied psychology with William James, brother of the novelist Henry James,
before going on to study medicine at Johns Hopkins University. After brief
spells in Bloomsbury, London, and New York, she moved to Paris in 1903
with her brother Leo, where she met her lifelong companion Alice B. Toklas.
Stein's first book, *Three Lives* (1909), was heavily influenced by the cubist
practice of Picasso and Cézanne. Edith Sitwell reviewed *Geography and Plays*
in *The Nation* in 1923. They met in Paris in 1924, and in 1925, Sitwell wrote
in *Vogue* that 'in the future it is evident that no history of the English litera-
ture of our time could be of any worth without a complete survey of the work
Gertrude Stein is doing for our language'. Despite being Jewish, Stein remained
in France with Toklas during the German occupation. Mina Loy writes: 'Mod-
ernism has democratised the subject-matter and *la belle matière* of art; through
cubism the newspaper has assumed an aesthetic quality, through Cézanne a
plate has become more than something to put an apple upon, Brancusi has
given an evangelistic import to eggs, and Gertrude Stein has given us the Word,
in and for itself [...] Stein leaves grammatical lacuna among her depictions and
the mind trips up and fall through into the subconscious source of associated
ideas.' (*Gender of Modernism*, p.244). Stein's works include *Tender Buttons* (1914),
The Making of Americans (1925), *How to Write* (1931), *The Autobiography of
Alice B. Toklas* (1933), *Bee Time Vine and Other Pieces 1913-1927* (1953) and
Stanzas in Meditation and Other Poems [1929-1933] (1956). In the prose poems
here, we see Stein exploring objects, attempting to shape and interrogate the
material through disruptive syntax much in the way that the cubist painter
offers several dimensions simultaneously to the eye.

from Tender Buttons

A CARAFE, THAT IS A BLIND GLASS

A kind in glass and a cousin, a spectacle and nothing strange a single hurt color and an arrangement in a system to pointing. All this and not ordinary, not unordered in not resembling. The difference is spreading.

A BOX

A large box is handily made of what is necessary to replace any substance. Suppose an example is necessary, the plainer it is made the more reason there is for some outward recognition that there is a result.

A box is made sometimes and them to see to see to it neatly and to have the holes stopped up makes it necessary to use paper.

A custom which is necessary when a box is used and taken is that a large part of the time there are three which have different connections. The one is on the table. The two are on the table. The three are on the table. The one, one is the same length as is shown by the cover being longer. The other is different there is more cover that shows it. The other is different and that makes the corners have the same shade the eight are in singular arrangement to make four necessary.

Lax, to have corners, to be lighter than some weight, to indicate a wedding journey, to last brown and not curious, to be wealthy, cigarettes are established by length and by doubling.

Left open, to be left pounded, to be left closed, to be circulating in summer and winter, and sick color that is grey that is not dusty and red shows, to be sure cigarettes do measure an empty length sooner than a choice in color.

Winged, to be winged means that white is yellow and pieces pieces that are brown are dust color if dust is washed off, then it is choice that is to say it is fitting cigarettes sooner than paper.

An increase why is an increase idle, why is silver cloister, why is the spark brighter, if it is brighter is there any result, hardly more than ever.

A LONG DRESS

What is the current that makes machinery, that makes it crackle, what is the current that presents a long line and a necessary waist. What is this current.

What is the wind, what is it.

Where is the serene length, it is there and a dark place is not a dark place, only a white and red are black, only a yellow and green are blue, a pink is scarlet, a bow is every color. A line distinguishes it. A line just distinguishes it.

A RED HAT

A dark grey, a very dark grey, a quite dark grey is monstrous ordinarily, it is so monstrous because there is no red in it. If red is in everything it is not necessary. Is that not an argument for any use of it and even so is there any place that is better, is there any place that has so much stretched out.

A MOUNTED UMBRELLA

What was the use of not leaving it there where it would hang what was the use if there was no chance of ever seeing it come there and show that it was handsome and right in the way it showed it. The lesson is to learn that it does show it, that it shows it and that nothing, that there is nothing, that there is no more to do about it and just so much more is there plenty of reason for making an exchange.

1911 [1914]

MINA LOY
(1882-1966)

Born in London, Loy moved to the States in 1916, where she later took US citizenship. Trained as a painter, her work achieved some success, and was included in the Salon d'Automne show in Paris in 1905. She was strongly affected by the artist Marinetti's futurist principles, but abhorred his gender politics. She was also influenced by the writing and thinking of Gertrude Stein. By 1914 her writing was becoming well-known in experimental poetry circles in New York. She married the poet and boxer Arthur Cravan in 1918. *Lunar Baedecker* was published in 1923, followed a quarter of a century later by *Lunar Baedeker & Time-tables* (1958), edited by Roger L. Conover, who also produced two posthumous selections, *The Last Lunar Baedeker* (1985) and *The Lost Lunar Baedeker* (1996/1997). Reclusive in her later years, Loy worked on an unfinished biography of Isadora Duncan, and left behind unpublished poems from the 1940s as well as a novel, *Insel*, finally published in 1991.

Her work often addresses "taboo" subjects: she has written about childbirth, prostitution, sex, and drugs. In her 'Feminist Manifesto' she demands that gender roles be radically rethought: 'The man who lives a life in which his activities conform to a social code which is a protectorate of the feminine element – is no longer <u>masculine</u>. The women who adapt themselves to a theoretical valuation of their sex as a <u>relative impersonality</u>, are not yet <u>Feminine</u> Leave off looking to men to find out what you are not – seek within yourselves to find out what you <u>are</u>. As conditions are at present constituted – you have the choice between <u>Parasitism</u> & <u>Prostitution</u> – or Negation.' (*Lost Lunar Baedeker*, pp.153-54). In an essay, 'Modern Poetry', she writes: 'More than to read poetry we must listen to poetry. All reading is the evocation of speech; the difference in our approach, then, in reading a poem or a newspaper is that our attitude in reading a poem must be rather that of listening to and looking as a pictured song. Modern poetry, like music, has received a fresh impetus from contemporary life; they have both gained in precipitance of movement. The structure of all poetry is the movement that an active individuality makes in expressing itself. Poetic rhythm, of which we have all spoken so much, is the chart of a temperament.' (*Lost Lunar Baedeker*, p.157)

The Effectual Marriage
or The Inspid Narrative of GINA AND MIOVANNI

The door was an absurd thing
Yet it was passable
They quotidienly passed through it
It was this shape

Gina and Miovanni   who they were God knows
They knew   it was important to them
This being of who they were
They were themselves
Corporeally   transcendentally   consecutively
conjunctively   and they were quite   complete

In the evening they looked out of their two windows
Miovanni out of his library window
Gina from the kitchen window
From among his pots and pans

Where he so kindly kept her
Where she so wisely busied herself
Pots and Pans   she cooked in them
All sorts of sialagogues
Some say   that happy women are immaterial

So here we might dispense with her
Gina being a female
But she was more than that
Being an incipience   a correlative
an instigation of the reaction of man
From the palpable to the transcendent
Mollescent irritant of his fantasy
Gina had her use   Being useful
contentedly conscious
She flowered in Empyrean
From which no well-mated woman ever returns

Sundays   a warm light in the parlor
From the gritty road   on the white wall
anybody could see it
Shimmered a composite effigy
Madonna   crinolined   a man
hidden beneath her hoop
Ho for the blue and red of her
The silent eyelids of her
The shiny smile of her

Ding dong   said the bell
Miovanni   Gina called
Would it be fitting for you to tell
the time for supper
Pooh   said Miovanni   I am
Outside time and space

Patience said Gina   is an attribute
And she learned   at any hour to offer
The dish   appropriately delectable

What had Miovanni made of his ego
In his library
What had Gina wondered   among the pots and pans
One never asked the other
So they   the wise ones   eat their suppers in peace

Of what their peace consisted
We cannot say
Only that he was magnificently man
She insignificantly a woman who understood
Understanding   what is that
To Each   his entity   to others
their idiosyncrasies   to the free expansion
to the annexed their liberty
To man his work
To woman her love
Succulent meals   and an occasional caress
            So be it
                  It so seldom is

While Miovanni thought alone in the dark
Gina supposed that peeping   she might see
A round light   shining   where his mind was
She never opened the door
Fearing that this might blind her
Or even
That she should see   Nothing at all
So while he thought
She hung out of the window
Watching for falling stars
And when a star fell
She wished   that still
Miovanni would love her tomorrow
And as Miovanni
Never gave any heed to the matter
He did

Gina was a woman
Who wanted everything
To be everything in woman
Everything everyway at once
Diurnally variegate
Miovanni always knew her
She was Gina
Gina who lent monogamy
With her fluctuant aspirations
A changeant consistency
Unexpected intangibilities

Miovanni remained
Monumentally the same
The same Miovanni
If he had become anything else
Gina's world would have been at an end
Gina with no axis to revolve on
Must have dwindled to a full stop

In the mornings she dropped
Cool crystals
Through devotional fingers
Saccharine   for his cup
And marketed
With a Basket
Trimmed with a red flannel flower
When she was lazy
She wrote a poem on the milk bill
The first strophe   Good morning
The second   Good night
Something not too difficult to
Learn by heart

The scrubbed smell of the white-wood table
Greasy cleanliness   of the chopper board
The coloured vegetables
Intuited quality of flour
Crickly sparks of straw-fanned charcoal
Ranged themselves among her audacious happinesses
Pet simplicities of her Universe
Where circles were only round
                    Having no vices.

(This narrative halted when I learned that the
house which inspired it was the home of a mad
woman.
                    – Forte dei Marmi)

1915 [1917]

Brancusi's Golden Bird

The toy
become the aesthetic archetype

As if
some patient peasant God
had rubbed and rubbed
the Alpha and Omega
of Form
into a lump of metal

A naked orientation
unwinged   unplumed
  – the ultimate rhythm
has lopped the extremities
of crest and claw
from
the nucleus of flight

The absolute act
of art
conformed
to continent sculpture
– bare as the brow of Osiris –
this breast of revelation

an incandescent curve
licked by chromatic flames
in labyrinths of reflections

This gong
of polished hyperaesthesia

shrills with brass
as the aggressive light
strikes
its significance

The immaculate
conception

of the inaudible bird
occurs
in gorgeous reticence...

1922 [1923]

Gertrude Stein

Curie
of the laboratory
of vocabulary
   she crushed
the tonnage
of consciousness
congealed to phrases
   to extract
a radium of the word

1924 [1924/1982]

ANNA WICKHAM
(1884-1947)

Edith Alice Mary Harper was born in Wimbledon, London, and moved to
Brisbane, Australia when she was six. She returned to England in 1904, married
in 1905, and gave birth to four children. She lived in Bloomsbury and Highgate
and included amongst her friends Dylan Thomas, Ezra Pound, D.H. Lawrence
and Natalie Barney, with whom she had a long correspondence. Writing under
several pseudonyms, she published *Songs of John Oland* (as John Oland) in 1911,
followed by (as Anna Wickham) *The Contemplative Quarry* (1915), *The Man
with a Hammer* (1916), *The Little Old House* (1921), and in 1936 a selected in
the Richard's Shilling Selections of Edwardian poets. She writes: 'The creative
consciousness of a pure artist is bisexual. There is a marriage in the house of
the soul. The female principle produces the myth from some source within
herself, and fertilises it with her essential energy. The male principle is intel-
lectual, ranging the world to select material. He is critic and scholar, and
master of characterisation. He fertilises his wife from what he knows, and the
result is a work of pure imagination.' (*The Writings of Anna Wickham*, p.368).
Perhaps because of her humour and the resonant off-key rhymes, R.D. Smith
has compared her writing with that of Stevie Smith. Wickham's engagement
with women's issues and sexual politics also bear interesting comparison with

that of women writing during the second wave of feminism in the 1970s and 1980s. Wickham spent six weeks in a mental institution in 1911, which she attributed to her husband's attempts to prevent her from writing; she committed suicide in 1947. A posthumous *Selected Poems* appeared in 1971, and *The Writings of Anna Wickham: Freewoman and Poet* in 1984. A biography by Jennifer Vaughan Jones, *Anna Wickham: A Poet's Daring Life*, was published in 2003.

The Egoist

(FROM *The Contemplative Quarry*)

Shall I write pretty poetry
Controlled by ordered sense in me
With an old choice of figure and of word,
So call my soul a nesting bird?

Of the dead poets I can make a synthesis,
And learn poetic form that in them is;
But I will use the figure that is real
For me, the figure that I feel.

And now of this matter of ear-perfect rhyme,
My clerk can list all language in his leisure time;
A faulty rhyme may be a well-placed microtone,
And hold a perfect imperfection of its own.

A poet rediscovers all creation;
His instinct gives him beauty, which is sensed relation.
It was as fit for one man's thoughts to trot in iambs, as it is for me,
Who live not in the horse-age, but in the day of aeroplanes, to
            write my rhythms free.

[1915]

Nervous Prostration

I married a man of the Croydon class
When I was twenty-two.
And I vex him, and he bores me
Till we don't know what to do!

It isn't good form in the Croydon class
To say you love your wife,
So I spend my days with the tradesmen's books
And pray for the end of life.

In green fields are blossoming trees
And a golden wealth of gorse,
And young birds sing for joy of worms:
It's perfectly clear, of course,
That it wouldn't be taste in the Croydon class
To sing over dinner or tea:
But I sometimes wish the gentleman
Would turn and talk to me!

But every man of the Croydon class
Lives in terror of joy and speech.
'Words are betrayers', 'joys are brief' –
The maxims their wise ones teach –
And for all my labour of love and life
I shall be clothed and fed,
And they'll give me an orderly funeral
When I'm still enough to be dead.

I married a man of the Croydon class
When I was twenty-two.
And I vex him, and he bores me
Till we don't know what to do!
And as I sit in his ordered house,
I feel I must sob or shriek,
To force a man of the Croydon class
To live, or to love, or to speak!

[1915]

FRANCES CORNFORD

(1886-1960)

The granddaughter of Charles Darwin, Frances Cornford was also related to
William Wordsworth. Her books include *Poems* (1910), *Autumn Midnight* (1923),
Different Days (1928), *Mountains and Molehills* (1934), *Collected Poems* (1954)
and, posthumously, *Fifteen Poems from the French* (1976) and *Selected Poems*
(1996). She had five children with her husband, Francis Cornford; the eldest,

John, also a poet, was killed at the age of 21 fighting for the Republican cause during the Spanish Civil War. Praised by Naomi Mitchison and Sylvia Townsend Warner, she often writes about domestic life, children and childhood, from surprising angles unafraid of voicing the difficulties and anxieties of motherhood. Frances Cornford was given the Queen's Gold Medal for Poetry in 1959.

The New-Born Baby's Song

When I was twenty inches long,
I could not hear the thrushes' song;
The radiance of morning skies
Was most displeasing to my eyes.

For loving looks, caressing words,
I cared no more than sun or birds;
But I could bite my mother's breast,
And that made up for all the rest.

[1923]

The Sick Queen

I hear my children come. They trample with their feet,
Fetched from their play to kiss my thin-boned hands lying on the
      sheet,
Fresh as young colts with every field before them,
With gazing apple-faces. Can it be this body bore them?
(This poor body like an outworn glove,
That yet subdues a spirit which no more knows that it can love.)
All day is theirs. I belong to night,
The brown surrounding caverns made of dream. The long failing
      fight,
On and on with pain. Theirs is sweet sleep
And morning breakfast with bright yellow butter. They can laugh
      and weep
Over a tiny thing – a toy, a crumb, a letter.
Tomorrow they will come again and say: *Now* are you better?'
'Better, my lords, today', the Chamberlain replies;
And I shall be too tired and too afraid to cry out that he lies.

[1928]

Ode on the Whole Duty of Parents

The spirits of children are remote and wise,
They must go free
Like fishes in the sea
Or starlings in the skies,
Whilst you remain
The shore where casually they come again.
But when there falls the stalking shade of fear,
You must be suddenly near,
You, the unstable, must become a tree
In whose unending heights of flowering green
Hangs every fruit that grows, with silver bells;
Where heart-distracting magic birds are seen
And all the things a fairy-story tells;
Though still you should possess
Roots that go deep in ordinary earth,
And strong consoling bark
To love and to caress.

Last, when at dark
Safe on the pillow lies an up-gazing head
And drinking holy eyes
Are fixed on you,
When, from behind them, questions come to birth
Insistently,
On all the things that you have ever said
Of suns and snakes and parallelograms and flies,
Then for a while you'll need to be no more
That sheltering shore
Or legendary tree in safety spread,
No, then you must put on
The robes of Solomon,
Or simply be
Sir Isaac Newton sitting on the bed.

[1934]

HILDA DOOLITTLE [H.D]

(1886-1961)

Born into a Moravian household in Bethlehem, Pennsylvania, Doolittle moved to London in 1911. Her early writing, which was originally heavily edited by Ezra Pound, who "created" her persona H.D, was included in early Imagist manifestos. Her first book, *Sea Garden*, was published in 1916. Her daughter was born in 1919. *Sea Garden* was followed by *Hymen* in 1921, the year when she published Marianne Moore's first book, in London, without her knowing. Moore, in a review of H.D.'s *Hymen*, writes: 'Talk of weapons and the tendency to match one's intellectual and emotional rigor with the violence of nature, give a martial, an apparently masculine tone to such writing as H.D.'s.' (*Gender of Modernism*, p.352) Her *Collected Poems* appeared in 1925. She briefly underwent analysis with Freud in 1933 and 1934, an account of which she published as *Tribute to Freud* (1956). Noted for her engagement with classical imagery, she wrote her long poem *Trilogy* (1946) during the Blitz in London (comprising *The Walls Do Not Fall* [1944], *Tribute to the Angels* [1945] and *The Flowering of the Rod* [1946]), moving away then from the classical references and the imagism that had preoccupied her in her early work. Doolittle's novels include *HERmione* (written 1927, published 1981) and *Bid Me to Live* (1960), which give thinly veiled accounts of her relationships with, amongst others, Pound, her husband Richard Aldington, and D.H. Lawrence. She featured in two films, *Foothills* (1927) and *Borderline* (1930), and lived with and was supported by one of the major patrons of Modernism, Winifred Ellerman, known as Bryher. She lived in Switzerland until her death in 1984, the year when her final collection of poems, *Helen in Egypt*, was published. *Collected Poems 1912-44* was published in 1984. The poems included here show her continuing to experiment with the image, from the flower poems of *Sea Garden*, to the longer sequences of the 1940s. *Trilogy* can be usefully compared with Sheila Wingfield's three-part poem of the 1940s, *Beat Drum Beat Heart*, Lynette Roberts' *Gods with Stainless Ears* and T.S. Eliot's *Four Quartets*.

Oread

Whirl up, sea –
whirl your pointed pines.
splash your great pines
on our rocks,
hurl your green over us,
cover us with your pools of fir.

[1915]

Sea Rose

Rose, harsh rose
marred and with stint of petals,
meagre flower, thin,
sparse of leaf,

more precious
than a wet rose
single on a stem –
you are caught in the drift.

Stunted, with small leaf,
you are flung on the sand,
you are lifted
in the crisp sand
that drives in the wind.

Can the spice-rose
drip such acrid fragrance
hardened in a leaf?

1915 [1916]

Sea Violet

The white violet
is scented on its stalk,
the sea-violet
fragile as agate,
lies fronting all the wind
among the torn shells
on the sand-bank.

The greater blue violets
flutter on the hill,
but who would change for these
who would change for these
one root of the white sort?

Violet
your grasp is frail
on the edge of the sand-hill,
but you catch the light –
frost, a star edges with its fire.

1915 [1916]

from Tribute to the Angels

(FROM *Trilogy*)

28

I had been thinking of Gabriel,
of the moon-cycle, of the moon-shell,

of the moon-crescent
and the moon at full:

I had been thinking of Gabriel,
the moon-regent, the Angel,

and I had intended to recall him
in the sequence of candle and fire

and the law of the seven;
I had not forgotten

his special attribute
of annunciator; I had thought

to address him as I had the others,
Uriel, Annael;

how could I imagine
the Lady herself would come instead?

29

We have seen her
the world over,

Our Lady of the Goldfinch,
Our Lady of the Candelabra,

Our Lady of the Pomegranate,
Our Lady of the Chair;

we have seen her, an empress,
magnificent in pomp and grace,

and we have seen her
with a single flower

or a cluster of garden-pinks
in a glass beside her;

we have seen her snood
drawn over her hair,

or her face set in profile
with the blue hood and stars;

we have seen her head bowed down
with the weight of a domed crown,

or we have seen her, a wisp of a girl
trapped in a golden halo;

we have seen her with arrow, with doves
and a heart like a valentine;

we have seen her in fine silks imported
from all over the Levant,

and hung with pearls brought
from the city of Constantine;

we have seen her sleeve
of every imaginable shade

of damask and figured brocade;
it is true,

the painters did very well by her;
it is true, they missed never a line

of the suave turn of the head
or subtle shade of lowered eye-lid

or eye-lids half-raised; you find
her everywhere (or did find),

in cathedral, museum, cloister,
at the turn of the palace stair.

30

We see her hand in her lap,
smoothing the apple-green

or the apple-russet silk;
we see her hand at her throat,

fingering a talisman
brought by a crusader from Jerusalem;

we see her hand unknot a Syrian veil
or lay down a Venetian shawl

on a polished table that reflects
half a miniature broken column;

we see her stare past a mirror
through an open window,

where boat follows slow boat on the lagoon;
there are white flowers on the water.

[1945]

ELIZABETH DARYUSH

(1887-1977)

The daughter of the poet Robert Bridges, Daryush published her first collection of poems, *Charitessi 1911*, anonymously in 1912, the year before her father became the Poet Laureate. *Verses* was published in 1916, and *Sonnets from Hafez and Other Verses* in 1921, under the name Elizabeth Bridges. She married Ali Akbar Daryush in 1926 and they moved to Persia before returning to Britain in 1929. Disowning her first three collections of poems, she wrote prolifically after the death of her father during the 1930s, publishing *Verses* (1930), *Verses: Second Book* (1932), *Verses: Third Book* (1933), *Verses: Fourth Book* (1934), *Selected Poems* (1935), *The Last Man and Other Verses*

(1936) and *Verses: Sixth Book* (1938). A later *Selected Poems*, with an intro-
duction by Yvor Winters, appeared in 1948. Daryush described her use of
syllabics in 1934: 'The poems without line-capitals are written in syllabic
metres (by which I mean metres governed only by the number of syllables to
the line, and in which the number and position of the stresses may be varied
at will) and are so printed as a reminder to the reader to follow strictly the
natural speech-rhythm and not to look for stresses where there are none
intended.' (Appendix, *Selected Poems*, 1972).

Verses: Seventh Book was published in 1971, and *Selected Poems: Verses 1-VI*
in 1972. Donald Davie, in an article in *Poetry Nation* in 1975, praises Daryush,
demanding a reevaluation of her work, comparing her at times with Thomas
Hardy. Roy Fuller has connected her work with that of her exact contemporary
Marianne Moore, while Jane Dowson has suggested that her work 'paved the
way for the metrical ranges of Auden and other poets who popularised syllabic
metre after 1939' (*Women Poets of the 1930s*, p.57). Her *Collected Poems*, with
an introduction by Davie, was published in 1976.

'You should at times go out...'

You should at times go out
    from where the faithful kneel,
visit the slums of doubt
    and feel what the lost feel;

you should at times walk on,
    away from your friends' ways,
go where the scorned have gone,
    pass beyond blame and praise;

and at times you should quit
    (ah yes) your sunny home,
sadly awhile should sit,
    even, in wrong's dark room,

or ever, suddenly
    by simple bliss betrayed,
you shall be forced to flee,
    unloved, alone, afraid.

[1934]

Still-Life

Through the open French window the warm sun
lights up the polished breakfast-table, laid
round a bowl of crimson roses, for one –
a service of Worcester porcelain, arrayed
near it a melon, peaches, figs, small hot
rolls in a napkin, fairy rack of toast,
butter in ice, high silver coffee-pot,
and, heaped on a salver, the morning's post.

She comes over the lawn, the young heiress,
from her early walk in her garden-wood
feeling that life's a table set to bless
her delicate desires with all that's good,

that even the unopened future lies
like a love-letter, full of sweet surprise.

[1936]

'Children of wealth in your warm nursery...'

Children of wealth in your warm nursery,
Set in the cushioned window-seat to watch
The volleying snow, guarded invisibly
By the clear double pane through which no touch
Untimely penetrates, you cannot tell
What winter means; its cruel truths to you
Are only sound and sight; your citadel
Is safe from feeling, and from knowledge too.

Go down, go out to elemental wrong,
Waste your too round limbs, tan your skin too white;
The glass of comfort, ignorance, seems strong
Today, and yet perhaps this very night

You'll wake to horror's wrecking fire – your home
Is wired within for this, in every room.

[1938]

47

MARIANNE MOORE

(1887-1972)

Marianne Moore was born near St Louis, Missouri, and in 1896 moved to Pennsylvania, where her mother was a teacher. Her father, whom she never met, spent his life after her birth in psychiatric care. Moore studied Biology and Histology at Bryn Mawr College, graduating in 1909, and after a brief spell in New Jersey moved to New York City with her mother in 1918, where she worked as a librarian. Her first collection, *Poems*, published in 1921, was followed by *Observations* (1924). She joined *The Dial* in 1925, and was its final editor from 1926 to 1929, publishing Eliot, Pound, Hart Crane and Valéry. Her *Selected Poems*, with an introduction by T.S. Eliot, appeared in 1935, and was followed by several books, including *Collected Poems* (1951) and *Complete Poems* (1968), as well as a translation of La Fontaine's *Fables* (1954). Grace Schulman's definitive edition *The Poems of Marianne Moore* was published in 2003.

Moore is a key figure within Modernism and of particular importance to the women who write after her. Sylvia Plath, for example, when trying to place herself within a female poetic lineage in her journals, refers to Moore, along with Edith Sitwell, as a 'poetic fairy godmother'. Moore had a long friendship with the poet Elizabeth Bishop, whom she met in 1934. In her memoir of Moore, 'Efforts of Affection', Bishop wonders whether 'the feminist critics' had read Moore's poem 'Marriage', which says 'everything Virginia Woolf has said? It is a poem which transforms a justified sense of injury into a work of art'. Or whether they knew that Moore had 'paraded with the suffragettes, led by Inez Milholland on her white horse, down Fifth Avenue? Once, Marianne told me, she "climbed a lamppost" in a demonstration for votes for women... in long skirt and petticoats and a large hat. Perhaps it was pride or vanity that kept her from complaints, and that put her sense of injustice through the prisms dissected by "those various scalpels" into poetry (*Collected Prose*, pp.144-45). Joanne Feit Diehl offers the relationship between Moore and Bishop as 'an alternative paradigm to male, modernist tradition...acknowledging the primary importance of the literary foremother' and showing how 'the daughter-poet learns to express her own word, how she comes to differentiate herself from her mother while dealing with her own feelings of aggression, loss and anxiety' (*Elizabeth Bishop and Marianne Moore*, p.110).

Marriage

This institution,
perhaps one should say enterprise
out of respect for which
one says one need not change one's mind
about a thing one has believed in,

requiring public promises
of one's intention
to fulfill a private obligation:
I wonder what Adam and Eve
think of it by this time,
this fire-gilt steel
alive with goldenness;
how bright it shows –
'of circular traditions and impostures,
committing many spoils,'
requiring all one's criminal ingenuity
to avoid!
Psychology which explains everything
explains nothing,
and we are still in doubt.
Eve: beautiful woman –
I have seen her
when she was so handsome
she gave me a start,
able to write simultaneously
in three languages –
English, German, and French –
and talk in the meantime;
equally positive in demanding a commotion
and in stipulating quiet:
'*I* should like to be alone';
to which the visitor replies,
'I should like to be alone;
why not be alone together?'
Below the incandescent stars
below the incandescent fruit,
the strange experience of beauty;
its existence is too much;
it tears one to pieces
and each fresh wave of consciousness
is poison.
'See her, see her in this common world,'
the central flaw
in that first crystal-fine experiment,
this amalgamation which can never be more
than an interesting impossibility,
describing it
as 'that strange paradise

unlike flesh, stones,
gold or stately buildings,
the choicest piece of my life:
the heart rising
in its estate of peace
as a boat rises
with the rising of the water';
constrained in speaking of the serpent –
shed snakeskin in the history of politeness
not to be returned to again –
that invaluable accident
exonerating Adam.
And he has beauty also;
it's distressing – the O thou
to whom from whom,
without whom nothing – Adam;
'something feline,
something colubrine' – how true!
a crouching mythological monster
in that Persian miniature of emerald mines,
raw silk – ivory white, snow white,
oyster white, and six others –
that paddock full of leopards and giraffes –
long lemon-yellow bodies
sown with trapezoids of blue.
Alive with words,
vibrating like a cymbal
touched before it has been struck,
he has prophesied correctly –
the industrious waterfall,
'the speedy stream
which violently bears all before it,
at one time silent as the air
and now as powerful as the wind.'
'Treading chasms
on the uncertain footing of a spear,'
forgetting that there is in woman
a quality of mind
which is an instinctive manifestation
is unsafe,
he goes on speaking
in a formal customary strain
of 'past states, the present state,

seals, promises,
the evil one suffered,
the good one enjoys,
hell, heaven,
everything convenient
to promote one's joy.'
In him a state of mind
perceives what it was not
intended that he should;
'he experiences a solemn joy
in seeing that he has become an idol.'
Plagued by the nightingale
in the new leaves,
with its silence –
not its silence but its silences,
he says of it:
'It clothes me with a shirt of fire.'
'He dares not clap his hands
to make it go on
lest it should fly off;
if he does nothing, it will sleep;
if he cries out, it will not understand.'
Unnerved by the nightingale
and dazzled by the apple,
impelled by 'the illusion of a fire
effectual to extinguish fire,'
compared with which
the shining of the earth
is but deformity – a fire
'as high as deep
as bright as broad
as long as life itself,'
he stumbles over marriage,
'a very trivial object indeed'
to have destroyed the attitude
in which he stood –
the ease of the philosopher
unfathered by a woman.
Unhelpful Hymen!
a kind of overgrown cupid
reduced to insignificance
by the mechanical advertising
parading as involuntary comment,

by that experiment of Adam's
with ways out but no way in –
the ritual of marriage,
augmenting all its lavishness;
its fiddlehead ferns,
lotus flowers, opuntias, white dromedaries,
its hippopotamus –
nose and mouth combined
in one magnificent hopper –
its snake and the potent apple.
He tells us
that 'for love that will
gaze an eagle blind,
that is with Hercules
climbing the trees
in the garden of the Hesperides,
from forty-five to seventy
is the best age,'
commending it
as a fine art, as an experiment,
a duty or as merely recreation.
One must not call him ruffian
nor friction a calamity –
the fight to be affectionate:
'no truth can be fully known
until it has been tried
by the tooth of disputation.'
The blue panther with blue eyes,
entirely graceful –
one must give them the path –
the black obsidian Diana
who 'darkeneth her countenance
as a bear doth,'
the spiked hand
that has an affection for one
and proves it to the bone,
impatient to assure you
that impatience is the mark of independence
not of bondage.
'Married people often look that way' –
'seldom and cold, up and down,
mixed and malarial
with a good day and bad.'

We Occidentals are so unemotional,
self lost, the irony preserved
in 'the Ahasuerus *tête-à-tête* banquet'
with its small orchids like snakes' tongues,
with its 'good monster, lead the way,'
with little laughter
and munificence of humor
in that quixotic atmosphere of frankness
in which 'four o'clock does not exist,
but at five o'clock
the ladies in their imperious humility
are ready to receive you';
in which experience attests
that men have power
and sometimes one is made to feel it.
He says, 'What monarch would not blush
to have a wife
with hair like a shaving brush?'
The fact of woman
is 'not the sound of the flute
but very poison.'
She says, 'Men are monopolists
of "stars, garters, buttons
and other shining baubles" –
unfit to be the guardians
of another person's happiness.'
He says, 'These mummies
must be handled carefully –
'the crumbs from a lion's meal,
a couple of shins and the bit of an ear';
turn to the letter M
and you will find
that 'a wife is a coffin,'
that severe object
with the pleasing geometry
stipulating space and not people,
refusing to be buried
and uniquely disappointing,
revengefully wrought in the attitude
of an adoring child
to a distinguished parent.'
She says, 'This butterfly,
this waterfly, this nomad

that has "proposed
to settle on my hand for life" –
What can one do with it?
There must have been more time
in Shakespeare's day
to sit and watch a play.
You know so many artists who are fools.'
He says, 'You know so many fools
who are not artists.'
The fact forgot
that 'some have merely rights
while some have obligations,'
he loves himself so much,
he can permit himself
no rival in that love.
She loves herself so much,
she cannot see herself enough –
a statuette of ivory on ivory,
the logical last touch
to an expansive splendor
earned as wages for work done:
one is not rich but poor
when one can always seem so right.
What can one do for them –
these savages
condemned to disaffect
all those who are not visionaries
alert to undertake the silly task
of making people noble?
This model of petrine fidelity
who 'leaves her peaceful husband
only because she has seen enough of him' –
that orator reminding you,
'I am yours to command.'
'Everything to do with love is mystery;
it is more than a day's work
to investigate this science.'
One sees that it is rare –
that striking grasp of opposites
opposed each to the other, not to unity,
which in cycloid inclusiveness
have dwarfed the demonstration
of Columbus with the egg –

a triumph of simplicity –
that charitive Euroclydon
of frightening disinterestedness
which the world hates,
admitting:

    'I am such a cow,
    if I had a sorrow,
    I should feel it a long time;
    I am not one of those
    who have a great sorrow
    in the morning
    and a great joy at noon';

which says: 'I have encountered it
among those unpretentious
protégés of wisdom,
where seeming to parade
as the debater and the Roman,
the statesmanship
of an archaic Daniel Webster
persists to their simplicity of temper
as the essence of the matter:

    'Liberty and union
    now and forever;'

the Book on the writing-table;
the hand in the breast-pocket.'

[1924]

EDITH SITWELL

(1887-1964)

Born in Scarborough, Yorkshire, Edith Sitwell, with her brothers Osbert and Sacherevell, was at the centre of London literary life for over 40 years. Yeats, in his preface to the *Oxford Book of Modern Verse* in 1936, writes astutely of Sitwell's work: 'In its first half, through separated metaphor, through mythology, she creates, amid crows and scenery that suggest the Russian ballet and Aubrey Beardsley's final phase, a perceptual metamorphosis that seems an elegant artificial childhood; in the other half... A nightmare vision, like that of Webster, of the emblems of mortality.'

Sitwell's first book, *The Mother and Other Poems*, was published in 1915, followed by a dozen collections before her first *Collected Poems* (1930). *Façade* (1922), which was set to music by the young William Walton, remains her most popular work. Later selections included *The Canticle of the Rose: Selected Poems 1920-1947* (1949), *Façade and Other Poems 1920-1935* (1950), and further editions of her *Collected Poems* in 1954, 1993 and 2005. She edited the anthology *Wheels* from 1916 to 1921.

The butt of many jokes, Sitwell was set up as the antithesis of the Auden group in the 1930s. Her most anthologised pieces from the 40s, written during the London Blitz, show her increasing interest in religion; she converted to Catholicism in 1955. Sitwell is a more socially aware poet than she has been given credit for. Her *Elegy on Dead Fashion* (1926) and, particularly, *Gold Coast Customs* (1929), offer a blistering attack on the wealthy and vacuous upper classes. In a letter to Robert Nichols in 1918, Sitwell draws attention to a debate about the difference between men and women's poetry: 'They grumble,' she writes, 'because they say women will try to write like men and can't – then if a woman tries to invent a female poetry, and uses every feminine characteristic for the making of it, she is called trivial. It has made me furious, not because it is myself, but because it is unjust' (cited by John Pearson, in *Facades*, p.132). In a later article, 'Some Observations on Women's Poetry', published in *Vogue* in 1925, she urges that 'women's poems should above all things, be eloquent as a peacock, and there should be a fantastic element, a certain strangeness to their beauty' (cited by Anthea Trodd, *Women's Writing in English 1900-1945*, p.87).

The Mother

I

Our dreams create the babes we bear;
Our beauty goes to make them fair.
We give them all we have of good,
Our blood to drink, our hearts for food;

And in our souls they lie and rest
Until upon their mother's breast
So innocent and sweet they lie.
They live to curse us; then they die.

When he was born, it seemed the spring
Had come again with birds to sing
And blossoms dancing in the sun
Where streams released from winter run.

His sunlit hair was all my gold;
His loving eyes my wealth untold.
All heaven was hid within the breast
Whereon my child was laid to rest.

He grew to manhood. Then one came
False-hearted as Hell's blackest shame,
To steal my child from me, and thrust
The soul I loved down to the dust.

Her hungry, wicked lips were red
As that dark blood my son's hand shed;
Her eyes were black as Hell's own night,
Her ice-cold breast was winter-white. –

I had put by a little gold
To bury me when I was cold.
Her fangèd, wanton kiss to buy
My son's love willed that I should die.

The gold was hid beneath my bed;
So little, and my weary head
Was all the guard it had. They lie
So quiet and still who soon must die.

He stole to kill me while I slept –
The little son, who never wept
But that I kissed his tears away
So fast, his weeping seemed but play.

So light his footfall. Yet I heard
Its echo in my heart, and stirred
From out my weary sleep to see
My child's face bending over me.

The wicked knife flashed serpent-wise. –
Yet I saw nothing but his eyes,
And heard one little word he said
Go echoing down among the Dead.

II

They say the Dead may never dream.
But yet I heard my pierced heart scream
His name within the dark. They lie
Who say the Dead can ever die.

For in the grave I may not sleep
For dreaming that I hear him weep.
And in the dark, my dead hands grope
In search of him. O barren hope!

I cannot draw his head to rest
Deep down upon my wounded breast...
He gave the breast that fed him well
To suckle the small worms of Hell.

The little wicked thoughts that fed
Upon the weary, helpless Dead...
They whispered o'er my broken heart,
They stuck their fangs deep in the smart.

'The child she bore with bloody sweat
And agony has paid his debt.
Through that bleak face the stark winds play;
The crows have chased his soul away.

'His body is a blackened rag
Upon the tree – a monstrous flag.'
Thus one Worm to the other saith.
Those slow mean servitors of Death,

They chuckling said: 'Your soul grown blind
With anguish, is the shrieking Wind
That blows the flame that never dies
About his empty, lidless eyes.'

I tore them from my heart. I said:
'The life-blood that my son's hand shed,
That from my broken heart outburst
I'd give again, to quench his thirst.

He did no sin. But cold blind earth
The body was that gave him birth.
All mine, all mine the sin; the love
I bore him was not deep enough.'

[1915]

Waltz

Daisy and Lily,
Lazy and silly,
Walk by the shore of the wan grassy sea, –
Talking once more 'neath a swan-bosomed tree.
Rose castles,
Tourelles,
Those bustles
Where swells
Each foam-bell of ermine,
They roam and determine
What fashions have been and what fashions will be, –
What tartan leaves born,
What crinolines worn.
By Queen Thetis,
Pelisses
Of tarlatine blue,
Like the thin plaided leaves that the castle crags grew;
Or velours d'Afrande:
On the water-gods' land
Her hair seemed gold trees on the honey-cell sand
When the thickest gold spangles, on deep water seen,
Were like twanging guitar and like cold mandoline,
And the nymphs of great caves,
With hair like gold waves,
Of Venus, wore tarlatine.
Louise and Charlottine
(Boreas' daughters)

And the nymphs of deep waters,
The nymph Taglioni, Grisi the ondine,
Wear plaided Victoria and thin Clementine
Like the crinolined waterfalls;
Wood-nymphs wear bonnets, shawls,
Elegant parasols
Floating are seen.
The Amazons wear balzarine of jonquille
Beside the blond lace of a deep-falling rill;
Through glades like a nun
They run from and shun
The enormous and gold-rayed rustling sun;
And the nymphs of the fountains
Descend from the mountains
Like elegant willows
On their deep barouche pillows,
In cashmere Alvandar, barège Isabelle,
Like bells of bright water from clearest wood-well.
Our élégantes favouring bonnets of blond,
The stars in their apiaries,
Sylphs in their aviaries,
Seeing them, spangle these, and the sylphs fond
From their aviaries fanned
With each long fluid hand
The manteaux espagnols,
Mimic the waterfalls
Over the long and the light summer land.

.   .   .   .   .

So Daisy and Lily,
Lazy and silly,
Walk by the shore of the wan grassy sea,
Talking once more 'neath a swan-bosomed tree.
Rose castles,
Tourelles,
Those bustles!
Mourelles
Of the shade in their train follow.
Ladies, how vain, – hollow, –
Gone is the sweet swallow, –
Gone, Philomel!

1923 [1926]

Sir Beelzebub

When
Sir
Beelzebub called for his syllabub in the hotel in Hell
        Where Proserpine first fell,
Blue as the gendarmerie were the waves of the sea,
        (Rocking and shocking the barmaid).

Nobody comes to give him his rum but the
Rim of the sky hippopotamus-glum
Enhances the chances to bless with a benison
Alfred Lord Tennyson crossing the bar laid
With cold vegetation from pale deputations
Of temperance workers (all signed In Memoriam)
Hoping with glory to trip up the Laureate's feet,
        (Moving in classical metres)...

Like Balaclava, the lava came down from the
Roof, and the sea's blue wooden gendarmerie
Took them in charge while Beelzebub roared for his rum.
        ...None of them come!

1922 [1922]

Still Falls the Rain
The Raids, 1940. Night and Dawn

Still falls the Rain –
Dark as the world of man, black as our loss –
Blind as the nineteen hundred and forty nails
Upon the Cross.

Still falls the Rain
With a sound like the pulse of the heart that is changed to the
        hammer-beat
In the Potter's Field, and the sound of the impious feet

On the Tomb:
　　　　Still falls the Rain
In the Field of Blood where the small hopes breed and the human
　　　　brain
Nurtures its greed, that worm with the brow of Cain.

Still falls the Rain
At the feet of the Starved Man hung upon the Cross.
Christ that each day, each night, nails there, have mercy on us –
On Dives and on Lazarus:
Under the Rain the sore and the gold are as one.

Still falls the Rain –
Still falls the Blood from the Starved Man's wounded Side:
He bears in His Heart all wounds, – those of the light that died,
The last faint spark
In the self-murdered heart, the wounds of the sad uncomprehending
　　　　dark,
The wounds of the baited bear, –
The blind and weeping bear whom the keepers beat
On his helpless flesh...the tears of the hunted hare.

Still falls the Rain –
Then – O Ile leape up to my God: who pulles me doune –
See, see where Christ's blood streames in the firmament:
It flows from the Brow we nailed upon the tree
Deep to the dying, to the thirsting heart
That holds the fires of the world, – dark-smirched with pain
As Caesar's laurel crown.

Then sounds the voice of One who like the heart of man
Was once a child who among beasts has lain –
'Still do I love, still shed my innocent light, my Blood, for thee.'

1940 [1942]

EDNA ST VINCENT MILLAY

(1892-1950)

Born in Rockland, Maine, Millay came to attention when her poem 'Renascence' was published in 1912. After a preparatory period at Barnard College, she attended Vassar in 1913, studying languages and literature. During this period she also acted and wrote plays. Her first collection, *Renascence and Other Poems*, appeared in 1917. Millay moved to New York where she earned her living as an actor and writer. *A Few Figs from Thistles* was published in 1920 and *Second April* in 1921. In 1923 she published *The Harp-Weaver and Other Poems* and was the first woman to receive the Pulitzer Prize for poetry.

In 1923 she married Eugen Jan Boissevain, widower of Inez Milholland, and they set up home near Austerlitz, New York in 1925. *The Buck in the Snow* was published in 1928, and followed by *Fatal Interview* (1931), a sequence of 52 sonnets recounting her affair with a much younger man, George Dillon, with whom she later translated Baudelaire's *Les Fleurs du Mal* (1936). Her other books include *Wine from These Grapes* (1934), *Conversation at Midnight* (1937), *Huntsman, What Quarry?* (1939), *Make Bright the Arrows: 1940 Notebook* (1940), and the long poem *The Murder of Lidice* (1942). Millay was a close friend of the American poet Elinor Wylie (1885-1928).

'When I too long have looked upon your face...'

When I too long have looked upon your face,
Wherein for me a brightness unobscured
Save by the mists of brightness has its place,
And terrible beauty not to be endured,
I turn away reluctant from your light,
And stand irresolute, a mind undone,
A silly, dazzled thing deprived of sight
From having looked too long upon the sun.
Then is my daily life a narrow room
In which a little while, uncertainly,
Surrounded by impenetrable gloom,
Among familiar things grown strange to me
Making my way, I pause, and feel, and hark,
Till I become accustomed to the dark.

[1921]

Wild Swans

I looked in my heart while the wild swans went over.
And what did I see I had not seen before?
Only a question less or a question more;
Nothing to match the flight of wild birds flying.
Tiresome heart, forever living and dying,
House without air, I leave you and lock your door.
Wild swans, come over the town, come over
The town again, trailing your legs and crying!

[1921]

The Buck in the Snow

White sky, over the hemlocks bowed with snow,
Saw you not at the beginning of evening the antlered buck and his doe
Standing in the apple-orchard? I saw them. I saw them suddenly go,
Tails up, with long leaps lovely and slow,
Over the stone-wall into the wood of hemlocks bowed with snow.

Now lies he here, his wild blood scalding the snow.

How strange a thing is death, bringing to his knees, bringing to his
          antlers
The buck in the snow.
How strange a thing, – a mile away by now, it may be,
Under the heavy hemlocks that as the moments pass
Shift their loads a little, letting fall a feather of snow –
Life, looking out attentive from the eyes of the doe.

[1928]

SYLVIA TOWNSEND WARNER
(1893-1978)

Novelist, short story writer, biographer, and translator of Proust, Warner published her first collection of poems, *The Espalier*, in 1925. Her other books of poetry include *Time Importuned* (1928), *Opus 7* (1931), *Rainbow* (1932), *Boxwood*

(1960), *King Duffus and Other Poems* (1968), *Twelve Poems* (1980), and the posthumously published *Collected Poems* (1982) and *Selected Poems* (1985). Also a highly respected musicologist, she studied composition with Vaughan Williams and was the editor of a ten-volume series, *Tudor Church Music* (1917-1927). From the early 1930s she was closely connected, with her partner Valentine Ackland, with the Communist Party, the Left Book Club and the Association of Writers for Intellectual Liberty, and during the Spanish Civil War she was a volunteer in Spain. With Ackland she co-authored a collection of poems, *Whether a Dove or a Seagull* (1933).

Jane Dowson has commented on Warner's awareness 'of the double restraints of the lesbian existence and, of the pressures upon the single woman; she was also acutely aware of the frustrations of the housewife' (*Women's Poetry of the 1930s*, p.152). John Lucas connects her work, via Vaughan Williams, with Whitman and Charlotte Mew, through her interest in 'writing about marginal figures who shun or are shunned from conventional communities' (*Starting to Explain*, p.189).

In a lecture delivered to the Royal Society in 1959 Warner declares the woman writer to be 'obstinate and sly...[t]hough a woman writing today is not hampered by an attribute of innate moral superiority, she has to reckon with an attribution of innate physical superiority; and this too can be cumbersome. There is for instance bi-location. It is well-known that a woman can be in two places at once; at her desk and her washing machine...' [...] '[W]omen have entered literature – breathless, inequipped, and with nothing but their wits to trust to. A few minutes ago, or a few centuries ago, they were writing a letter about apoplexy, or a recipe for custard, now they are inside the palace writing with great clearness...' (*Collected Poems*, pp.267-68; 271). Warner sees the dualities associated with middle-class women of 'good taste, prudence, acceptance of limitations, compliance with standards and that typically middle-class merit of making the most of what one's got' (*CP*, p.274) as ultimately limiting, suggesting that the lack of great women writers is due to social not sexual disadvantage.

Waiting at Cerbere

And on the hillside
That is the colour of peasant's bread,
Is the rectangular
White village of the dead.

No one stirs in those streets,
Out of those dark doorways no one comes,
At the tavern of the Black Cross
Only the cicada strums.

And below, where the headland
Strips into rock, the white mane
Of foam like a quickened breath
Rises and falls again;

And above, the road
Zigzagging tier on tier
Above the terraced vineyards,
Goes on to the frontier.

[1939]

In April

I am come to the threshold of a spring
Where there will be nothing
To stand between me and the smite
Of the martin's scooping flight,
Between me and the halloo
Of the first cuckoo.
'As you hear the first cuckoo,
So you will be all summer through.'
This year I shall hear it naked and alone;
And lengthening days and strengthening sun will show
Me my solitary shadow,
My cypressed shadow – but no,
My Love, I was not alone; in my mind I was talking with you
When I heard the first cuckoo,
And gentle as thistledown his call was blown.

[1980]

RUTH PITTER
(1897-1992)

Pitter grew up in Ilford, Essex. Her parents were teachers in the East End of London, and her earliest poems were published while she was still at school. She left her studies at the University of London to work in the War Office in 1914. With the help of Hilaire Belloc, *First Poems* was published in 1920. It was followed by many books, including *First and Second Poems* (1927), *Persephone in Hades* (1931), *A Mad Lady's Garland* (1934), *The Spirit Watches* (1939), *The Rude Potato* (1941), *The Bridge: Poems 1939-1944* (1945), *On Cats* (1947), *Urania* (1950), *The Ermine: Poems 1942-1952* (1953), *Still by Choice* (1966), *End of Drought* (1975) and *A Heaven to Find* (1987), as well as three editions of *Collected Poems* in 1969, 1990 and 1996. In her introduction to the *Collected Poems* (1996), Elizabeth Jennings praises Pitter for her 'comic spirit' as well for her nature poetry: 'As she becomes more adept at making her subjects and themes inseparable from form and music, so her observations of Nature appear more exact and simple...Perhaps paradoxically, the closer she keeps to the life of natural creatures, the more frequent does the visionary element in her work appear' (p.17). Pitter earned her living as a painter of furniture and after her retirement took up gardening. She had a successful television career on the 'Brains Trust' and in 1955 became the first woman to receive the Queen's Gold Medal for Poetry.

The Coffin Worm

which consider

The Worm unto his love: lo, here's fresh store;
Want irks us less as men are pinched the more.
Why dost thou lag? thou pitiest the man?
Fall to, the while I teach thee what I can.
Men in their lives full solitary be:
We are their last and kindest company.
Lo, where care's claws have been! those marks are grim;
Go, gentle Love, erase the scar from him.

Hapless perchance in love (most men are so),
Our quaint felicity he could not know:
We and our generation shall sow love
Throughout that frame he was not master of;
Flatter his wishful beauties; in his ear
Whisper he is at last beloved here;
Sing him (and in no false and siren strain)
We will not leave him while a shred remain
On his sweet bones: then shall our labour cease,
And the imperishable part find peace
Even from love; meanwhile how blest he lies,
Love in his heart, his empty hands, his eyes.

[1934]

Love and the Child

Like mist in the holy morning, the thin veil of love
Mantles him over, and colours all he is conscious of;
Till time like the mounting sun rolling the mist to the crests
Bares all but the secret parts and the lips and the breasts.

Leave him the light shade, leave him his rosy tent;
Rend not the thin stuff, for death enters in at the rent:
Touch him but lightly, and see that you speak only truth,
For the sake of the secret parts and the breast and the mouth.

[1939]

The Bat

Lightless, unholy, eldritch thing,
Whose murky and erratic wing
Swoops so sickeningly, and whose
Aspect to the female Muse
Is a demon's, made of stuff
Like tattered, sooty waterproof,
Looking dirty, clammy, cold.

Wicked, poisonous, and old:
I have maligned thee!... for the Cat
Lately caught a little bat,
Seized it softly, bore it in.
On the carpet, dark as sin
In the lamplight, painfully
It limped about, and could not fly.

Even fear must yield to love,
And pity makes the depths to move.
Though sick with horror, I must stoop,
Grasp it gently, take it up,
And carry it, and place it where
It could resume the twilight air.

Strange revelation! warm as milk,
Clean as a flower, smooth as silk!

O what a piteous face appears,
What great fine thin translucent ears!
What chestnut down and crapy wings,
Finer than any lady's things –
And O a little one that clings!

Warm, clean, and lovely, though not fair,
And burdened with a mother's care:
Go hunt the hurtful fly, and bear
My blessing to your kind in air.

[1945]

NAOMI MITCHISON
(1897-1999)

Born in Edinburgh, Naomi Haldane grew up in a wealthy family; her brother
was the biologist J.B.S. Haldane. She married Richard (later Baron) Mitchison,
a Labour MP, in 1916. Having begun to study for a science degree at Oxford,
she left to train as a nurse. She published four books of poetry: *The Laburnum
Branch* (1926), *The Delicate Fire: Short Stories and Poems* (1933), *The Alban
Goes Out* (1939) and *The Cleansing of the Knife and Other Poems* (1978). Extra-
ordinarily prolific, she published at least one book, sometimes as many as three,
nearly every year, across a wide range of genres: autobiography, science fiction,
historical fiction, drama, essays and biography. A deeply committed socialist
and feminist, she kept a diary for the Mass Observation movement, and pub-
lished a book, *Comments on Birth Control* (1930), working in the early days at
the North Kensington family planning clinic. She also wrote a book of advice
for children and parents, and appeared in a film for the Socialist Film Council in
1933 called *The Road to Hell* (1933). She stood as a Labour candidate in 1935,
and was active in local politics in Scotland from 1947 to 1976. In the 1960s she
became an advisor to the Bakgatha tribe in Botswana, a country she visited many
times. Mitchison also bore seven children. She was friendly with Auden, and
particularly close to Stevie Smith, with whom she enjoyed a long correspondence.

Dick and Colin at the Salmon Nets

Outside, in the rain, on the edge of evening,
   There are men netting salmon at the mouth of the Tweed;
Two men go out of the house to watch this thing,
     Down the steep banks and field tracks to their minds' and
      bodies' need.

How can I, being a woman, write all that down?
How can I see the quiet pushing salmon against the net?
How can I see behind the sticks and pipe-smoke, the intent frown,
And the things speech cannot help with on which man's heart is set?

Must we be apart always, you watching the salmon nets, you in the rain,
　　Thinking of love or politics or what I don't know,
While I stay in with the children and books, and never again
　　Haul with the men on the fish nets, or walking slow
Through the wet grass in fields where horses have lain,
　　Be as sure of my friends as I am of the long Tweed's flow?

[1933]

The House of the Hare

At the time I was four years old
I went to glean with the women,
Working the way they told;
My eyes were blue like bluebells,
Lighter than oats my hair;
I came from the house of the Haldanes
Of work and thinking and prayer
To the God who is crowned with thorn,
The friend of the Boar and the Bear,
But oh when I went from there,
In the corn, in the corn, in the corn,
I was married young to a hare!

We went to kirk on the Sunday
And the Haldanes did not see
That a Haldane had been born
To run from the Boar and the Bear,
And the thing had happened to me
The day that I went with the gleaners,
The day that I built the corn-house,
That is not built with prayer.
For oh I was clean set free,
In the corn, in the corn, in the corn,
I had lived three days with the hare!

[1978]

70

FRANCES BELLERBY

(1899-1975)

Frances Bellerby was born Mary Eirene Frances Parker in Bristol. Her father was a clergyman, and her mother a nurse, who later committed suicide, while her only brother was killed in the First World War. In the mid 1920s, she suffered a fall which damaged her spine, an injury which was to affect her for the rest of her life. A teacher, writer and journalist, she married the socialist John Bellerby in 1929, but left him temporarily in 1934, before finally ending the marriage in 1942. At this point she began to write poetry again, and her first collection *Plash Mill and Other Poems* was published in 1946 and followed by *The Brightening Cloud* (1949), *The Stone Angel and the Stone Man* (1957), *The Stuttering Water* (1970) and *The First Known and Other Poems* (1975). Two editions of *Selected Poems* have been published, edited first by Charles Causley (1970) and later by Anne Stevenson (1986). In 1950 Bellerby was diagnosed with breast cancer, and struggled with mental and physical illness until the end of her life. Her other books include the novels *Shadowy Bricks* (1932) and *Hath the Rain a Father?* (1946), and two collections of short stories, *Come to an End* (1939) and *The Acorn and the Cup* (1948); Jeremy Hooker edited her *Collected Short Stories* in 1986.

Voices

I heard those voices today again:
Voices of women and children, down in that hollow
Of blazing light into which swoops the tree-darkened lane
Before it mounts up into the shadow again.

I turned the bend – just as always before
There was no one at all down there in the sunlit hollow;
Only ferns in the wall, foxgloves by the hanging door
Of that blind old desolate cottage. And just as before

I noticed the leaping glitter of light
Where the stream runs under the lane; in that mine-dark archway
– Water and stones unseen as though in the gloom of night –
Like glittering fish slithers and leaps the light.

I waited long at the bend of the lane,
But heard only the murmuring water under the archway.
Yet I tell you, I've been to that place again and again,
And always, in summer weather, those voices are plain,
Down near that broken house, just where the tree-darkened lane
Swoops into the hollow of light before mounting to shadow again...

Night

Behind the silence is sound,
Rhythmic orchestral background:
Chuckle rattle thud of winter water
Swirling hurling, froth-sudded brim-levelled, after
Dark-faced weeks of rain.
Now sharp-blade yelps the owl close by;
Again; and, further off, again
Although without softest whisper of flight –
And at once the moonlight-frozen night
Hollows undinted round the sword-slash lightning-flash cry.

Am I the dreamer or the dream?...
There's something now half-heard
Under the winter symphony of the stream,
And close behind that shock of flashing cry –
And now in the hiss of rain's quick violence,
Not a sound in silence leaves the heart undisturbed.
But *what* do I half-sense?
Someone commenting? Calling?
Who? Is it I?
Or am I myself called, from far, always too far, away,
The voice lost swiftly as a wild star seen falling, falling,
Like the bright brief ghost of a shot bird?...

[1947]

LAURA (RIDING) JACKSON
(1901-91)

Laura Riding was born Laura Reichenthal in New York City, attended Cornell University, and was briefly married to a teacher, Louis Gottschalk. She published her first work as Laura Riding Gottschalk and was associated initially with writers such as John Crowe Ransom, Allen Tate, Merrill Moore and others who contributed to the magazine *The Fugitive*, published in Nashville between 1922 and 1925, and who were known collectively as 'The Fugitives'. Laura Riding left for Britain at the end of 1925 at the invitation of Robert Graves and his wife Nancy Nicholson, and lived in Egypt, England and Majorca before returning to the States in 1939. Her first collection, *The Close Chaplet*, was published in 1926. She wrote, with Graves, *A Survey of Modernist Poetry* (1927), and their *A Pamphlet Against Anthologies* appeared in 1928. She published several collections followed by a *Collected Poems* in 1938, but stopped writing poetry in 1940 because she felt there was nowhere further toward truthfulness to go with the form. Editions of her work include *The Poems of Laura Riding* (1980 & 1986), *First Awakenings: The Early Poems of Laura Riding* (1992), *Selected Poems* (1994), and *The Laura Riding Jackson Reader* (2005), which includes her 'Introduction to a Broadcast', from a radio programme she made for the BBC in 1962. The programme was heard by Sylvia Plath, who noted after her poem 'Little Fugue', 'on listening to Laura Riding'. Riding's broadcast included this comment: '...there is no vital connection between the verbal successes of poetry and our actual speaking needs – they are no more than dramatic effects produced with words. I have learned that language does not lend itself naturally to the poetic style, but is warped in being fitted into it; that the only style that can yield a natural and happy use of words is the style of truth, a rule of trueness of voice and mind sustained in every morsel of one's speech; that for the practice of the style of truth to become a thing of the present, poetry must become a thing of the past.' In *The Enemy Self* (1990), Barbara Adams suggests convincingly that Riding's 'The Virgin' and 'The Tiger' were influential to Plath's later work.

The Tiger

The tiger in me I know late, not burning bright.
Of such women as I am, they say,
'Woman, many women in one,' winking.
Such women as I say, thinking,
'A procession of one, reiteration
Of blinking eyes and disentangled brains
Measuring their length in love.
Each yard of thought is an embrace.
To these I have charms.
Shame, century creature.'
To myself, hurrying, I whisper,
The lechery of time greases their eyes.
Lust, earlier than time,
Unwinds their minds.
The green anatomy of desire
Plain as through glass
Quickens as I pass.'

Earlier than lust, not plain,
Behind a darkened face of memory,
My inner animal revives.

Beware, that I am tame.
Beware philosophies
Wherein I yield.

They cage me on three sides.
The fourth is glass.
Not to be image of the beast in me,
I press the tiger forward.
I crash through.
Now we are two.
One rides.

And now I know the tiger late,
And now they pursue:
'A woman in a skin, mad at her heels
With pride, pretending chariot wheels –
Fleeing our learned days,
She reassumes the brute.'

The first of the pursuers found me.
With lady-ears I listened.
'Dear face, to find you here
After such tiger-hunt and pressing of
Thick forest, to find you here
In high house in a jungle,
To brave as any room
The tiger-cave and as in any room
Find woman in the room
With dear face shaking her dress
To wave like any picture queen...'
'Dear pursuer, to find me thus
Belies no tiger. The tiger runs and rides,
But the lady is not venturous.
Like any picture queen she hides
And is unhappy in her room,
Covering her eyes against the latest year,
Its learning of old queens,
Its death to queens and pictures,
Its lust of century creatures,
And century creatures as one woman,
Such a woman as I,
Mirage of all green forests –
The colour of the season always
When hope lives of abolished pleasures.'

So to the first pursuer I prolonged
Woman's histories and shames,
And yielded as became a queen
Picture-dreaming in a room
Among silk provinces where pain
Ruined her body without stain –
So white, so out of time, so story-like.
While woman's pride escaped
In tiger stripes.

Hymn to the hostage queen
And her debauched provinces.
Down fell her room,
Down fell her high couches.
The first pursuer rose from his hot cloak.

'Company,' he cried, 'the tiger made magic
While you slept and I dreamt of ravages.
The queen was dust.'
And Queen, Queen, Queen,
Crowded the Captain's brain.
And Queen, Queen, Queen,
Spurred the whole train
With book-thoughts
And exploits of queen's armies
On gold and silver cloth.
Until they stumbled on their eyes,
Read the number of the year,
Remembered the fast tiger.

The tiger recalled man's fear
Of beast, in man-sweat they ran back,
Opened their books at the correct pages.
The chapter closed with queens and shepherdesses.
'Peace to their dim tresses,'
Chanted the pious sages.

And now the tiger in me I knew late.
'O pride,' I comforted, 'rest.
The mischief and the rape
Cannot come through.
We are in the time of never yet
Where bells peal backward,
Peal "forget, forget".'

Here am I found forgotten.
The sun is used. The men are in the book.
I, woman, have removed the window
And read in my high house in the dark,
Sitting long after reading, as before,
Waiting, as in the book, to hear the bell,
Though long since has fallen away the door,
Long since, when like a tiger I was pursued '
And the first pursuer, at such and such a date,
Found how the tiger takes the lady
Far away where she is gentle.
In the high forest she is gentle.

She is patient in a high house.
Ah me, ah me, says every lady in the end,
Putting the tiger in its cage
Inside her lofty head.
And weeps reading her own story.
And scarcely knows she weeps,
So loud the tiger roars.
Or thinks to close her eyes,
Though surely she must be sleeping,
To go on without knowing weeping,
Sleeping or not knowing,
Not knowing weeping,
Not knowing sleeping.

[1928]

The Troubles of a Book

The trouble of a book is first to be
No thoughts to nobody,
Then to lie as long unwritten
As it will lie unread,
Then to build word for word an author
And occupy his head
Until the head declares vacancy
To make full publication
Of running empty.

76

The trouble of a book is secondly
To keep awake and ready
And listening like an innkeeper,
Wishing, not wishing for a guest,
Torn between hope of no rest
And hope of rest.
Uncertainly the pages doze
And blink open to passing fingers
With landlord smile, then close.

The trouble of a book is thirdly
To speak its sermon, then look the other way,
Arouse commotion in the margin,
Where tongue meets the eye,
But claim no experience of panic,
No complicity in the outcry.
The ordeal of a book is to give no hint
Of ordeal, to be flat and witless
Of the upright sense of print.

The trouble of a book is chiefly
To be nothing but book outwardly;
To wear binding like binding,
Bury itself in book-death,
Yet to feel all but book;
To breath live words, yet with the breath
Of letters; to address liveliness
In reading eyes, be answered with
Letters and bookishness.

[1928]

You or You

How well, you, you resemble!
Yes, you resemble well enough yourself
For me to swear the likeness
Is no other and remarkable
And matchless and so that

I love you therefore.
And all else which is very like,
Perfect counterfeit, pure almost,
Love, high animation, loyal unsameness –
To the end true, unto
Unmasking, self.

I am for you both sharp and dull.
I doubt thoroughly
And thoroughly believe.
I love you doubly,
How well, you, you deceive,
How well, you, you resemble.
I love you therefore.

[1930]

STEVIE SMITH

(1902-71)

Born in Hull, Florence Smith moved to Palmers Green, London, with her mother and her aunt when she was three, and lived in the family house for the rest of her life. She worked for most of her life as a private secretary at Newnes-Pearson, finally leaving to look after her bedridden aunt. *Novel on Yellow Paper*, her first novel, was published in 1936 and followed in 1937 by her first book of poems, *A Good Time Was Had By All*. She published two further novels, *Over the Frontier* (1938) and *The Holiday* (1949). Her second book of poems, *Tender Only to One* (1938), was followed by *Mother, What Is Man?* (1942), *Harold's Leap* (1950), *Not Waving but Drowning* (1957), *Selected Poems* (1962) [with 11 new poems], *The Frog Prince and Other Poems* (1966), *Two in One* (1971) [*Selected Poems* and *The Frog Prince*], and *Scorpion and Other Poems* (1972). She received the Queen's Gold Medal for Poetry in 1969.

Many of her poems are accompanied by what she calls her 'doodling', and it could be argued that these oblique 'supplements' to the poems are as essential to interpretation as the illustrations of Blake, whom she greatly admired. Smith has been championed by writers as different as Larkin and Heaney. Her quirky "dialogic" poems which so often revise the work of male writers to her own ends, and her interest and transformation of fairytale and myth, make her an essential, if inimitable, figure in the development of women's poetry. Smith herself did not consider gender an important factor in poetry: 'Differences between men and women poets are best seen when the poets are bad...But neither odd lives nor sex really signify, it is a person's poems that stand to be judged.' (*Me Again*, p.181). Later editions of her work include *Collected Poems* (1975), *Selected Poems* (1978), *Me Again: The Uncollected Writings of Stevie Smith* (1981) and *Stevie Smith: A Selection* (1983).

Souvenir de Monsieur Poop

I am the self-appointed guardian of English literature,
I believe tremendously in the significance of age;
I believe that a writer is wise at 50,
Ten years wiser at 60, at 70 a sage.
I believe that juniors are lively, to be encouraged with discretion
and snubbed,
I believe also that they are bouncing, communistic, ill mannered
and, of course, young.
But I never define what I mean by youth
Because the word undefined is more useful for general purposes
of abuse.
I believe that literature is a school where only those who apply
themselves diligently to their tasks acquire merit.
And only they after the passage of a good many years (see above).
But then I am an old fogey.
I always write more in sorrow than in anger.
I am, after all, devoted to Shakespeare, Milton,
And, coming to our own times,
Of course
Housman.
I have never been known to say a word against the established
classics,
I am in fact devoted to the established classics.
In the service of literature I believe absolutely in the principle of
division;
I divide into age groups and also into schools.
This is in keeping with my scholastic mind, and enables me to
trounce
Not only youth
(Which might be thought intellectually frivolous by pedants) but
also periodical tendencies,
To ventilate, in a word, my own political and moral philosophy.
(When I say that I am an old fogey, I am, of course, joking.)
English literature, as I see it, requires to be defended
By a person of integrity and essential good humour
Against the forces of fanaticism, idiosyncrasy and anarchy.
I perfectly apprehend the perilous nature of my convictions
And I am prepared to go to the stake
For Shakespeare, Milton,
And, coming to our own times,

Of course
Housman.
I cannot say more than that, can I?
And I do not deem it advisable, in the interests of the editor to
        whom I am spatially contracted,
To say less.

[1938]

The River God

I may be smelly and I may be old,
Rough in my pebbles, reedy in my pools,
But where my fish float by I bless their swimming
And I like the people to bathe in me, especially women.
But I can drown the fools
Who bathe too close to the weir, contrary to rules.
And they take a long time drowning
As I throw them up now and then in a spirit of clowning.
Hi yih, yippity-yap, merrily I flow,
O I may be an old foul river but I have plenty of go.
Once there was a lady who was too bold
She bathed in me by the tall black cliff where the water runs cold,
So I brought her down here
To be my beautiful dear.
Oh will she stay with me will she stay
This beautiful lady, or will she go away?
She lies in my beautiful deep river bed with many a weed
To hold her, and many a waving reed.
Oh who would guess what a beautiful white face lies there
Waiting for me to smooth and wash away the fear
She looks at me with. Hi yih, do not let her
Go. There is no one on earth who does not forget her
Now. They say I am a foolish old smelly river
But they do not know of my wide original bed
Where the lady waits, with her golden sleepy head.
If she wishes to go I will not forgive her.

[1950]

The After-thought

Rapunzel Rapunzel let down your hair
It is I your beautiful lover who am here
And when I come up this time I will bring a rope ladder with me
And then we can both escape into the dark wood immediately.
This must be one of those things, as Edgar Allan Poe says
        somewhere in a book,
Just because it is perfectly obvious one is certain to overlook.

I wonder sometimes by the way if Poe isn't a bit introspective,
One can stand about getting rather reflective,
But thinking about the way the mind works, you know,
Makes one inactive, one simply doesn't know which way to go;
Like the centipede in the poem who was corrupted by the toad
And ever after never did anything but lie in the middle of the road,
Or the old gurus of India I've seen, believe it or not,
Standing seventy-five years on their toes until they dropped.
Or Titurel, for that matter, in his odd doom
Crying: I rejoice because by the mercy of the Saviour I continue
        to live in the tomb.

What is that darling? You cannot hear me?
That's odd. I can hear you quite distinctly.

[1950]

Not Waving but Drowning

Nobody heard him, the dead man,
But still he lay moaning:
I was much further out than you thought
And not waving but drowning.

81

Poor chap, he always loved larking
And now he's dead
It must have been too cold for him his heart gave way,
They said.

Oh, no no no, it was too cold always
(Still the dead one lay moaning)
I was much too far out all my life
And not waving but drowning.

1953 [1957]

A Dream of Comparison
After reading Book Ten of 'Paradise Lost'.

Two ladies walked on the soft green grass
On the bank of a river by the sea
And one was Mary and the other Eve
And they talked philosophically.

'Oh to be Nothing,' said Eve, 'oh for a
Cessation of consciousness
With no more impressions beating in
Of various experiences.'

'How can Something envisage Nothing?' said Mary,
'Where's your philosophy gone?'
'Storm back through the gates of Birth,' cried Eve,
'Where were you before you were born?'

Mary laughed: 'I love Life,
I would fight to the death for it,
That's a feeling you say? I will find
A reason for it.'

They walked by the estuary,
Eve and the Virgin Mary,
And they talked until nightfall,
But the difference between them was radical.

[1957]

A House of Mercy

It was a house of female habitation,
Two ladies fair inhabited the house,
And they were brave. For although Fear knocked loud
Upon the door, and said he must come in,
They did not let him in.

There were also two feeble babes, two girls,
That Mrs S. had by her husband had,
He soon left them and went away to sea,
Nor sent them money, nor came home again
Except to borrow back
Her Naval Officer's Wife's Allowance from Mrs S.
Who gave it him at once, she thought she should.

There was also the ladies' aunt
And babes' great aunt, a Mrs Martha Hearn Clode,
And she was elderly.
These ladies put their money all together
And so we lived.

I was the younger of the feeble babes
And when I was a child my mother died
And later Great Aunt Martha Hearn Clode died
And later still my sister went away.

Now I am old I tend my mother's sister
The noble aunt who so long tended us,
Faithful and True her name is. Tranquil.
Also Sardonic. And I tend the house.

It is a house of female habitation
A house expecting strength as it is strong
A house of aristocratic mould that looks apart
When tears fall; counts despair
Derisory. Yet it has kept us well. For all its faults,
If they are faults, of sternness and reserve,
It is a Being of warmth I think; at heart
A house of mercy.

[1966]

The Word

My heart leaps up with streams of joy,
My lips tell of drouth;
Why should my heart be full of joy
And not my mouth?

I fear the Word, to speak or write it down,
I fear all that is brought to birth and born;
This fear has turned my joy into a frown.

[1972]

UNA MARSON
(1905-65)

Born in Jamaica, the daughter of a Baptist minister, Marson attended Hampton High School. She then went on to work for the Salvation Army and the YMCA. She left for England in 1932 in the same year as her play *At What Price* was performed. *Tropic Reveries*, her first book of poems, was self-published in 1930. It was followed by *Heights and Depths* (1931) and *The Moth and the Star* (1937), both self-published. Marson was a committed feminist and campaigned on behalf of women, particularly highlighting discrimination against black women. She became the personal secretary of Haile Selassie and in 1936 travelled to the United Nations to plead on behalf of Abyssinia (now Ethiopia) when it was attacked by Italy. The first black woman broadcaster in Britain, she was employed by the BBC in 1941 to develop the *Calling the West Indies* broadcasts. She appears in the film *West Indies Calling* (1943), an account of the black war effort, with Learie Constantine and Ulric Cross. She contributed twice to George Orwell's poetry programme, *Voice*, which was edited by George Orwell, reading poetry alongside T.S. Eliot and William Empson, amongst others. Her radio programme *Caribbean Voices* provided a platform for emerging Caribbean poets. Her poetic influences included Langston Hughes, James Weldon Johnson and Bessie Smith. Also influenced by jazz and the blues, Marson was one of the first women to use Jamaican dialect in poetry. Her final collection of poems, *Towards the Stars*, was published by the University of London Press in 1945. Marson returned to Jamaica in the same year, continuing in her successful career as a journalist, and lived in the US from 1952 to 1960. She did not return to Britain until 1964.

Getting de Spirit

Lord gie you chile de spirit
Let her shout
Lord gie you chile de power
An' let her pray –
Hallelujah – Amen –
Shout sister – shout
God is sen' you His spirit
Shout sister – shout.

Shout sister – shout –
Hallelujah – Amen.
Can't you feel de spirit
Shout sister – shout
Hallelujah – Amen.

Join de chorus,
We feel it flowing o'er us –
You is no chile of satan
So get de spirit
And shout – sister – shout –
Hallelujah – Amen.
Shout – Sister – shout!

[1937]

Kinky Hair Blues

Gwine find a beauty shop
Cause I ain't a belle.
Gwine find a beauty shop
Cause I ain't a lovely belle.
The boys pass me by,
They say I's not so swell.

See oder young gals
So slick and smart.
See dose oder young gals
So slick and smart.
I jes gwine die on de shelf
If I don't mek a start.

I hate dat ironed hair
And dat bleaching skin.
Hate dat ironed hair
And dat bleaching skin.
But I'll be all alone
If I don't fall in.

Lord 'tis you did gie me
All dis kinky hair.
'Tis you did gie me
All dis kinky hair,
And I don't envy gals
What got dose locks so fair.

I like me black face
And me kinky hair.
I like me black face
And me kinky hair.
But nobody loves dem,
I jes don't tink it's fair.

Now I's gwine press me hair
And bleach me skin.
I's gwine press me hair
And bleach me skin.
What won't a gal do
Some kind a man to win.

[1937]

SHEILA WINGFIELD
(1906-92)

Born in Hampshire to an English father and an Irish mother, Wingfield (*née* Beddington) spent much of her married life in Ireland. She attended Roedean School and a finishing school in Paris before marrying the Viscount of Powerscourt, who lived at Powerscourt House, near Enniskerry, Co. Wicklow, Ireland. She wrote secretly at first and her poems were initially published in the *Dublin Magazine* in the 1930s. Her first 'imagistic' collection (though she claimed never to have heard the term), *Poems*, appeared in 1938. Her most ambitious and successful work, *Beat Drum, Beat Heart*, was published in 1946, though it had been written prior to the war. *Beat Drum, Beat Heart* draws on the writing of Whitman and D.H. Lawrence to examine the gender divide in wartime. Her later books were *A Cloud Across the Sun* (1949), *A Kite's Dinner* (1954), *The Leaves Darken* (1964), *Her Storms* (1977) and *Admissions* (1977). Her memoirs are *Real People* (1952) and *Sun Too Fast* (1974). Her work was widely praised, notably by Yeats, who admired it for its 'style distinction...precise and subtle vocabulary', as well as by Elizabeth Bowen. Her *Collected Poems 1938-1983* was published by Enitharmon in 1983.

Winter

The tree still bends over the lake,
And I try to recall our love,
Our love which had a thousand leaves.

[1938]

A Bird

Unexplained
In the salt meadow
Lay the dead bird.
The wind
Was fluttering its wings.

[1938]

from Beat Drum, Beat Heart

FROM PART THREE: *Women in Love*

Where is the lumber-room of what was important?
The bric-à-brac of old feelings? Finished, put away.
And where the motes of ideas we breathed for our *now*?
Lost corridors, stray paths in the woods to our *here*?
Forgotten, of no account. In me, I feel
New space, new time, strangely askew and on whose
Axes spin my world, as you and I –
The man, the woman – tremble face-to-face.
The air is filled with power, hesitancy,
And awareness sharp as a blade's edge:
The lightest gesture, the least sign, can alter
Our whole fate. Opposed like this, we know,
We two, the other's soul is the most threatening
And immediate fact there's ever been –
You are so whole and real, he says, and keeps
Back tears; she, Nothing can stop the force
Of this great hour: I, as a woman, know
That from this confrontation a momentous
Grace or plight will come. It is the reason
I was born a peasant in the rain
Or one who trails her mantle through the hall;
Centuries have waited and prepared
For, with mimed passion and mock battles –
Yes, for this one and overpowering cause:
A cause whose glare lights up the skies and roofs,
Streets, spires and alleys of the mind

With an intensity so sacrificial
That its blazing flash and burning shadow
Fill with unseen, heroic acts. What
Can profane, he thinks, such faith as this? And she:
In finding you, I find myself, will cry.

For now I understand all twofold things;
How dark and light, matter and spirit, gut
And brain can be acquainted, how they accord:
Angel and beast in me are one because
The midway heart is held between
What's private, base, and what's diffused and rare,
Binding the two as the sun's power can weld
The soil, where his foot rests, into quick life
With upper levels of the air. Through me
All contraries of grief and joy are strung:
I am rage and mercy, impulse and slow patience,
Folly and wisdom; I am the rain-filled wind,
The blade that suffers drought. I've tolled
A bell of duty harshly; groaned and wept
For mercy like a saint on a stone floor.
Some fear me, and of one I go in terror;
I am those Fates with scant hair and red eyes
And brittle bones, who so disdain the young;
I am the thread that stretches to be nicked.
I am a parody and extreme, but round me
Natural things are stupid, without substance:
People with idiot faces, in nameless houses,
Going on errands that can have no meaning.
Aloof from others, I still speak for them
And must fulfil them. Bending my ear to catch
The oracle, at the same time it's I,
Fume-crazy croaking sibyl, who predict it.
[…]

Should anyone ask, Where are these battlefields?
Perhaps in the country house
Where a clammy mist falls over the garden,
Fills muddied lanes
And surges into an empty room.

Perhaps in some Park.
Municipal ducks, freezing lake,

Reeds like straw,
And an old bottle caught in the ice.

Perhaps by sand near prickled,
Sea-pitted coral rocks,
Where fond hope and insufficiency
Are the same as anywhere else;
While in the heat
Roads blind you with whiteness.

These are my Flanders, Valley Forge, Carthage.

Late 1930s [1946]

Back

The dark-breasted flesh of a swan
Needing much blood to beat its great wings
How fiercely I wish it would
Carry me

Not away from death
In whose fist I've been held
Too often to be afraid
Of the last clenching

Nor towards that vigour of passion
Where fate speaks directly
To each person in a marble theatre
Perhaps at Epidavros
And gods and goddesses are vengeful or petulant
Bullying us then
As now

But back
          to those pleasant places
Where surprise was quick as nettle-stings
And amazement blushed from the dog-rose
And somewhere in the hedge was a little
Uptailed wren.

[1974]

In a Dublin Museum

No clue
About the use or name
Of these few
Bronze Age things,
Rare
And in gold,
Too wide for finger-rings.
Till some old epic came
To light, which told
Of a king's
Daughter: how she slid them on to hold
The tail ends of her plaited hair.

[1974]

E.J. SCOVELL
(1907-99)

Edith Joy Scovell was born in Sheffield and studied at Somerville College, Oxford. Her poems appeared in *Oxford Poetry* and she edited the Oxford magazine *Fritillary*. She married the ecologist Charles Sutherland Elton in 1937 and spent time working in the south and central American rainforests. Her first collection, published in 1944, was *Shadows of Chrysanthemums*. It was followed by *The Midsummer Meadow* (1946), *The River Steamer* (1956), *The Space Between* (1982) and *Listening to Collared Doves* (1986). Scovell is perhaps best known for her poems about infancy, motherhood, and old age. Her poems on motherhood are remarkable for the intimacy and detail of their focus as they search for an idiom through which to explore the daily rituals and ordinary joys of parenting. She writes in 'Two Notes on Parenthood': 'I did not know I was to be / Built into a wall and weathered like a stone / To an anonymous ripeness of tone / And with the valerian and toadflax grown / And all the future rest on me.' In 'The First Year' Scovell charts the relationship between mother and baby in a world where there is no language, the mother 'absorbed and clouded by a sensual love' as she realises that in this limbo experience of watching and feeding she is 'less than I was on my own...not what I was'. While Scovell could not be thought of as a political poet in the wider sense, her articulation of rarely spoken maternal experience is clearly important, prefiguring work by later women writing about motherhood. Scovell was a close friend of Anne Ridler. Her *Collected Poems* was published in 1988 and *Selected Poems* in 1991.

Light the Fire

Light the fire when night is near,
A little flame to span the night.
He will not feel the winds of fear
In the curved glades of firelight.

And sing smoothly if you sing,
Lest he should hear between the stresses
The insensible cold rain falling
In unpeopled wildernesses.

With your song and vaulted light
Build his brittle starless ark.
With a curtain on the night
Overthrow the wild and dark.

Child Waking

The child sleeps in the daytime,
With his abandoned, with his jetsam look,
On the bare mattress, across the cot's corner;
Covers and toys thrown out, a routine labour.

Relaxed in sleep and light,
Face upwards, never so clear a prey to eyes;
Like a walled town surprised out of the air –
All life called in, yet all laid bare

To the enemy above –
He has taken cover in daylight, gone to ground
In his own short length, his body strong in bleached
Blue cotton and his arms outstretched.

Now he opens eyes but not
To see at first; they reflect the light like snow,
And I wait in doubt if he sleeps or wakes, till I see
Slight pain of effort at the boundary

And hear how the trifling wound
Of bewilderment fetches a caverned cry
As he crosses out of sleep – at once to recover
His place and poise, and smile as I lift him over.

But I recall the blue-
White snowfield of his eyes empty of sight
High between dream and day, and think how there
The soul might rise visible as a flower.

[1956]

The Space Between

From this high window best, you see the briar rose
In its short flowering – how the yellow one has spread
Rangy above the white on the deep-sea garden bed;
As clouds lie over clouds in archipelagos,
But small as petals on the grass, under the wing
Of the soaring plane. And are they clouds or can they be,
Those deepest down, foam flecks or mountain waves of sea?
Our eyes are dazed by nature's see-through curtaining,

Layer upon layer stretched, woven to all degrees
Of part-transparency: the rose, knotted like lace
To a star pattern, thins between to stellar space.
Though eyes before they learn level the galaxies,
It is not the flowers' selves only, webbed in their skies of green,
It is depth they grant to sight; it is the space between.

[1982]

KATHLEEN RAINE
(1908-2003)

Raine grew up in Ilford, Essex, in a socialist Methodist family. Her mother was
Scottish and from her she inherited 'Scotland's songs and ballads – lowland
Scots, not the Gaelic Highlands...sung or recited by my mother, aunts and
grandmothers, who had learned them from *their* mothers and grandmothers
before universal literacy destroyed an oral tradition and culture that scarcely

any longer exists' (in Couzyn, *Contemporary Women Poets*, p.57). Her father, from Co. Durham, was a teacher from whom, she writes, 'I learned to regard the words of the great poets as expressions of the same order of truth (though in a lesser degree) as we found in the Bible. Both were "inspired" from beyond the everyday human mind, and were expressions of a knowledge different in kind from the natural knowledge we gather from everyday experience or scientific experiment' (Couzyn, p.57). In 1926 Raine went to study Botany and Zoology at Girton College, Cambridge, and converted to Catholicism. *Stone and Flower: Poems 1935-1943* was published in 1943, followed by many other collections. Editions of her *Collected Poems* were published in 1956, 1981 and 2000, and she received the Queen's Gold Medal for Poetry in 1992.

Raine wrote critical work on Blake and Yeats and her *Defending Ancient Springs* was published in 1967 in which she writes 'I am one of those who hold the unfashionable belief that talent cannot make a poet, and that the what of art is more important than the how.' She continues: 'technique: does not exist in itself but only as a means to an end, an idea that is to be realised. Nor are all poetic ideas of equal value. Donne or Dryden cannot be as great as Milton or Dante because these poets do not attempt themes that bring into play so great a range of imaginative experience. The themes of major poetry are epic, and cosmic' (p.15). Jane Dowson writes of the apparent contradiction in her 'denunciation of the "woman poet" as a valid category and her claims that "men and women are different" or that she herself is "as good as any woman poet who's written in the English Language"' (*Women's Poetry of the 1930s*, p.94).

The Moment

To write down all I contain at this moment
I would pour the desert through an hour-glass,
The sea through a water-clock,
Grain by grain and drop by drop
Let in the trackless, measureless, mutable seas and sands.

For earth's days and nights are breaking over me,
The tides and sands are running through me,
And I have only two hands and a heart to hold the desert and the sea.

What can I contain of it? It escapes and eludes me,
The tides wash me away,
The desert shifts under my feet.

[1945]

The Star

I thought because I had looked into your eyes
And on our level eyebeams the world at rest
In motion turned upon its steady pole
That I had passed beyond the places and the times of sorrow.
My soul said to me, 'You have come home to here and now:
Before all worlds this beam of love began, and it runs on
And we and worlds are woven of its rays.'
But after I am in absence as before,
And my true love proved false as any other.
We looked away, and never looked again
Along the gaze that runs from love to love for ever:
So far? I wondered, looking at a star
Tonight above my house.

[1964]

LYNETTE ROBERTS
(1909-95)

Born Evelyn Beatrice in Buenos Aires, of parents of Welsh descent, Roberts
was Spanish speaking when she left Argentina and came to Britain at the end
of the First World War. She attended the Central School of Art and married
Kiedrych Rhys in 1939 with whom she had two children. She was closely
associated with Dylan and Caitlin Thomas when they were neighbours in
1939-40. *An Introduction to Village Dialect, an essay on dialect and seven short
stories* was published in 1944, in the same year as T.S. Eliot – then poetry
editor at Faber – published her *Poems*. Roberts was also closely connected with
Robert Graves, and supplied much research for his study *The White Goddess*,
later important to Sylvia Plath and Ted Hughes. *Gods with Stainless Ears*, which
was written between 1941 and 1943, was finally published in its entirety in
1951, the fifth section having appeared earlier in *Poems*. In a brief introduction
to the book-length poem, Roberts writes: 'Not liking varied metre forms in a
long poem, short-lipped lyrics interspersed with heavy marching strides, and
not feeling too comfortable within the strict limits of the heroic couplet (wanting
elbow room and breathing space), I decide to use the same structure through-
out, changing only the rhythm, texture, and tone internally. The use of congested
words, images, and certain hard metallic lines are introduced with deliberate
emphasis to represent a period of muddle and intense thought...' Despite many
differences, and although it is not a drama as such, with its 'cadence of sight
and sound', its Laugharne setting, and its incorporation of many voices, *Gods*

with *Stainless Ears* can be compared with Thomas's *Under Milk Wood* (1956). *Gods with Stainless Ears* was followed by *The Fifth Pillar of Song*, which was rejected by Eliot. Roberts also wrote *Nesta*, a novel now lost. A posthumous *Selected Poems*, edited by Patrick McGuinness, was published in 2005.

from Gods with Stainless Ears

PART IV

CRI MADONNA	(THE CRY OF THE MADONNA)
Un eich amynedd un ddi-feth,	(The same your patience unfailing,
Un yn eich croes a'ch cri,	The same your cross and your cry,
Mair, mam Iesu o Nasareth	Mary, mother of Nazareth
A' Mari o Llanybri.	And Mary of Llanybri)

    – DYFNALLT

ARGUMENT

Of birth. Of uneventful birth. Owing to lack of money and to emotional strain death cuts in, double death, loss of lover and child. The struggle for birth under these conditions suggests a comparison with the Madonna, which becomes the nucleus and theme of the whole poem. *That the birth of flesh and blood is everywhere a noble event and that lives of all nationalities must be considered sacred – not to be callously destroyed.* Of the girl's distraction. Humiliation at her double loss. Stanzas of discordant fifths prevail. Cherubs weep, and a desolation and deadness of spirit is felt as after raids. The uselessness of the soldiers' jobs is intensified as they empty latrine buckets in the rain. Making them, since to rebel at this particular time would bring about the country's defeat, *our heroes. The heroes unknown who braved and bore, each a private crucifix.*

I, rimmeled, awake before the dressing sun:
Alone I, pent up incinerator, serf of satellite gloom
Cower around my cradled self; find crape-plume
In a work-basket cast into swaddling clothes
Forcipated from my mind after the foetal fall:

Rising ashly, challenge blood to curb – compose –
Martial mortal, face a red mourning alone.
To the star of the third magnitude O my God,
Shriek, sear my swollen breasts, send succour
To sift and settle me. – This the labour of it...

But reality worse than the pain intrudes,
And no near doctor for six days. This
Also is added truth. Razed for lack of
Incomputable finance. For womb was
Fresh as the day and solid as your hand.

BLOOD OF ALL MEN. DRENCHED ANCESTORS OF WAR
WHETHER GERMAN. BRITISH. RUSSIAN. OR HIDE
FROM SOME OTHER FOREIGN FIELD: REMEMBER AGAIN
BLOOD IS HUMAN. BORN AT COST. REMEMBER THIS
ESPECIALLY YOU TAWDRY LAIRDS AND JUGGLERS OF MINT.

So double hurt was hard to console. Heart hatched
Shrived nerves each day in valley clove. Stretched
Mind tight into scarlet umbrella. Slatched
Nowhere the deflated ropes of blood. Wrenched
Harbouring heartbreak that is a crack grailed.

O where was my consoler. Where O where
You double beast down. Callous Cymru.
O love beaten. By loss humiliated.
Stretched out in muslin distress. Bound
By an iron wreath scattered with coloured beads.

O my people immeasurably alone.
No ringfinger: with the tips of my nails glazed
With sorrow with solemn gravity. Crown tipped sideways;
Ears blown back like lilac; with set face
And dry lids, waiting for Love's Arcade.

O LOVE was there no barddoniaeth?
No billing birds to be – coinheritor?

The night sky is braille in a rock of frost.

Why wail ribbon head. Crystallised cherubic
Cluster of stars. Why weep spilling splints to
Steelgraze the sky. Why shrillcold cerulean
Flesh with identity tacked hot on your wing.
Why dribble prick-ears, scintillating in an up

And down nailmourn. Tumbling to earth an icy precision
Of pins, distilling flies and peacock fins,
Tears in flames on fire, scorching air as they
Splash into heavier spills of quavering
Silver, drops, seels resinate woe, chills hedge and

Chilblain glades. Grisaille freezes the sense; crines
The gills into a drill motion; stills-shrills
The singing birds to kill; Drips rills
From envelopes, pustule eyes and hat. With
Urinal taint instils mind with a perilled dampness;

Fells skilled discipline to halls of humidity
Engraving clothes to trail balustrades without
Flesh; to a wilderness of pavements blue crayoned
With telegrams, where by a trick of air, owners
And cats remain, trying in mid-air to force riseup

Their own smashed brick. These men have brothers,
Are wived. And in dredging buckets of steam
Through stable-showers, men sway with the slush,
Dreamwhile teeming out cables and rope
Stretch barb wire tight across the crimped moon.

Wringing out moisture from mind and mouth,
Pulverising a haze to gauze their contorted feature,
Inebriate mouths cratered: others with lime fresh
On briared cheeks cut Easter Island shadows, elongating
Into weathered struts that strain all clouds for height.

On the lowering of the Dandelion Sun brail umbrage
For their pall: for those hovering above us tall as a
Siren's wail...pocked and pale as pumice stone...
Mother-shrivelled with tansy tears: and those from
Accumulators, with eyes vacant as motor horns

Who shutter out the bleakness and blink in their
Own way. In quiet corners men yawn out death.
Commiserately sodden. Here rain contravariant:
Here in discord and disobedience:
Probable mutiny and desertion: night splashes up

Mullions in heavy hayloads: lights up shiny
Pailettes on rawset faces: spits up frogs
And tins to fidget their bowels. Dodging
Pillars of rain; pails overbrimming swishswashing,
Drenching rifty suits, their steel shoulders subscribing

Thin laminations of grief. O my people here
With labour illused and minds deranged....
Through rivets of light; *Here are your Heroes.*
While high up, swallowsoft....
Marine butterflies flood out the whole estuary.

1941-43 [1951]

ELIZABETH BISHOP
(1911-79)

Elizabeth Bishop was born in Worcester, Massachusetts. After the death of
her father and her mother's committal to a mental asylum, Bishop moved to
Nova Scotia to live with her grandparents. She studied at Vassar College. Her
first collection *North and South* was published in 1946. It was followed by *A
Cold Spring* (1955), *Questions of Travel* (1965), *The Ballad of the Burglar of
Babylon* (1968) (for children), *The Complete Poems* (1969), and her final col-
lection, *Geography III* (1976). Later editions include *The Complete Poems 1927-
1979* (1983) and *Edgar Allan Poe & The Juke-Box: Uncollected Poems, Drafts,
and Fragments* (2006). Her prose works are *Brazil* (1962), *The Collected Prose*
(1984) and *One Art: Selected Letters* (1994), and her art is published in *Exchang-
ing Hats: Paintings* (1996). She was also the editor of *The Diary of "Helena
Morley"* (1957). Bishop moved to Brazil in 1951 where she lived with Lota
de Macedo Soares, returning to the States in the late 1960s.

Although I have been unable to include Bishop's poems here because of her
wish not to be included in women-only anthologies, her position as a central
figure to both male and female writers in the later part of the 20th century is
irrefutable. Bishop's close friends and influences included writers with char-
acters and poetic styles as diverse as Marianne Moore, Robert Lowell and
Randall Jarrell. Most notably among contemporary British women poets,
Lavinia Greenlaw and Jo Shapcott have spoken of her importance to their
development; indeed it might be argued that for British women coming to
writing in the early 1980s Bishop's detached persona and cool and detailed
poetics did much to counter the image of the woman poet which had grown
up in the wake of Sylvia Plath's death in 1962.

Recommended poems for new readers might include: 'The Man-Moth' [1946],
'The Fish' [1946], 'Roosters' [1946], 'The Shampoo' [1955], 'The Moose' [1976],
'Crusoe in England' [1976], 'In the Waiting Room' [1976], 'One Art' [1976].

ANNE RIDLER

(1912-2001)

Educated in Italy and at Kings College London, Ridler worked for a while as assistant to T.S. Eliot at Faber. Her first book *Poems* (1939) was followed by *A Dream Observed* (1941), *The Nine Bright Shiners* (1943), *The Golden Bird and Other Poems* (1951), *A Matter of Life and Death* (1959), *Selected Poems* (1961), *Who is My Neighbour and How Bitter the Bread* (1963), *Some Time After and Other Poems* (1972), *Dies Natalis: Poems of Birth and Infancy* (1980), *New and Selected Poems* (1988) and *Collected Poems* (1994).

In an interview with Carole Satyamurti she discusses the idea of the "woman poet". 'You do need staying power and that can be sapped away by everyday jobs, but being a woman poet, that was a more tiresome thing. You were always reviewed first and foremost as a woman and that was irksome to a degree. You could say it was my fault for writing about childbirth and that kind of thing, but it always seemed to be the subject that the critics fastened on in this tedious way, as if I'd never written about anything else and other things that interested me. Poetry itself was an absorbing interest quite apart from my sex or the experiences of my sex…some reviewers seemed to have a kind of resentment of the fact that there could be poetry written by a woman, from a woman's point of view…I don't feel much sympathy with the feminist movement… because again it seems to me to be distracting our attention from things that are more important, to the fact of the differences between men and women. I wanted above everything to be judged just as a poet, and with nothing to do with which sex I happened to belong to.' (*A Taste for the Truth*, pp.8-9)

The Images that Hurt…

> *The images that hurt and that connect*
> W.H. AUDEN

All the materials of a poem
Are lying scattered about, as in this garden
The lovely lumber of spring.
All is profusion, confusion: hundred-eyed
The primulae in crimson pink and purple,
Golden at the pupil;
Prodigal the nectarine and plum
That fret their petals against a rosy wall.
Flame of the tulip, fume of the blue anemone,
White Alps of blossom in the giant pear tree,
Peaks and glaciers, rise from the same drab soil.

Far too much joy for comfort:
The images hurt because they won't connect.
No poem, no possession, therefore pain.
And struggling now to use
These images that bud from the bed of my mind
I grope about for a form,
As much in the dark, this white and dazzling day,
As the bulb at midwinter; as filled with longing
Even in this green garden
As those who gaze from the cliff at the depths of sea
And know they cannot possess it, being of the shore
And severed from that element for ever.

[1959]

Corneal Graft

And after fifty years of blindness
The hand of science touched him, and he saw.

A face was a blur, poised on a stalk of speech;
Colour meant simply red; all planes were flat,
Except where memory, taught by his learnèd fingers,
Spoke to his 'prentice sight.
                                    As for the moon,
The Queen of heaven, she was a watery curd
Spilt on his window-pane,
For height, more than his stick could measure,
Was a senseless word.
The splendours of the morning gave no pleasure,
But he would rise at dawn to see
Distant cars and lorries, moving divinely
Across his strange horizon, stranger by far
Than the Pacific to the old explorers.

And is the patient grateful, subject of a miracle?

Blind, he was confident, forging through his twilight,
Heedless of dangers he had never seen.
As a dreamer on the brink of a ravine
Walks fearlessly, but waking, totters and falls,

So now the surging traffic appals him,
Monsters menace, he dare not cross:
A child, long past the childhood season;
A prince in darkness, but in the light a prisoner.

And if, after this five-sense living,
The hand of God should touch us to eternal light –
Not saints, well practised in that mode of seeing,
But grown-up babies, with a world to unlearn,
Menaced by marvels, how should we fare?
Dense, slow of response, only at the fingertips
Keeping some fragments of truth –
What could that heaven bring us but despair?

[1972]

GWENDOLYN BROOKS
(1917-2000)

Born in Topeka, Kansas, Gwendolyn Brooks grew up in Chicago where she
lived throughout her life. She graduated from Wilson Junior College in 1936
and worked variously as a domestic help, and secretary, before becoming the
publicity director of the Youth Council of the National Association for he
Advancement of Colored People. In 1941, with her husband the poet Henry
L. Blakely, she attended a poetry workshop and in 1945 she published her
first book, *A Street in Bronzeville* (1945). This was followed by *Annie Allen*
(1949), *The Bean Eaters* (1960), *Selected Poems* (1963), *We Real Cool* (1966),
The Wall (1967) and *In the Mecca* (1968). *Family Pictures* (1970) was pub-
lished by Broadside, a new publisher committed to the work of black writers.
With the exception of *The World of Gwendolyn Brooks* (1971), she published
with Broadside for the remainder of her life: *Riot* (1969), *Black Steel: Joe
Frazier and Muhammad Ali* (1971), *Aloneness* (1971), *Aurora* (1972), *Beckonings*
(1975), *Black Love* (1981), *To Disembark* (1981), *The Near-Johannesburg Boy
and Other Poems* (1986), *Blacks* (1987), *Winnie* (1988) and *Children Coming
Home* (1991).

In 1950 Brooks was the first black author to win a Pulitzer Prize, which was
to be the first of many accolades, which included the post of Poetry Consultant
to the Library of Congress, the Poetry Society of America's Frost Medal, and
a Lifetime Achievement Award from the National Endowment for the Arts.
Brooks stated that her aim as a poet was 'to write poems that will somehow
successfully "call"...all black people...in gutters, in schools, offices factories,
prisons, the consulate...in mines, on farms, on thrones' (*Selected Poems*). She
also wrote a novel, *Maud Martha* (1953), and *Report from Part One: An Auto-
biography* (1972).

the mother

Abortions will not let you forget.
You remember the children you got that you did not get,
The damp small pulps with a little or with no hair,
The singers and workers that never handled the air.
You will never neglect or beat
Them, or silence or buy with a sweet.
You will never wind up the sucking-thumb
Or scuttle off ghosts that come.
You will never leave them, controlling your luscious sigh,
Return for a snack of them, with gobbling mother-eye.

I have heard in the voices of the wind the voices of my dim
        killed children.
I have contracted. I have eased
My dim dears at the breasts they could never suck.
I have said, Sweets, if I sinned, if I seized
Your luck
And your lives from your unfinished reach,
If I stole your births and your names,
Your straight baby tears and your games,
Your stilted or lovely loves, your tumults, your marriages, aches,
        and your deaths,
If I poisoned the beginnings of your breaths,
Believe that even in my deliberateness I was not deliberate.
Though why should I whine,
Whine that the crime was other than mine? –
Since anyhow you are dead.
Or rather, or instead,
You were never made.
But that too, I am afraid,
Is faulty: oh, what shall I say, how is the truth to be said?
You were born, you had body, you died.
It is just that you never giggled or planned or cried.

Believe me, I loved you all.
Believe me, I knew you, though faintly, and I loved, I loved you
All.

[1945]

103

The Bean Eaters

They eat beans mostly, this old yellow pair.
Dinner is a casual affair.
Plain chipware on a plain and creaking wood,
Tin flatware.

Two who are Mostly Good.
Two who have lived their day,
But keep on putting on their clothes
And putting things away.

And remembering...
Remembering, with twinklings and twinges,
As they lean over the beans in their rented back room that is full
    of beads and receipts and dolls and cloths, tobacco crumbs,
    vases and fringes.

[1960]

MURIEL SPARK

(*b*. 1918)

Muriel Spark was born Muriel Sarah Camberg, in Edinburgh, of Jewish Lith-
uanian and English Presbyterian parents. After her marriage, she lived in
Rhodesia from 1937 to 1944 where her son was born. She worked for the
Foreign Office in Political Intelligence from 1944 to 1945. She was General
Secretary of the Poetry Society from 1947 to 1949 and the editor of *Poetry
Review* in 1949, and also founded the literary magazine, *Forum*. She converted
to Catholicism in 1954. Her first collection of poems *The Fanfarlo and Other
Verse* was published in 1952 and followed by *Collected Poems 1* (1967), *Going
up to Sotheby's and Other Poems* (1982) and *All the Poems of Muriel Spark* (2004).
A biographer and critic, Spark is best known as a novelist, and her first work
of fiction, *The Comforters*, was published in 1957; her most famous novel, *The
Prime of Miss Jean Brodie* appeared in 1961. Spark moved to Italy in 1967 and
now lives in Rome and New York.

Elementary

Night, the wet, the onyx-faced
Over the street was shining where
I saw an object all displaced
In black water and black air.

Was it myself? If so I found
An odd capacity for vision.
Capacity, I understand
Is limited by fixed precision,

Being the measure of displacement:
The void exists as bulk defined it,
The cat subsiding down a basement
Leaves a catlessness behind it.

That vision then, shall I concede is
Proved by a void capacity?
What's good enough for Archimedes
Ought to be good enough for me.

But knowing little of natural law
I can't describe what happens after
You weigh a body such as I saw,
First in air and then in water.

c. 1951 [1952]

Evelyn Cavallo

This person never came to pass,
Being the momentary name I gave
To a slight stir in a fictitious grave
Wherein I found no form and face, alas
Of Evelyn Cavallo, Evelyn of grass.

Therefore, therefore, Evelyn,
Why do you assert your so non-evident history
While all your feminine motives make a mystery

Which, to resolve, arise your masculine?
Why will you not lie down

At the back of the neither here not there
Where lightly I left you, Evelyn of guile?
But no, you recur in the orgulous noonday style,
Or else in your trite, your debonair
Postprandial despair.

c. 1952 [1952]

ELMA MITCHELL
(1919-2004)

Mitchell was born in Airdrie in Scotland and trained as a librarian. Her first collection, *The Poor Man in the Flesh*, was published in 1976, when she was 57, and was followed by *The Human Cage* (1979) and *Furnished Rooms* (1983), *People Etcetera: New and Selected Poems* (1987); her work also featured, with that of U.A Fanthorpe and Charles Causley, in *Penguin Modern Poets 6* (1996). Mitchell's is a voice which, like that of Elizabeth Bartlett, is able to carry the experience of the disappointed or disaffected with energy and verve. She is a very social poet, interested in drawing our attention to the lives of women, particularly the intense experiences of older women, as well as to difficulties between men and women.

Thoughts After Ruskin

Women reminded him of lilies and roses.
Me they remind rather of blood and soap,
Armed with a warm rag, assaulting noses,
Ears, neck, mouth and all the secret places:

Armed with a sharp knife, cutting up liver,
Holding hearts to bleed under a running tap,
Gutting and stuffing, pickling and preserving,
Scalding, blanching, broiling, pulverising,
– All the terrible chemistry of their kitchens.

Their distant husbands lean across mahogany
And delicately manipulate the market,
While safe at home, the tender and the gentle

Are killing tiny mice, dead snap by the neck,
Asphyxiating flies, evicting spiders,
Scrubbing, scouring aloud, disturbing cupboards,
Committing things to dustbins, twisting, wringing,
Wrists red and knuckles white and fingers puckered,
Pulpy, tepid. Steering screaming cleaners
Around the snags of furniture, they straighten
And haul out sheets from under the incontinent
And heavy old, stoop to importunate young,
Tugging, folding, tucking, zipping, buttoning,
Spooning in food, encouraging excretion,
Mopping up vomit, stabbing cloth with needles,
Contorting wool around their knitting needles,
Creating snug and comfy on their needles.

Their huge hands! their everywhere eyes! their voices
Raised to convey across the hullabaloo,
Their massive thighs and breasts dispensing comfort,
Their bloody passages and hairy crannies,
Their wombs that pocket a man upside down!

And when all's over, off with overalls,
Quickly consulting clocks, they go upstairs,
Sit and sigh a little, brushing hair,
And somehow find, in mirrors, colours, odours,
Their essences of lilies and of roses.

[1976]

Alice Uglier

Alice is uglier now by several years.
   Her eyes
Are sunk and fortified against surprise,
   Humiliations, tears.
Sensible to the bone, her gait proclaims.
   Her cut
Of coal disdains the sympathiser, but
   Her mouth is restless: tensions dug
    These trenches in her throat.

She wasn't bred on love or promises,
    Lonely, never alone,
Her future was provided for, not cherished.
    She nursed
Her nearest through senility and worse.
    Placid in gratitude, dumb to abuse,
    She kept
The business out of debt, the books in order,
    But now, it seems, the monkey's loose,
And something's tearing papers in the cellar
    Far down.

While habit, like a well-maintained machine,
    Keeps up the play of knife and fork
And answers questions in between –
    Her sturdy tree is withered to a rod.
She's given up her country walks,
    (Too stiff to stoop for primroses)
Under the table, foot and fist
    Tap out their private messages –
She wakes in darkness to her bath of flames
    And wonders what became of God.

Still
She must get back, or she'll be missed.
    Over the coffee, she'll insist
We should go fifty-fifty on the bill.
This is a block that salts will not remove.
    I pour out coffee, and retain
Her drowning image, and my useless love.

[1976]

AMY CLAMPITT
(1920-94)

The first of five children, Amy Clampitt was born and brought up in New Providence, Iowa. She graduated from Grinnell College and moved to New York City, where she was a secretary at Oxford University Press, a librarian and a freelance editor. Her first full-length collection, *The Kingfisher*, appeared in 1983, when she was 63, followed by *What the Light was Like* (1985), *Archaic Figure* (1987), *Westward* (1990) and her final volume *A Silence Opens* (1994).

The Collected Poems of Amy Clampitt was published in 1998. Clampitt is in many ways the natural inheritor of Marianne Moore and Elizabeth Bishop. A near contemporary of Bishop, the hallmark of her poetry is the almost exhaustive detail with which she views the world, a detail which celebrates consciousness at its most alert and which becomes in its proliferations, the basis of her style. Clampitt married her partner of 25 years, Harold Korn, only several months before her death. Her prose includes *Homage to John Keats* (1984), *The Essential Donne*, selected and introduced by Amy Clampitt (1988), and *Predecessors, Et Cetera: Essays* (1991).

Beach Glass

While you walk the water's edge,
turning over concepts
I can't envision, the honking buoy
serves notice that at any time
the wind may change,
the reef-bell clatters
its treble monotone, deaf as Cassandra
to any note but warning. The ocean,
cumbered by no business more urgent
than keeping open old accounts
that never balanced,
goes on shuffling its millenniums
of quartz, granite, and basalt.
                      It behaves
toward the permutations of novelty –
driftwood and shipwreck, last night's
beer cans, spilt oil, the coughed-up
residue of plastic – with random
impartiality, playing catch or tag
ot touch-last like a terrier,
turning the same thing over and over,
over and over. For the ocean, nothing
is beneath consideration.
                   The houses
of so many mussels and periwinkles
have been abandoned here, it's hopeless
to know which to salvage. Instead
I keep a lookout for beach glass –
amber of Budweiser, chrysoprase

of Almadén and Gallo, lapis
by way of (no getting around it,
I'm afraid) Phillips'
Milk of Magnesia, with now and then a rare
translucent turquoise or blurred amethyst
of no known origin.
                    The process
goes on forever: they came from sand,
they go back to gravel,
along with treasuries
of Murano, the buttressed
astonishments of Chartres,
which even now are readying
for being turned over and over as gravely
and gradually as an intellect
engaged in the hazardous
redefinition of structures
no one has yet looked at.

[1985]

A Silence

past parentage or gender
beyond sung vocables
the slipped-between
the so infinitesimal
fault line
a limitless
interiority

beyond the woven
unicorn   the maiden
(man-carved   worm-eaten)
God at her hip
incipient
the untransfigured
cottontail
bluebell and primrose
growing wild   a strawberry
chagrin   night terrors

past the earthlit
unearthly masquerade

(we shall be changed)

a silence opens

*

the larval feeder
naked   hairy   ravenous
inventing from within
itself its own
raw stuffs'
hooked silk-hung
relinquishment

behind the mask
the milkfat   shivering
sinew   isinglass
uncrumpling   transient
greed to reinvest

*

names have been
given (revelation
kif   nirvana
syncope)   for
whatever gift
unasked
gives birth to

torrents
fixities
reincarnations of
the angels
Joseph Smith
enduring
martyrdom

a cavernous
compunction driving

founder-charlatans
who saw in it
the infinite
love of God
and had
(George Fox
was one)
great openings

[1994]

DENISE LEVERTOV

(1923-97)

Denise Levertov grew up in Ilford, Essex, the daughter of a Russian Jewish
immigrant father, (who later became an Anglican priest) and a Welsh mother,
her first book of poems *The Double Image* was published in 1946. In 1948 she
moved to North America where she was included in Kenneth Rexroth's *The
New British Poets* (1949). Her books that followed were all subsequently pub-
lished in the US, including *Here and Now* (1957), *With Eyes at the Back of
our Heads* (1960), *O Taste and See* (1964), *Relearning the Alphabet* (1970), *To
Stay Alive* (1971), *Life in the Forest* (1978), *Candles in Babylon* (1982), *Oblique
Prayers* (1984/1986 UK), *Selected Poems* (UK 1986), *Breathing the Water* (1987/
1988 UK), *Sands of the Well* (1996/1998 UK), and posthumously, *This Great
Unknowing* (1999/2001 UK) and *New Selected Poems* (2002/2003 UK). She
also translated the work of Guillevic and Joubert from the French, and wrote
a prose memoir, *Tesserae: memories and suppositions* (1995/1997 UK).

Levertov managed to combine her largely image-driven poems with both
political commitment and spiritual awareness, two not necessarily contradictory
forces, but certainly elements difficult to balance within the framework of the
lyric. Her influences included Ezra Pound, William Carlos Williams and H.D.,
as well as Robert Creeley and Robert Duncan. Levertov later converted to
Catholicism under the influence of the feminist theologian Dorothy Rowe.

Laying the Dust

What a sweet smell rises
    when you lay the dust –
bucket after bucket of water thrown
on the yellow grass.

                    The water
flashes
each time you
make it leap –
          arching its glittering back.
The sound of
                    more water
pouring into the pail
almost quenches my thirst.
Surely when flowers
grow here, they'll not
smell sweeter than this
                    wet ground, suddenly black.

[1957]

Terror

Face-down; odor
of dusty carpet. The grip
of anguished stillness.

Then your naked voice, your
head knocking the wall, sideways,
the beating of trapped thoughts against iron.

If I remember, how is it
my face shows
barely a line? Am I
a monster, to sing
in the wind on this sunny hill

and not taste the dust always,
and not hear
that rending, that retching?
How did morning come, and the days
that followed, and quiet nights?

[1960]

Song for Ishtar

The moon is a sow
and grunts in my throat
Her great shining shines through me
so the mud of my hollow gleams
and breaks in silver bubbles

She is a sow
and I a pig and a poet

When she opens her white
lips to devour me I bite back
and laughter rocks the moon

In the black of desire
we rock and grunt, grunt and
shine

[1964]

A Woman Alone

When she cannot be sure
which of two lovers it was with whom she felt
this or that moment of pleasure, of something fiery
streaking from head to heels, the way the white
flame of a cascade streaks a mountainside
seen from a car across a valley, the car
changing gear, skirting a precipice,
climbing...
When she can sit or walk for hours after a movie
talking earnestly and with bursts of laughter
with friends, without worrying
that it's late, dinner at midnight, her time
spent without counting the change...
When half her bed is covered with books
and no one is kept awake by the reading light
and she disconnects the phone, to sleep till noon...

Then
selfpity dries up, a joy
untainted by guilt lifts her.
She has fears, but not about loneliness;
fears about how to deal with the aging
of her body – how to deal
with photographs and the mirror. She feels
so much younger and more beautiful
than she looks. At her happiest
– or even in the midst of
some less than joyful hour, sweating
patiently through a heatwave in the city
or hearing the sparrows at daybreak, dully gray,
toneless, the sound of fatigue –
a kind of sober euphoria makes her believe
in her future as an old woman, a wanderer,
seamed and brown,
little luxuries of the middle of life all gone,
watching cities and rivers, people and mountains,
without being watched; not grim nor sad
an old winedrinking woman, who knows
the old roads, grass-grown, and laughs to herself...
She knows it can't be:
that's Mrs Doasyouwouldbedoneby from
The Water-Babies –
no one can walk the world any more
a world of fumes and decibels.
But she thinks maybe
she could get to be tough and wise, some way,
anyway. Now at least
she is past the time of mourning,
now she can say without shame or deceit,
O blessed Solitude.

[1978]

The Métier of Blossoming

Fully occupied with growing – that's
the amaryllis. Growing especially
at night: it would take

only a bit more patience than I've got
to sit keeping watch with it till daylight;
the naked eye could register every hour's
increase in height. Like a child against a barn door,
proudly topping each year's achievement,
steadily up
goes each green stem, smooth, matte,
traces of reddish purple at the base, and almost
imperceptible vertical ridges
running the length of them:
Two robust stems from each bulb,
sometimes with sturdy leaves for company,
elegant sweeps of blade with rounded points.
Aloft, the gravid buds, shiny with fullness.
One morning – and so soon! – the first flower
has opened when you wake. Or you catch it poised
in a single, brief
moment of hesitation.
Next day, another,
shy at first like a foal,
even a third, a fourth,
carried triumphantly at the summit
of those strong columns, and each
a Juno, calm in brilliance,
a maiden giantess in modest splendor.
If humans could be
that intensely whole, undistracted, unhurried,
swift from sheer
unswerving impetus! If we could blossom
out of ourselves, giving
nothing imperfect, withholding nothing!

[1999]

PATRICIA BEER

(1924-99)

Beer was born in Exmouth, Devon, and lectured as Padua University, Italy
and Goldsmiths College before becoming a full-time writer in 1968. Some of
her early poems from *Loss of the Magyar* (1959) and *The Survivors* (1963) are
included in her *Collected Poems*. Her first mature collection, *Just Like Resurrection*,
appeared in 1967 and was followed by *The Estuary* (1971), *Driving West* (1975),
Selected Poems (1979), *The Lie of the Land* (1983), *Collected Poems* (1988), *Friend*

of *Heraclitus* (1993) and *Autumn* (1997). Beer frequently writes with a matter of fact melancholy. Her off-key tone arises from the disjuncture between poetic cadences and the more prose-inflected tone which often qualifies them. Like her heroine Stevie Smith, her poems depend on a performed voice, what the commentary on the back of her *Collected Poems* describes as 'a poetry of tones of voice, with her Devon accent audible in the texture of her language'. Beer was also the author of a novel set in 16th-century Devon, *Moon's Ottery* (1988). Her autobiography, *Mrs Beer's House*, was posthumously published in 2004.

In Memory of Stevie Smith

A goodbye said after a party, after the drive home,
Is often final, to be labelled
Months later as the last word, meaninglessly.
The one who goes inside, clicking
The door after a polite pause, and the one who drives
Off still have something to discuss.

There had been friendship, not close, coming late in the day
With darkness already tropically near.
I remember an outing through the lanes near Hereford
With Easter weather and a fantastic
Story about gold plate in a stately home
That made us laugh till the car swerved.

Mrs Arbuthnot, Phoebe and Rose, must have died
Long ago, and Mrs Courtley
Though she had a few years of conversation left.
Mrs Arbuthnot we know became
A wave, a long and curling wave that broke
Upon a shore she had not expected.

Muriel, dressed up to the nines, with even
Her tiara on, must in the end
Have heard death knock, and opened to her beau
With the black suit come to take her out.
The swimmer whose behaviour was so misinterpreted
At last stopped both waving and drowning.

A heroine is someone who does what you cannot do
For yourself and so is this poet. She discovered
Marvels: a cat that sings, a corpse that comes in

Out of the rain. She struck compassion
In strange places: for ambassadors to hell, for smelly
Unbalanced river gods, for know-all men.

[1975]

The Lost Woman

My mother went with no more warning
Than a bright voice and a bad pain.
Home from school on a June morning
And where the brook goes under the lane
I saw the back of a shocking white
Ambulance drawing away from the gate.

She never returned and I never saw
Her buried. So a romance began.
The ivy-mother turned into a tree
That still hops away like a rainbow down
The avenue as I approach.
My tendrils are the ones that clutch.

I made a life for her over the years.
Frustrated no more by a dull marriage
She ran a canteen through several wars.
The wit of a cliché-ridden village
She met her match at an extra-mural
Class and the OU summer school.

Many a hero in his time
And every poet has acquired
A lost woman to haunt the home,
To be compensated and desired,
Who will not alter, who will not grow,
A corpse they need never get to know.

She is nearly always benign. Her habit
Is not to stride at dead of night.
Soft and crepuscular in rabbit-
Light she comes out. Hear how they hate
Themselves for losing her as they did.
Her country is bland and she does not chide.

But my lost woman evermore snaps
From somewhere else: 'You did not love me.
I sacrificed too much perhaps,
I showed you the way to rise above me
And you took it. You are the ghost
With the bat-voice, my dear. *I* am not lost.'

[1983]

ELIZABETH BARTLETT
(*b*. 1924)

Born in Deal, Bartlett grew up in Kent. She left school at 15 to work in a
factory making hypodermic needles just before the outbreak of World War II
and continued to work variously as a medical secretary, home help service and
a tutor to support her family. Bartlett did not publish her first book *A Lifetime
of Dying* (1979) until she was in her 50s, although she was writing and pub-
lishing at an early age, with her first poem appearing in *Poetry London* when
she was 19. Her idiomatic use of language gives it a freshness and urgency: in
many ways she reads like a poet of the much younger generation with whom
she was publishing in the 1980s and 1990s. Perhaps what surprises most about
her poems is the way social conscience is brought to bear in the poems but
never seeks to exploit its subject or buttonhole the reader. Hers is a voice
which remains uncompromised, angry but unhectoring. Her other poetry books
are *Strange Territory* (1983), *The Czar is Dead* (1986), *Look No Face* (1991),
Two Women Dancing: New and Selected Poems (1995), *Appetites of Love* (2001)
and *Mrs Perkins and Oedipus* (2004). She lives in Burgess Hill, East Sussex.

Neurosis

I am a dark cypress driven in the wind,
And the quarrelling voices of children behind
The Sunday streets. I am the listener, waiting
In doorways for the sounds of struggle
And torment. I am the shock machine in the empty ward,
And the enemy soldier under the point of the sword.
I am a little boy crying out Dolore in his sleep,
And the dazed women in rusty black who weep
Outside provincial cemeteries, and a foetus taken piecemeal
From its mother, and an old woman dying
Of cancer in a back room. I am my own analyst lying

Dead in his bed with the marks of the syringe
Like a macabre tattoo on his white body.

In childhood I was the red lady of my own nightmares,
And the pursuing jeers, and the hostile stares.
I was Manuela dead in a German courtyard, and the open maw
Of the butcher boy's basket, and the threat of war.
I was the clinging Goodwins who sucked down the merry
Cricketers, and the drums at the tattoo, and the poisoned berry.
Did you see me lingering at the gates of Buchenwald,
Or running from Electra, or making friends with the bald
Syphilitic hawking laces on the sea-front?
I was all men collecting the dole in long lines
In bitter weather, and the accident siren shrieking from the mines.
You have heard my name called in the courts
Of law for perversion and murder, and malice aforethought.

Would you know me? I am also a young woman, growing
My flowers in season, feeding my cats, knowing
Little, but feeling everything, writing at all times
And in all places, working out rhythms and rhymes.
I make clothes for young children, a red kilt
Or a jacket for a newly-delivered child,
Assuaging my envy and covering my guilt.
Sometimes, from my husband's arms, I catch
A glimpse of the potency of love, like a mirage
Soon gone, and I wonder if I shall ever be whole,
Or always playing torturer and tortured in my double role.

1952 [1979]

Birth

When they gave you to me you were redolent
Of acrid badly-made soap and blood,
And indeed you were covered with a waxy layer,
Like rice-paper on a macaroon, or cottage cheese.
You had obviously done some very heavy laundry
In the womb, using soda, wringing your hands,
Purple and sodden like a washer-woman,
Whose feeble fingers have mandarin's nails

With which you scratched your face, adding
To the general air of wear and tear and age.
And yet you were so young, a few minutes,
And the placenta not yet flowering in the bowl,
Your doll's clothes still airing, your air-way
Choked with mucus. All night we drained
You like a boiled potato, tipping you up
And, newly-washed we looked upon your great
High forehead, and your thin crop of hair,
And marvelled that you had travelled so far
Through such a small tunnel, no cuts,
No stitches, no forceps, just a long journey
And a small body, like a fish, sliding neatly
Into a quiet house, and an old bed,
Where no other child had been born before.
You cried a little, and then, exhausted, fell
Into the deepest sleep there is, apart
From death, and I lay flat and empty
Awake all night, tired beyond sleep,
Fearing and hoping beyond all bounds
That you would not live to curse your birth
As many have done before you,
And will do again.

1956 [1979]

Stretchmarks

Lying awake in a provincial town
I think about poets. They are mostly
men, or Irish, turn out old yellow
photographs, may use four letter words,
stick pigs or marry twice, and edit
most of the books and magazines.

Most poets, who are men, and get to
the bar first at poetry readings,
don't like us fey or even feminist,
too old, too young, or too intense,
and monthlies to them are just the
times when very few need us.

Gowned like women in funereal black
they have friends who went punting
on the Cam. I'm not too clear
what others did in Oxford, except
avoid the traffic, bathe in fountains,
drunkenly, a different shade of blue.

Mostly they teach, and some must be
fathers, but they have no stretch marks
on their smooth stomachs to prove it.
At least we know our children
are our own. They can never really
tell, but poems they can be sure of.

[1986]

MAIRI MacINNES

(*b.* 1925)

Born in Co. Durham, MacInnes was educated in Yorkshire and at Somerville
College, Oxford. She moved to Berlin with her husband John McCormick, in
1954, and then spent 30 years in America before retiring to North Yorkshire.
Her poems first appeared in *Oxford Poetry* in 1948. Her books include *Splinters*
(1953), *The House on the Ridge Road* (1988), *Elsewhere & Back: New and Selected
Poems* (1993), *The Ghostwriter* (1999) and *The Pebble: Old and New Poems* (2000);
two novels, *Admit One* (1956) and *The Quondam Wives* (1993); and *Clearances:
A Memoir* (2002). The mother of three children, she writes here about the
poem 'I Object, said the Object' and the conflicts of being poet, wife and mother.
    'The woman I was depicting as a ravening force of nature, one who angered
and wore down the narrator (me as husband) became the Muse, she whom
though only an occasional visitor in our house I longed to have as a permanent
guest...the narrator here (me) turns into the poet, the woman poet as it happens.
The lambs are both her children and her poems...the self I'd objectified as
the maenad, the wild shouting woman and the Muse, assumed my mother's
face...It is very hard to write from the heart of your marriage. Sylvia Plath
did it, at terrible cost. Her accomplishment has made the task seem at least
possible, though her marriage was unique... Are we limited to celebration? To
write through difficulty made for better poems than to write through ease, not
because I despised the gracefulness of ready language, but because sometimes
I didn't know what the difficulty really was...I had to discover such knowledge
through the poem itself...such difficulty loaded the work with the life – even
my life then, trivialised with meeting the needs of my family and household,
and haunted by the demands of my job as an editor of medical publications;
and paradoxically tormented by the desire to put my own words on paper. The
hurt for the poet in me...was marriage, my excellent marriage.' (*The Ghostwriter*,
pp.74-75).

I Object, said the Object

Out of the habit, I remembered nothing,
  Till, like a drunkard beating on the door,
  She shrieked out, 'More!' and more
    She had to have.
It was our anniversary. The devil longed
For rings and songs and coloured rocks and tinsel.

I wish the police would fix her.
  They'd end her screams with an axe's chop.
  What bliss to hear that yell lopped off!
    Think of the blank
Flowering, and then her coiffed acquaintance
Relishing her visceral history and sad finis.

I wonder now just how I could have picked her.
  Liable, was she reward? Her loss leucotomy?
  Was she the fundamental shifting at the eye
    Of penetrating pain?
Do magical mischances falter without her, the needle
In vision, for earth to pivot on, like an apple?

Whatever she meant once, appreciation's over.
  Today was bad. Tomorrow will be worse.
  Some hormone malady has made her haggish,
    Storming the stairs,
Mouth agog to the quivering uvula,
Taut hands like blown-up gloves waggling disaster –

Day after day I send for the doctor,
  And let his hollow needle intercept the kill.
  Thankfully I watch the boggling congeal,
    The blubbering less.
Sobered, she recovers rapidly,
Her eyes awash like two great silly puddles.

And then she swears she's never loved me more.
  She takes me in her big caress,
  Delicate diva, apt to bless,
    Hand on my head,
As if through blubbing we grow richer and closer,
Instead of always poorer and more cold.

But soon high-horsed again, she hops away,
    And sorry that I've let her be ridiculous,
    And slow to monkey with the maladress
        That she displays,
I let her bolt and wander, and play herd
Upon the unsteady spending of her miscellaneous powers.

So it may happen, some night noble and serene,
    The last phut firework of her endeavour done,
    She'll turn, sane, cool, and say, 'Come,
        Bring down your sheep.
November's leaning on the fells, and Cassiopeia
Leans down to chant her song. Count your last lambs.'

Heart-full and grateful then I'll bid them come,
    Their mouths like filmstars' ravaged and remote
    Uttering sounds unchosen, spontaneous, not
        Chidden, flocking,
My lambs, crowding to me, a stranger that says,
'What is it that you want? Is it this? Or this?'

[1982]

Mass

1

Someone said in a dream, 'Flying's dead easy –
just give yourself to the air.'
It was true: I tripped on a top stair
and took off like a frisbee.
Stairs rivered beneath in the hall's arroyo,
suns flashed through windows,
and I saw that the carpet
approached like a rig of flowered silk
or the leaf canopy of a rain forest –
and I caught at a bough or strut banister
and dropped down unhurt.

Yet unexpectedly the forest
still went past, and how dense,
how weighty and immediate,

124

the outer world was!
I still floated, I did not exist
minute after minute but in a burst,
all at once, weightless, a rocket
that fired its stars before it fell.

2

Last night there was rain
after a summer of drought
and mushrooms cropped in old pasture.
Today I met women gathering them,
a line seen far-off climbing the hill,
their faces touched by the October sun,
strung out, stooped, companionable,
mothers and the mothers of mothers,
neighbours from the village.
I hailed them as a newcomer
out on my own, and they rose up
full height and gazed, gentle as giraffes,
and immediately from crammed baskets
offered me mushrooms...weightless
nothing food, food of the dead.
At its moist uncanny touch I felt
the skin on my fingertips to be
no less than the skin of my life,
so heavy and immediate I was,
so dense and full of earth.

[1993]

ELIZABETH JENNINGS
(1926-2001)

Born in Boston, Lincolnshire, Jennings studied English at St Anne's College, Oxford from 1945 to 1949. Her early poems were published in *Oxford Poetry* in 1948, edited by Kingsley Amis and James Michie. She was the only woman included in Robert Conquest's *New Lines* anthology (1956) and became associated with the so-called Movement poetry of Amis, Larkin, Thom Gunn and John Wain. She worked as a librarian in Oxford from 1950 to 1958. Her first collection, *Poems*, was published in 1953 and followed by numerous books including *A Way of Looking* (1955), *A Sense of the World* (1958), *Sonnets of Michelangelo* (1961), *Song for a Birth or a Death* (1961), *The Mind Has Mountains* (1966), *Collected Poems* (1967), *Growing Points* (1975), *Moments of Grace* (1980), *Celebrations and Elegies* (1982), *Collected Poems* (1987), *Times and Seasons* (1992), *Praises* (1998), and the posthumous *Timely Issues* (2001) and *New Collected Poems* (2002). She spoke of her early influences as Auden, Edwin Muir and Robert Graves. Jennings writes, often formally, with an elegiac turn. A practising Catholic, she also published *Every Changing Shape* (1961), a study of mystical poetry, *Christianity and Poetry* (1965), and *Seven Men of Vision* (1976). Like Elizabeth Bishop, she cites Hopkins and Herbert as poets important to her. Her explorations of mental illness and breakdown bear interesting if surprising comparison with the "confessional" poets of her generation, especially Robert Lowell and Anne Sexton.

Identity

When I decide I shall assemble you
Or, more precisely, when I decide which thoughts
Of mine about you fit most easily together,
Then I can learn what I have loved, what lets
Light through the mind. The residue
Of what you may be goes. I gather

Only as lovers or friends gather at all
For making friends means this –
Image and passion combined into a whole
Pattern within the loving mind, not her or his
Concurring there. You can project the full
Picture of lover or friend that is not either.

So then assemble me,
Your exact picture firm and credible,
Though as I think myself I may be free
And accurate enough.
That you love what is truthful to your will
Is all that ever can be answered for
And, what is more,
Is all we make each other when we love.

[1953]

A Fear

Always to keep it in and never spare
Even a hint of pain, go guessing on,
Feigning a sacrifice, forging a tear
For someone else's grief, but still to bear
Inward the agony of self alone –

And all the masks I carry on my face,
The smile for you, the grave considered air
For you and for another some calm grace
When still within I carry an old fear
A child could never speak about, disgrace
That no confession could assuage or clear.

But once within a long and broken night
I woke and threw the shutters back for air
(The sudden moths were climbing to the light)
And from another window I saw stare
A face like mine still dream-bereft and white
And, like mine, shaken by a child's nightmare.

[1958]

About These Things

About these things I always shall be dumb.
Some wear their silences as more than dress,
As more than skin-deep. I bear mine like some

Scar that is hidden out of shamefulness.
I speak from depths I do not understand
Yet cannot find the words for this distress.

So much of power is put into my hand
When words come easily. I sense the way
People are charmed and pause; I seem to mend

Some hurt. Some healing seems to make them stay.
And yet within the power that I use
My wordless fears remain. Perhaps I say

127

In lucid verse the terrors that confuse
In conversation. Maybe I am dumb
Because if fears were spoken I would lose

The lovely languages I do not choose
More than the darknesses from which they come.

[1961]

A Mental Hospital Sitting-Room

Utrillo on the wall. A nun is climbing
Steps in Montmartre. We patients sit below.
It does not seem a time for lucid rhyming;
Too much disturbs. It does not seem a time
When anything could fertilise or grow.

It is as if a scream were opened wide,
A mouth demanding everyone to listen.
Too many people cry, too many hide
And stare into themselves. I am afraid.
There are no life-belts here on which to fasten.

The nun is climbing up those steps. The room
Shifts till the dust flies in between our eyes.
The only hope is visitors will come
And talk of other things than our disease...
So much is stagnant and yet nothing dies.

[1966]

The Unknown Child

That child will never lie in me, and you
Will never be its father. Mirrors must
Replace the real image, make it true
So that the gentle love-making we do
Has powerful passions and a parents' trust.

That child will never lie in me and make
Our loving careful. We must kiss and touch
Quietly and watch our own reflexions break
As in a pool that is disturbed. Oh take
My watchful love; there must not be too much

A child lies within my mind. I see
The eyes, the hands. I see you also there,
I see you waiting with an honest care,
Within my mind, within me bodily,
And birth and death close to us constantly.

[1967]

The Lord's Prayer

'Give us this day.' Give us this day and night.
Give us the bread, the sky. Give us the power
To bend and not be broken by your light.

And let us soothe and sway like the new flower
Which closes, opens to the night, the day,
Which stretches up and rides upon a power

More than its own, whose freedom is the play
Of light, for whom the earth and air are bread.
Give us the shorter night, the longer day.

In thirty years so many words were spread
And miracles. An undefeated death
Has passed as Easter passed, but those words said

Finger our doubt and run along our breath.

[1975]

ANNE SEXTON

(1928-74)

Anne Gray Harvey grew up in Wellesley, Massachusetts, married at 19, took a modelling course, and had her first child in 1953. In 1954 she was hospitalised for her first nervous breakdown, and again in 1955, seven months after the birth of her second child. She attempted suicide in 1956 and began writing in 1957 at the instigation of her psychiatrist. Sexton forged a close friendship with the poet Maxine Kumin, who also attended a poetry workshop with John Holmes, and later made the acquaintance of Sylvia Plath. Her first collection of poems *To Bedlam and Part Way Back* was published in 1960 and followed by *All My Pretty Ones* (1962), and *Live or Die* (1966), which won the Pulitzer Prize; then *Love Poems* (1969), *Transformations* (1971), *The Book of Folly* (1972), *The Death Notebooks* (1974), *The Awful Rowing Toward God* (1975), and post-humously, *45 Mercy Street* (1976) and *Words for Dr. Y* (1978). She committed suicide in 1974. In her introduction to Sexton's *Complete Poems*, Maxine Kumin suggests that 'Women poets in particular owe a debt to Anne Sexton, who broke new ground, shattered taboos, and endured a barrage of attacks along the way because of the flamboyance of her subject-matter, which, 20 years later, seems far less daring. She wrote openly abut menstruation, abortion, masturbation, incest and adultery, and drug addiction at a time when the proprieties embraced none of these as proper topics for poetry...Anne delineated the problematic position of women – the neurotic reality of the time – though she was not able to cope in her own life with the personal trouble it created.' (p.xxxiv)

With Mercy for the Greedy

(for my friend Ruth, who urges me to make an
appointment for the Sacrament of Confession)

Concerning your letter in which you ask
me to call a priest and in which you ask
me to wear The Cross that you enclose;
your own cross,
your dog-bitten cross,
no larger than a thumb,
small and wooden, no thorns, this rose –

I pray to its shadow,
that gray place
where it lies on your letter...deep, deep.
I detest my sins and I try to believe
in The Cross. I touch its tender hips, its dark jawed face,
its solid neck, its brown sleep.

True. There is
a beautiful Jesus.
He is frozen to his bones like a chunk of beef.
How desperately he wanted to pull his arms in!
How desperately I touch his vertical and horizontal axes!
But I can't. Need is not quite belief.

All morning long
I have worn
your cross, hung with package string around my throat.
It tapped me lightly as a child's heart might,
tapping secondhand, softly waiting to be born.
Ruth, I cherish the letter you wrote.

My friend, my friend, I was born
doing reference work in sin, and born
confessing it. This is what poems are:
with mercy
for the greedy,
they are the tongue's wrangle,
the world's pottage, the rat's star.

[1962]

Consorting with Angels

I was tired of being a woman,
tired of the spoons and the pots,
tired of my mouth and my breasts,
tired of the cosmetics and the silks.
There were still men who sat at my table,
circled around the bowl I offered up.
The bowl was filled with purple grapes
and the flies hovered in for the scent
and even my father came with his white bone.
But I was tired of the gender things.

Last night I had a dream
and I said to it...
'You are the answer.
You will outlive my husband and my father.'

131

In that dream there was a city made of chains
where Joan was put to death in man's clothes
and the nature of the angels went unexplained,
no two made in the same species,
one with a nose, one with an ear in its hand,
one chewing a star and recording its orbit,
each one like a poem obeying itself,
performing God's functions,
a people apart.

'You are the answer,'
I said, and entered,
lying down on the gates of the city.
Then the chains were fastened around me
and I lost my common gender and my final aspect.
Adam was on the left of me
and Eve was on the right of me,
both thoroughly inconsistent with the world of reason.
We wove our arms together
and rode under the sun.
I was not a woman anymore,
not one thing or the other.

O daughters of Jerusalem,
the king has brought me into his chamber.
I am black and I am beautiful.
I've been opened and undressed.
I have no arms or legs.
I'm all one skin like a fish.
I'm no more a woman
than Christ was a man.

February 1963 [1966]

Briar Rose
(Sleeping Beauty)

Consider
a girl who keeps slipping off,
arms limp as old carrots,
into the hypnotist's trance,

into a spirit world
speaking with the gift of tongues.
She is stuck in the time machine,
suddenly two years old sucking her thumb,
as inward as a snail,
learning to talk again.
She's on a voyage.
She is swimming further and further back,
up like a salmon,
struggling into her mother's pocketbook.
Little doll child,
come here to Papa.
Sit on my knee.
I have kisses for the back of your neck.
A penny for your thoughts, Princess.
I will hunt them like an emerald.

Come be my snooky
and I will give you a root.
That kind of voyage,
rank as a honeysuckle.

Once
a king had a christening
for his daughter Briar Rose
and because he had only twelve gold plates
he asked only twelve fairies
to the grand event.
The thirteenth fairy,
her fingers as long and thing as straws,
her eyes burnt by cigarettes,
her uterus an empty teacup,
arrived with an evil gift.
She made this prophecy:
The princess shall prick herself
on a spinning wheel in her fifteenth year
and then fall down dead.
Kaputt!
The court fell silent.
The king looked like Munch's *Scream*,
Fairies' prophecies,
in times like those,
held water.

However the twelfth fairy
had a certain kind of eraser
and thus she mitigated the curse
changing that death
into a hundred-year sleep.

The king ordered every spinning wheel
exterminated and exorcised.
Briar Rose grew to be a goddess
and each night the king
bit the hem of her gown
to keep her safe.
He fastened the moon up
with a safety pin
to give her perpetual light
He forced every male in the court
to scour his tongue with Bab-o
lest they poison the air she dwelt in.
Thus she dwelt in his odor.
Rank as honeysuckle.

On her fifteenth birthday
she pricked her finger
on a charred spinning wheel
and the clocks stopped.
Yes indeed. She went to sleep.
The king and queen went to sleep,
the courtiers, the flies on the wall.
The fire in the hearth grew still
and the roast meat stopped crackling.
The trees turned into metal
and the dog became china.
They all lay in a trance,
each a catatonic
stuck in a time machine.
Even the frogs were zombies.
Only a bunch of briar roses grew
forming a great wall of tacks
around the castle.
Many princes
tried to get through the brambles
for they had heard much of Briar Rose
but they had not scoured their tongues

so they were held by the thorns
and thus were crucified.
In due time
a hundred years passed
and a prince got through.
The briars parted as if for Moses
and the prince found the tableau intact.
He kissed Briar Rose
and she woke up crying:
Daddy! Daddy!
Presto! She's out of prison!
She married the prince
and all went well
except for the fear –
the fear of sleep.

Briar Rose
was an insomniac...
She could not nap
or lie in sleep
without the court chemist
mixing her some knock-out drops
and never in the prince's presence.
If it is to come, she said,
sleep must take me unawares
while I am laughing or dancing
so that I do not know that brutal place
where I lie down with cattle prods,
the hole in my cheek open.
Further, I must not dream
for when I do I see the table set
and a faltering crone at my place,
her eyes burnt by cigarettes
as she eats betrayal like a slice of meat.

I must not sleep
for while I'm asleep I'm ninety
and think I'm dying.
Death rattles in my throat
like a marble.
I wear tubes like earrings.
I lie as still as a bar of iron.
You can stick a needle

through my kneecap and I won't flinch.
I'm all shot up with Novocain.
This trance girl
is yours to do with.
You could lay her in a grave,
an awful package,
and shovel dirt on her face
and she'd never call back: Hello there!
But if you kissed her on the mouth
her eyes would spring open
and she'd call out: Daddy! Daddy!
Presto!
She's out of prison.

There was a theft.
That much I am told.
I was abandoned.
That much I know.
I was forced backward.
I was forced forward.
I was passed hand to hand
like a bowl of fruit.
Each night I am nailed into place
and forget who I am.
Daddy?
That's another kind of prison.
It's not the prince at all,
but my father
drunkeningly bends over my bed,
circling the abyss like a shark,
my father thick upon me
like some sleeping jellyfish.
What voyage is this, little girl?
This coming out of prison?
God help –
this life after death?

[1971]

ADRIENNE RICH

(b. 1929)

Rich was born in Baltimore Maryland, the elder of two daughters. Her father, Arnold Rich, was a professor at Johns Hopkins University, and her mother Helen Jones, a pianist and composer. Rich's first book, *A Change of World* was published in 1951, the year she graduated from Radcliffe College. In 1953 she married Alfred Haskell Conrad (*d.* 1970) and had three sons. In 1966 she moved with her husband to New York and became deeply involved in the civil rights and the women's movement. Since 1976 she has lived with the writer Michelle Cliff, currently in northern California.

Her other books of poetry include: *The Diamond Cutters and Other Poems* (1955), *Snapshots of a Daughter-in-Law: Poems 1954-1962* (1963), *Necessities of Life: Poems 1962-1965* (1966), *Selected Poems* (1967), *Leaflets: Poems 1965-1968* (1969), *The Will to Change: Poems 1968-1970* (1972), *Diving into the Wreck: Poems 1971-1972* (1973), *The Dream of a Common Language: Poems 1974-1977* (1978) *The Fact of a Doorframe: Poems Selected and New 1950-1984* (1984); *Time's Power: Poems 1985-1988* (1989) *An Atlas of the Difficult World: Poems 1988-1991* (1991), *Collected Early Poems: 1950-1970* (1993) *Dark Fields of the Republic: Poems 1991-1995* (1995) *Midnight Salvage: Poems 1995-1998* (1999), *Fox: Poems 1998-2000* (2001) and *The School Among the Ruins: Poems 2000-2004* (2004).

A distinguished essayist and political activist her non-fiction prose includes: *Of Woman Born: Motherhood as Experience and Institution* (1986), *What is Found There: Notebooks on Poetry and Politics* (1993) and *Arts of the Possible: Essays and Conversations* (2001). She writes in the preface to *The Fact of a Doorframe*: 'To work in a medium which can be, has been, used as an instrument of trivialisation and deceit, not to mention colonisation and humiliation, is somewhat different from working in a medium like stone, clay, paint, charcoal, even iron or steel. A poet cannot refuse language, chose another medium. But the poem can re-fuse the language given to him or her, bend and torque it into an instrument for connection instead of dominance and apartheid toward what Edouard Glissant has wonderfully called "the poetics of relation".' Perhaps because of her desire to unite poetry and politics, Rich has an acute awareness of history: since 1956, all her poems have been individually dated.

Snapshots of a Daughter-in-Law

1

You, once a belle in Shreveport,
with henna-colored hair, skin like a peachbud,
still have your dresses copied from that time,
and play a Chopin prelude
called by Cortot: '*Delicious recollections
float like perfume through the memory.*'

Your mind now, moldering like wedding-cake,
heavy with useless experience, rich
with suspicion, rumor, fantasy,
crumbling to pieces under the knife-edge
of mere fact. In the prime of your life.

Nervy, glowering, your daughter
wipes the teaspoons, grows another way.

2

Banging the coffee-pot into the sink
she hears the angels chiding, and looks out
past the raked gardens to the sloppy sky.
Only a week since They said: *Have no patience.*

The next time it was: *Be insatiable.*
Then: *Save yourself; others you cannot save.*
Sometimes she's let the tapstream scald her arm,
a match burn to her thumbnail,

or held her hand above the kettle's snout
right in the woolly steam. They are probably angels,
since nothing hurts her anymore, except
each morning's grit blowing into her eyes.

3

A thinking woman sleeps with monsters.
The beak that grips her, she becomes. And Nature,
that sprung-lidded, still commodious
steamer-trunk of *tempora* and *mores*
gets stuffed with it all: the mildewed orange-flowers,
the female pills, the terrible breasts
of Boadicea beneath flat foxes' heads and orchids.

Two handsome women, gripped in argument,
each proud, acute, subtle, I hear scream
across the cut glass and majolica
like Furies cornered from their prey:
The argument *ad feminam*, all the old knives
that have rusted in my back, I drive in yours,
ma semblable, ma soeur!

4

Knowing themselves too well in one another:
their gifts no pure fruition, but a thorn,
the prick filed sharp against a hint of scorn...
Reading while waiting
for the iron to heat,
writing, *My Life had stood – a Loaded Gun –*
in that Amherst pantry while the jellies boil and scum,
or, more often,
iron-eyed and beaked and purposed as a bird,
dusting everything on the whatnot every day of life.

5

Dulce ridens, dulce loquens,
she shaves her legs until they gleam
like petrified mammoth-tusk.

6

When to her lute Corinna sings
neither words nor music are her own;
only the long hair dipping
over her cheek, only the song
of silk against her knees
and these
adjusted in reflections of an eye.

Poised, trembling and unsatisfied, before
an unlocked door, that cage of cages,
tell us, you bird, you tragical machine –
is this *fertillisante douleur*? Pinned down
by love, for you the only natural action,
are you edged more keen
to prise the secrets of the vault? has Nature shown
her household books to you, daughter-in-law,
that her sons never saw?

7

'To have in this uncertain world some stay
which cannot be undermined, is
of the utmost consequence.'
                          Thus wrote
a woman, partly brave and partly good,

139

who fought with what she partly understood.
Few men about her would or could do more,
hence she was labeled harpy, shrew and whore.

8

'You all die at fifteen,' said Diderot,
and turn part legend, part convention.
Still, eyes inaccurately dream
behind closed windows blankening with steam.
Deliciously, all that we might have been,
all that we were – fire, tears,
wit, taste, martyred ambition –
stirs like the memory of refused adultery
the drained and flagging bosom of our middle years.

9

Not that it is done well, but
that it is done at all? Yes, think
of the odds! or shrug them off forever.
This luxury of the precocious child,
Time's precious chronic invalid, –
would we, darlings, resign it if we could?
Our blight has been our sinecure:
mere talent was enough for us –
glitter in fragments and rough drafts.

Sigh no more, ladies.
                           Time is male
and in his cups drinks to the fair.
Bemused by gallantry, we hear
our mediocrities over-praised,
indolence read as abnegation,
slattern thought styled intuition,
every lapse forgiven, our crime
only to cast too bold a shadow
or smash the mold straight off.

For that, solitary confinement,
tear gas, attrition shelling.
Few applicants for that honor.

Well,
she's long about her coming, who must be
more merciless to herself than history.
Her mind full to the wind, I see her plunge
breasted and glancing through the currents,
taking the light upon her
at least as beautiful as any boy
or helicopter,
                    poised, still coming,
her fine blades making the air wince

but her cargo
no promise then:
delivered
palpable
ours.

1958-60 [1963]

Diving into the Wreck

First having read the book of myths,
and loaded the camera,
and checked the edge of the knife-blade,
I put on
the body-armor of black rubber
the absurd flippers
the grave and awkward mask.
I am having to do this
not like Cousteau with his
assiduous team
aboard the sun-flooded schooner
but here alone.

There is a ladder.
The ladder is always there
hanging innocently
close to the side of the schooner.
We know what it is for,
we who have used it.

Otherwise
it's a piece of maritime floss
some sundry equipment.

I go down.
Rung after rung and still
the oxygen immerses me
the blue light
the clear atoms
of our human air.
I go down.
My flippers cripple me,
I crawl like an insect down the ladder
and there is no one
to tell me when the ocean
will begin.

First the air is blue and then
it is bluer and then green and then
black I am blacking out and yet
my mask is powerful
it pumps my blood with power
the sea is another story
the sea is not a question of power
I have to learn alone
to turn my body without force
in the deep element.

And now: it is easy to forget
what I came for
among so many who have always
lived here
swaying their crenellated fans
between the reefs
and besides
you breathe differently down here.

I came to explore the wreck.
The words are purposes.
The words are maps.
I came to see the damage that was done
and the treasures that prevail.
I stroke the beam of my lamp

slowly along the flank
of something more permanent
than fish or weed

the thing I came for:
the wreck and not the story of the wreck
the thing itself and not the myth
the drowned face always staring
toward the sun
the evidence of damage
worn by salt and sway into this threadbare beauty
the ribs of the disaster
curving their assertion
among the tentative haunters.

This is the place.
And I am here, the mermaid whose dark hair
streams black, the merman in his armored body.
We circle silently
about the wreck
we dive into the hold.
I am she: I am he

whose drowned face sleeps with open eyes
whose breasts still bear the stress
whose silver, copper, vermeil cargo lies
obscurely inside barrels
half-wedged and left to rot
we are the half-destroyed instruments
that once held to a course
the water-eaten log
the fouled compass

We are, I am, you are
by cowardice or courage
the one who find our way
back to this scene
carrying a knife, a camera
a book of myths
in which
our names do not appear.

1972 [1973]

FREDA DOWNIE

(1929-93)

Born in Woolwich, Downie published two collections of poetry during her
lifetime, *A Stranger Here* (1977) and *Plainsong* (1981), as well as a string of
small press publications. In her posthumously published memoir, *There'll
Always Be an England* (2003), Downie recalls her poor, often disrupted child-
hood, which included evacuation, London in the Blitz, and a hazardous
wartime sea voyage to Australia. She worked first as a secretary at Novello's
music publishers in London, and then later in a library, followed by a series
of part-time jobs after her marriage. Downie suffered a succession of nervous
breakdowns before her death from a blood disorder.

Her *Collected Poems*, edited and with an introduction by George Szirtes,
was published in 1995. Szirtes writes: 'She had little faith in practical politics:
nothing could be achieved by any -ism, whether this be socialism, toryism or
feminism. Such things made her angry...The trick was to see people in the
round and to understand their – and the poet's own – distress. But one had
to achieve this with tact, without egotism, without drawing attention to the
melodramatic self. She was a sublimator, not a confessor...One may usefully
think of the poems as a single drama of confrontation with the tragic muse.
Downie was in many ways a muse poet in the Gravesian sense. She could
describe the goddess and continually presented her magical island. She also
knew the goddess was dangerous: that she fed – to be absolutely plain about it
– on her depressions. At the same time it was important that the goddess be
confronted, that one's tragic mask should not be ridiculous; that it was only
right to have a slightly arch expression because this made the mask human.
She hated bombast and rhetoric, what she referred to as the "I, I, I... me, me,
me" of more strident poets.' (*Collected Poems*, p.19; p.21).

Some Poetry

Poetry is a loose term and only
A fool would offer a definition.
Those not concerned with the form
At all usually refer to some
Beautiful manifestation or the other.

Chopin, dying in hellish foggy London,
Wrote to say he was leaving for
Paris to finish the ultimate act,
Begging Grzymala to make his room ready
And not to forget a bunch of violets
So that he would have a little poetry
Around him when he returned.

I like to think the violets were
Easily obtainable and that the poetry
Was there, on the table, breathing
Wordless volumes for one too tired
To turn pages while moving swiftly
Towards an inevitable incomprehensible form.

[1977]

O Mary

O Mary
The girls in the convent
Are performing Die Fledermaus tonight.
Their faces are painted as beautifully as yours
And their borrowed dress is as long as yours.
They are very excited, but you remain calm
With your dolly blue glass eyes turned to God
In the solid resignation of your unmoving face.
It is the interval now and they decorate doorways.
The red headed girl in the black cape and top hat
Is handsome enough to escort me around the dusk
Of the damp grounds and empty swimming pool,
But she is very popular.
And Mary,
Although they promenade beyond the delicate
Blue light cast about you by a glass cupola heaven,
They appear to bear a life as charmed as your own.

[1977]

U.A. FANTHORPE

(*b*. 1929)

Born in Kent, Ursula Fanthorpe read English at St Anne's College, Oxford,
and then trained to teach at the University of London's Institute of Education.
She worked at Cheltenham Ladies College from 1962 to 1970, and then left
to take a diploma in counselling at University College, Swansea. She took on
a series of temporary jobs in order to concentrate on her writing, including

working as a hospital receptionist in Bristol. Her first collection, *Side Effects*, was published in 1978, and followed by *Standing To* (1982), *Voices Off* (1984), *Selected Poems* (1986), *A Watching Brief* (1987), *Neck-Verse* (1992), *Safe as Houses* (1995), *Consequences* (2000), *Christmas Poems* (2002), *Queuing for the Sun* (2003) and *Collected Poems 1978-2003* (2005). In 1994, she was the first woman to be nominated as Oxford Professor of Poetry, and in 2003 received the Queen's Gold Medal for Poetry, only the fifth woman to receive this honour.

Her early work made extensive use of the dramatic monologue, and she has spoken of feeling closest to the work of Anna Akhmatova, Elma Mitchell, Wendy Cope and Robert Browning. 'Mother-in-law' is one of four poems in a series titled 'Only Here for the Bier', written, she notes, 'because I was interested to see how the masculine world of Shakespeare's tragedies would look from the woman's angle. In fact, women exist in this world only to be killed, as sacrificial victims. So I imagined Gertrude...having a chat with some usual female confidante, like a hairdresser, or a telephone.' (*Standing To*, 1982)

Not My Best Side

(Uccello: S. George and the Dragon, The National Gallery)

I

Not my best side, I'm afraid.
The artist didn't give me a chance to
Pose properly, and as you can see,
Poor chap, he had this obsession with
Triangles, so he left off two of my
Feet. I didn't comment at the time
(What, after all, are two feet
To a monster?) but afterwards
I was sorry for the bad publicity.
Why, I said to myself, should my conqueror
Be so ostentatiously beardless, and ride
A horse with a deformed neck and square hoofs?
Why should my victim be so
Unattractive as to be inedible,
And why should she have me literally
On a string? I don't mind dying
Ritually, since I always rise again,
But I should have liked a little more blood
To show they were taking me seriously.

II

It's hard for a girl to be sure if
She wants to be rescued. I mean, I quite
Took to the dragon. It's nice to be
Liked, if you know what I mean. He was
So nicely physical, with his claws
And lovely green skin, and that sexy tail,
And the way he looked at me,
He made me feel he was all ready to
Eat me. And any girl enjoys that.
So when this boy turned up, wearing machinery,
On a really *dangerous* horse, to be honest,
I didn't much fancy him. I mean,
What was he like underneath the hardware?
He might have acne, blackheads or even
Bad breath for all I could tell, but the dragon –
Well, you could see all his equipment
At a glance. Still, what could I do?
The dragon got himself beaten by the boy,
And a girl's got to think of her future.

III

I have diplomas in Dragon
Management and Virgin Reclamation.
My horse is the latest model, with
Automatic transmission and built-in
Obsolescence. My spear is custom-built,
And my prototype armour
Still on the secret list. You can't
Do better than me at the moment.
I'm qualified and equipped to the
Eyebrow. So why be difficult?
Don't you want to be killed and/or rescued
In the most contemporary way? Don't
You want to carry out the roles
That sociology and myth have designed for you?
Don't you realise that, by being choosy,
You are endangering job-prospects
In the spear- and horse-building industries?
What, in any case, does it matter what
You want? You're in my way.

[1978]

147

from Stations Underground

1 *Fanfare*

*(for Winifrid Fanthorpe, born 5 February 1895,
died 13 November 1978)*

You, in the old photographs, are always
The one with the melancholy half-smile, the one
Who couldn't quite relax into the joke.

My extrovert dog of a father,
With his ragtime blazer and his swimming togs
Tucked like a swiss roll under his arm,
Strides in his youth towards us down some esplanade,

Happy as Larry. You, on his other arm,
Are anxious about the weather forecast,
His overdraft, or early closing day.

You were good at predicting failure: marriages
Turned out wrong because you said they would.
You knew the rotations of armistice and war,
Watched politicians' fates with gloomy approval.

All your life you lived in a minefield,
And were pleased, in a quiet way, when mines
Exploded. You never actually said
I told you so, but we could tell you meant it.

Crisis was your element. You kept your funny stories
Your music-hall songs for doodlebug and blitz-nights.
In the next cubicle, after a car-crash, I heard you
Amusing the nurses with your trench wit through the blood.

Magic alerted you. Green, knives and ladders
Will always scare me through your tabus.
Your nightmare was Christmas; so much organised
Compulsory whoopee to be got through.

You always had some stratagem for making
Happiness keep its distance. Disaster

148

Was what you planned for. You always
Had hoarded loaves or candles up your sleeve.

Houses crumbled around your ears, taps leaked,
Electric light bulbs went out all over England,
Because for you homes were only provisional,
Bivouacs on the stony mountain of living.

You were best at friendship with chars, gypsies,
Or very far-off foreigners. Well-meaning neighbours
Were dangerous because they lived near.

Me too you managed best at a distance. On the landline
From your dugout to mine, your nightly
Pass, friend was really often quite jovial.

You were the lonely figure in the doorway
Waving goodbye in the cold, going back to a sink-full
Of crockery dirtied by those you loved. We
Left you behind to deal with our crusts and gristle.

I know why you chose now to die. You foresaw
Us approaching the Delectable Mountains,
And didn't feel up to all the cheers and mafficking.

But how, dearest, will even you retain your
Special brand of hard-bitten stoicism
Among the halleluyas of the triumphant dead?

[1982]

from **Only Here for the Bier**

1 *Mother-in-law*

Such a nice girl. Just what I wanted
For the boy. Not top drawer, you know,
But so often, in our position, that
Turns out to be a mistake. They get
The ideas of their station, and that upsets
So many applecarts. The lieges, of course,

Are particularly hidebound, and the boy,
For all his absentminded ways, is a great one
For convention. Court mourning, you know...
Things like that. We don't want a Brunhilde
Here. But she was so suitable. Devoted
To her father and brother, and,
Of course, to the boy. And a very
Respectable, loyal family. Well, loyal
To number two, at any rate. Number one,
I remember, never quite trusted... Yes,
And had just the right interests. Folk song, for instance,
(Such a sweet little voice), and amateur
Dramatics. Inherited *that* taste
From her father. Dear old fellow, he'd go on
For hours about his college drama group.
And the boy's so keen on the stage. It's nice
When husband and wife have a shared interest,
Don't you think? Then botany. Poor little soul,
She was really keen. We'd go for trips
With the vasculum, and have such fun
Asking the lieges their country names for flowers.
Some of them, my dear, were scarcely delicate
(The names, I mean), but the young nowadays
Don't seem to notice. Marriage
Would have made her more innocent, of course.
I can't think who will do for the boy now.
I seem to be the only woman left round here.

[1982]

Women Laughing

Gurgles, genderless,
Inside the incurious womb.

Random soliloquies of babies
Tickled by everything.

Undomesticated shrieks
Of small girls. Mother prophesies
You'll be crying in a minute.

150

Adolescents wearing giggles
Like chain-mail, against embarrassment,
Giggles formal in shape as
Butterpats, or dropped stitches.

Young women anxious to please,
Laughing eagerly before the punchline
(Being too naïve to know which it is).

Wives gleaming sleekly in public at
Husbandly jokes, masking
All trace of old acquaintance.

Mums obliging with rhetorical
Guffaws at the children's riddles
That bored their parents.

Old women, unmanned, free
Of children, embarrassment, desire to please
Hooting grossly, without explanation.

[1984]

ELAINE FEINSTEIN
(*b*. 1930)

Born in Liverpool to Jewish immigrants from Odessa, Feinstein studied at
Newnham College, Cambridge. Her books include *In a Green Eye* (1966),
The Magic Apple Tree (1971), *The Celebrants* (1973), *Some Unease and Angels*
(1977), *The Feast of Eurydice* (1980), *Badlands* (1986), *City Music* (1990),
Daylight (1997), *Gold* (2000) and *Collected Poems and Translations* (2002). She
has translated many Russian writers, notably Marina Tsveteyeva and other
Russian women poets, but also Pushkin, whose biography she published in
1998. Her other biographies include *A Captive Lion: The Life of Marina
Tsveteyeva* (1987), *Lawrence's Women* (1993), *Ted Hughes: The Life of a Poet*
(2001) and *Anna of All the Russias: A Life of Anna Akhmatova* (2005). Her
influential translations of Tsvetayeva were first published in 1971, followed
by four enlarged later editions, the latest in 1999. She has also written plays
for radio and published 14 novels since 1970.

She writes: 'For a time, I was drawn to Black Mountain poets, particularly
Charles Olsen, and shared that enthusiasm with followers of J.H. Prynne...It
was translation, however, that helped me to find my own voice and the great
Russian poet Marina Tsvetaeva who proved to be the most important single
influence on my poetry... She was a dangerous example, since in both of us

domestic impracticality meant the usual tensions of wife, mother and poet were horrifyingly large. She taught me to be unafraid of exposing my least dignified emotions, as well as the technical discipline of a rhythm flowing down a page even when held in stanzas. After that, I rarely used completely open forms' (Preface to *Collected Poems*).

Patience

In water nothing is mean. The fugitive
enters the river, she is washed free;
her thoughts unravel like weeds of
green silk, she moves downstream
as easily as any cold-water creature.

can swim between furred stones, brown
fronds, boots and tins the river holds equally.
The trees hiss overhead. She feels their shadows.
She imagines herself clean as a fish,
evasive, solitary, dumb. Her prayer:
to make peace with her own monstrous nature.

[1977]

Infidelities

Last night she ran out barefoot over
the wet gravel to call him back
from the street. This morning,
in the tranquillity of bath water,

she wonders when it was she first shivered
with the wish for more than ordinary happiness.
How did she fall in love with poetry
that clear eyed girl she was?

Late at night, by a one-bar heater,
her unpainted lips parted
on the words of dead poets.
She was safer in the dance hall.

'And if you can't love poetry,'
she muses. 'What was there of me
all those years ago, apart from
that life of which it is made?

Only an inhospitable hostess,
a young woman in an old dress.'

[1990]

Aviation

Tonight our bodies lie unused like clothes flung
    over a bed. I can taste brown rain.
Flat land, wet land, I can feel your winter
    seeping into my blood like an old sickness.
This is your season of waiting and warm convalescence
    when restful spirits can be quiet and gentle.
Why am I feverish then, what are these
    troubled insomniac beckonings?
What are they to me, the islands where
    falcons breed, or green rivers
where red mullet and shad swim up from the sea?

I have a monster in my head, yellow
    and surly as a camel, an old woman
clutching a hot bottle against the damp,
    and I recognise her face. She frightens me,
more than the loneliness of being awake in the dark.
    And so I put on skinny leather wings and my
home-made cage of basket wear and start
    my crazy flapping run. In this light
I must look like an old enthusiast in
    daguerreotype. These marshlands
clog the feet. I know, but then
    I may not rise, but all night long I run.

[1990]

153

Versions of Marina Tsvetayeva:

Verses

written so long ago, I didn't even
    know I was a poet,
my words fell like spray from a fountain
    or flashes from a rocket,

like brats, they burst into sanctuaries
    asleep and filled with incense,
to speak of youth and mortality.
    And now my unread pages

lie scattered in dusty bookshops
    where nobody even lifts them
to examine. And yet, like expensive wines,
    your time will come, my lines.

May 1913 [trs. 1993]

'I opened my veins...'

I opened my veins.   Unstoppably
life spurts out with no remedy.
Now I set out bowls and plates.
Every bowl will be shallow.
Every plate will be small.
            And overflowing their rims,
into the black earth, to nourish
the rushes unstoppably
without cure, gushes
poetry...

1934 [trs. 1993]

RUTH FAINLIGHT

(*b*. 1931)

Born in New York, the daughter of an English father and an Austro-Hungarian mother, Ruth Fainlight has lived in England since she was 15. She married the writer Alan Sillitoe in 1959, and they live in London. Her books of poems include *Cages* (1966), *To See the Matter Clearly* (1968), *The Region's Violence* (1973), *Another Full Moon* (1976), *Sibyls and Others* (1980), *Fifteen to Infinity* (1983) *Climates* (1983), *Selected Poems* (1987), *The Knot* (1990), *This Time of Year* (1993), *Sugar-Paper Blue* (1997), *Burning Wire* (2002) and *Moon Wheels* (2006). She has also published two collections of short stories, and numerous libretti. On the relationship between gender and poetry, she wrote in 1985: 'The problem of the Muse: Is she mother sister, lover, oneself? Easy enough for a man to project the anima outward, but the animus, as is implicit in the more general use of the word to denote a hostile reaction, can become a repressive manifestation that muffles and paralyses with self doubt. It took me a long time to understand that my poem "The Other" is about the Muse' (Couzyn, p.131); and 'St Teresa said "To be a woman is to feel your wings droop." A specifically female anger has been the impetus for many of my poems. Nevertheless, I am convinced that the "negative capability" of the poet extends beyond/ below/ above gender. I am a poet who is a woman, not a woman poet' (Couzyn, p.130).

from Sheba and Solomon

V *The Invitation*

Sheba worshipped the sun,
but sight of the rising god
was blocked that day by the hoopoe
who perched in her eastern window
bearing Solomon's letter,
an invitation – or command –
to visit him. How could
a woman so sceptical
worship what disappears each
night, is eclipsed by a bird?

Sheba got her husband drunk
on their wedding night, then cut off his head
and hung it from the palace gate.
She had no problem after that –

until Solomon's hoopoe opened its beak
and dropped a letter on her neck
in the same place the sword had struck.
His words were as smooth as his penmanship,
but she sensed a threat. She sought advice
from her wisest men – and then ignored it.

VI *Sheba's Tests*

First she sent him treasure.
If he kept it, like any lesser king,
that would prove her the stronger.
When he sent it back, she understood
he was a man of power.
Yet she had to test him further.

*

She sent five hundred girls
five hundred boys, dressed in each others' clothes
to try his subtlety and intuition
to see if he would notice.

She sent an unpierced pearl
a moonstone hollowed in a twisted spiral.
Was one a symbol of virginity
the other, of violation?

*

When he solved her riddles –
could not be deceived by disguise, but recognised
the difference between the children,
the essence of male and female

and, to meet her challenge,
commanded that an earthworm and a fruitworm
pierce the pearl and thread the moonstone –
she confirmed his wisdom
                              and went herself.

[2002]

156

SYLVIA PLATH

(1932-63)

Born in Boston, Massachusetts, Sylvia Plath was educated at Wellesley and
Smith Colleges before studying in England at Cambridge University for two
years on a Fulbright scholarship. With Anne Sexton, Plath attended poetry
workshops with Robert Lowell. She settled in Britain with her husband, the
poet Ted Hughes, whom she married in 1956 and with whom she had two
children. Plath was very much aware of the scarcity of women poets on whom
to model herself, and saw herself in a journal entry of 1958 as in direct com-
petition with her female contemporaries. She writes: 'Arrogant, I think I have
written lines that will qualify me as The Poetess of America...Who rivals? Well,
in history – Sappho, Elizabeth Barrett Browning, Christina Rossetti, Amy Lowell,
Emily Dickinson, Edna St Vincent Millay – all dead. Now: Edith Sitwell &
Marianne Moore, the ageing giantesses & poetic godmothers. Phyllis McGinley
is out – light verse: she's sold herself. Rather: May Swenson, Isabella Gardner,
and most close, Adrienne Cecile Rich.' Plath wrote a long essay on the work
of Edith Sitwell in 1953 and later became interested in the work of Stevie
Smith. In a letter to Smith, she described herself a 'a desperate Smith addict'.
Plath was also influenced in important ways by Virginia Woolf, Theodore
Roethke, Dylan Thomas, Robert Graves and Laura (Riding) Jackson.

Her first book, *The Colossus*, was published in 1960, followed by a semi-
autobiographical novel, *The Bell Jar* (1962), published under the name Victoria
Lucas. *Ariel* was published posthumously in 1965, followed by *Winter Trees*
and *Crossing the Water* (1971), in addition to three pamphlets, *Crystal Gazer and
Other Poems, Fiesta Melons* and *Lyonesse: Poems* (1971). *Sylvia Plath: Selected
Poems* was published in 1985. Because of the circumstances of her death, and
her separation from Ted Hughes, Plath's life has in some ways come to over-
shadow her poetry. Plath was keen to find a way of writing that did not pigeon-
hole her as a woman writer. In 'A Comparison' she writes about the difference
between poetry and prose, describing a prose as an open hand, poetry as a
clenched fist. In 2004 *Ariel* was reissued in its original order, with facsimile
drafts of poems, and an introduction by her daughter, the poet and artist
Frieda Hughes.

The Colossus

I shall never get you put together entirely,
Pieced, glued, and properly jointed.
Mule-bray, pig-grunt and bawdy cackles
Proceed from your great lips.
It's worse than a barnyard.

Perhaps you consider yourself an oracle,
Mouthpiece of the dead, or of some god or other.
Thirty years now I have labored
To dredge the silt from your throat.
I am none the wiser.

Scaling little ladders with gluepots and pails of Lysol
I crawl like an ant in mourning
Over the weedy acres of your brow
To mend the immense skull-plates and clear
The bald, white tumuli of your eyes.

A blue sky out of the Oresteia
Arches above us. O father, all by yourself
You are pithy and historical as the Roman Forum.
I open my lunch on a hill of black cypress.
Your fluted bones and acanthine hair are littered

In their old anarchy to the horizon-line.
It would take more than a lightning-stroke
To create such a ruin.
Nights, I squat in the cornucopia
Of your left ear, out of the wind,

Counting the red stars and those of plum-color.
The sun rises under the pillar of your tongue.
My hours are married to shadow.
No longer do I listen for the scrape of a keel
On the blank stones of the landing.

1959 [1960]

Mirror

I am silver and exact. I have no preconceptions.
Whatever I see I swallow immediately
Just as it is, unmisted by love or dislike.
I am not cruel, only truthful –
The eye of a little god, four-cornered.
Most of the time I meditate on the opposite wall.

It is pink, with speckles. I have looked at it so long
I think it is a part of my heart. But it flickers.
Faces and darkness separate us over and over.

Now I am a lake. A woman bends over me,
Searching my reaches for what she really is.
Then she turns to those liars, the candles or the moon.
I see her back, and reflect it faithfully.
She rewards me with tears and an agitation of hands.
I am important to her. She comes and goes.
Each morning it is her face that replaces the darkness.
In me she has drowned a young girl, and in me an old woman
Rises toward her day after day, like a terrible fish.

23 October 1961 [1971]

Daddy

You do not do, you do not do
Any more, black shoe
In which I have lived like a foot
For thirty years, poor and white,
Barely daring to breathe or Achoo.

Daddy, I have had to kill you.
You died before I had time –
Marble-heavy, a bag full of God,
Ghastly statue with one gray toe
Big as a Frisco seal

And a head in the freakish Atlantic
Where it pours bean green over blue
In the waters off beautiful Nauset.
I used to pray to recover you.
Ach, du.

In the German tongue, in the Polish town
Scraped flat by the roller
Of wars, wars, wars.
But the name of the town is common.
My Polack friend

Says there are a dozen or two.
So I never could tell where you
Put your foot, your root,
I never could talk to you.
The tongue stuck in my jaw.

It stuck in a barb wire snare.
Ich, ich, ich, ich,
I could hardly speak.
I thought every German was you.
And the language obscene

An engine, an engine
Chuffing me off like a Jew.
A Jew to Dachau, Auschwitz, Belsen.
I began to talk like a Jew.
I think I may well be a Jew.

The snows of the Tyrol, the dear beer of Vienna
Are not very pure or true.
With my gipsy ancestress and my weird luck
And my Taroc pack and my Taroc pad
I may be a bit of a Jew.

I have always been scared of *you*,
With your Luftwaffe, your gobbledygoo.
And your neat mustache
And your Aryan eye, bright blue.
Panzer-man, panzer-man, O You –

Not God but a swastika
So black no sky could squeak through.
Every woman adores a Fascist,
The boot in the face, the brute
Brute heart of a brute like you.

You stand at the blackboard, daddy,
In the picture I have of you,
A cleft in your chin instead of your foot
But no less a devil for that, no not
Any less the black man who

Bit my pretty red heart in two.
I was ten when they buried you.
At twenty I tried to die
And get back, back, back to you.
I thought even the bones would do.

But they pulled me out of the sack,
And they stuck me together with glue.
And then I knew what to do.
I made a model of you,
A man in black with a Meinkampf look

And a love of the rack and the screw.
And I said I do, I do.
So daddy, I'm finally through.
The black telephone's off at the root,
The voices just can't worm through.

If I've killed one man, I've killed two –
The vampire who said he was you
And drank my blood for a year,
Seven years, if you want to know.
Daddy, you can lie back now.

There's a stake in your fat black heart
And the villagers never liked you.
They are dancing and stamping on you.
They always *knew* it was you.
Daddy, daddy, you bastard, I'm through.

12 October 1962 [1965]

Cut
(for Susan O'Neill Roe)

What a thrill –
My thumb instead of an onion.
The top quite gone
Except for a sort of a hinge

Of skin,
A flap like a hat,

Dead white.
Then that red plush.

Little pilgrim,
The Indian's axed your scalp.
Your turkey wattle
Carpet rolls

Straight from the heart.
I step on it,
Clutching my bottle
Of pink fizz.

A celebration, this is.
Out of a gap
A million soldiers run,
Redcoats, every one.

Whose side are they on?
O my
Homunculus, I am ill.
I have taken a pill to kill

The thin
Papery feeling.
Saboteur,
Kamikaze man –

The stain on your
Gauze Ku Klux Klan
Babushka
Darkens and tarnishes and when

The balled
Pulp of your heart
Confronts its small
Mill of silence

How you jump –
Trepanned veteran,
Dirty girl,
Thumb stump.

24 October 1962 [1965]

Lady Lazarus

I have done it again.
One year in every ten
I manage it –

A sort of walking miracle, my skin
Bright as a Nazi lampshade,
My right foot

A paperweight,
My face a featureless, fine
Jew linen.

Peel off the napkin
O my enemy.
Do I terrify? –

The nose, the eye pits, the full set of teeth?
The sour breath
Will vanish in a day.

Soon, soon the flesh
The grave cave ate will be
At home on me

And I a smiling woman.
I am only thirty.
And like the cat I have nine times to die.

This is Number Three.
What a trash
To annihilate each decade.

What a million filaments.
The peanut-crunching crowd
Shoves in to see

Then unwrap me hand and foot –
The big strip tease.
Gentlemen, ladies

These are my hands
My knees.
I may be skin and bone,

Nevertheless, I am the same, identical woman.
The first time it happened I was ten.
It was an accident.

The second time I meant
To last it out and not come back at all.
I rocked shut

As a seashell.
They had to call and call
And pick the worms off me like sticky pearls.

Dying
Is an art, like everything else.
I do it exceptionally well.

I do it so it feels like hell.
I do it so it feels real.
I guess you could say I've a call.

It's easy enough to do it in a cell.
It's easy enough to do it and stay put.
It's the theatrical

Comeback in broad day
To the same place, the same face, the same brute
Amused shout:

'A miracle!'
That knocks me out.
There is a charge

For the eyeing of my scars, there is a charge
For the hearing of my heart –
It really goes.

And there is a charge, a very large charge
For a word or a touch
Or at bit of blood

Or a piece of my hair or my clothes.
So, so, Herr Doktor.
So, Herr Enemy.

I am your opus,
I am your valuable,
The pure gold baby

That melts to a shriek.
I turn and burn.
Do not think I underestimate your great concern.

Ash, ash –
You poke and stir.
Flesh, bone, there is nothing there –

A cake of soap,
A wedding ring,
A gold filling.

Herr God, Herr Lucifer
Beware
Beware.

Out of the ash
I rise with my red hair
And I eat men like air.

23-29 October 1962 [1965]

Kindness

Kindness glides about my house.
Dame Kindness, she is so nice!
The blue and red jewels of her rings smoke
In the windows, the mirrors
Are filling with smiles.

What is so real as the cry of a child?
A rabbit's cry may be wilder

But it has no soul.
Sugar can cure everything, so Kindness says.
Sugar is a necessary fluid,

Its crystals a little poultice.
O kindness, kindness
Sweetly picking up pieces!
My Japanese silks, desperate butterflies,
May be pinned any minute, anesthetised.

And here you come, with a cup of tea
Wreathed in steam.
The blood jet is poetry,
There is no stopping it.
You hand me two children, two roses.

1 February 1963 [1965]

The Night Dances

A smile fell in the grass.
Irretrievable!

And how will your night dances
Lose themselves. In mathematics?

Such pure leaps and spirals –
Surely they travel

The world forever, I shall not entirely
Sit emptied of beauties, the gift

Of your small breath, the drenched grass
Smell of your sleeps, lilies, lilies.

Their flesh bears no relation.
Cold folds of ego, the calla,

And the tiger, embellishing itself –
Spots, and a spread of hot petals.

166

The comets
Have such a space to cross,

Such coldness, forgetfulness.
So your gestures flake off –

Warm and human, then their pink light
Bleeding and peeling

Through the black amnesias of heaven.
Why am I given

These lamps, these planets
Falling like blessings, like flakes

Six-sided, white
On my eyes, my lips, my hair

Touching and melting.
Nowhere.

6 November 1962 [1965]

JENNY JOSEPH

(*b.* 1932)

Born in Birmingham, of Jewish parentage, Jenny Joseph grew up in Buckingham-
shire. After studying English at St Hilda's College, Oxford, she worked as a
reporter in Bedford and Oxford, spending 18 months in South Africa in the
mid 50s before she was asked to leave by the government. Her poetry books
include *The Unlooked-for Season* (1960), *Rose in the Afternoon* (1974), *The
Thinking Heart* (1978), *Beyond Descartes* (1983), *Selected Poems* (1992), *Ghosts
and Other Company* (1995) and *Extreme of things* (2006). Her other books
include *Persephone* (1986), a story in prose and verse, which won the James
Tait Black Memorial Prize for fiction; *Beached Boats* (1991), with photographer
Robert Mitchell; *Extended Similes* (1997), prose fictions; and *Led by the Nose*
(2002), a prose work which goes through the months in the garden by smell.

She writes on poetry: 'It is one of the most impersonal things. It has nothing
to do with self-expression or identity. It is an extension of the paltry self into
the things that are interesting to learn and to be with – an escape into reality'
(Couzyn, p.170). Her poem 'Warning' is perhaps one of the best-known poems
by a 20th-century British woman writer. Originally part of a three-part set of
monologues, it is representative of only one strand of this wide-ranging poet's
work, although over the years Joseph has made use of the monologue and
acknowledges Browning as an influence.

Warning

When I am an old woman I shall wear purple
With a red hat which doesn't go, and doesn't suit me.
And I shall spend my pension on brandy and summer gloves
And satin sandals, and say we've no money for butter.
I shall sit down on the pavement when I'm tired
And gobble up samples in shops and press alarm bells
And run my stick along the public railings
And make up for the sobriety of my youth.
I shall go out in my slippers in the rain
And pick the flowers in other people's gardens
And learn to spit.

You can wear terrible shirts and grow more fat
And eat three pounds of sausages at a go
Or only bread and pickle for a week
And hoard pens and pencils and beermats and things in boxes.

But now we must have clothes that keep us dry
And pay our rent and not swear in the street
And set a good example for the children.
We must have friends to dinner and read the papers.

But maybe I ought to practise a little now?
So people who know me are not too shocked and surprised
When suddenly I am old, and start to wear purple.

[1974]

The inland sea

Did I tell you of a strange dream I had?
I was in the upper country, mule country,
The track twisting, dust, stone; sometimes,
Standing rare and beautiful, a thistle
On a cliff edge. White sky behind it.

Suddenly, singing
Was coming up the valley; and as it neared –
The little group, you could see that it travelled with them –

168

The green carpet of the valley floor:
Grasses and fronds with hanging heads, and mosses.

The fore man stood by me on the cliff
A Chinese ivory sage that fits in the palm
With every thousand hair in his beard distinct
And wrinkles lining a face as smooth as a pebble
But complete and whole; and this man spoke to me.

'It is the inland sea we seek,' he said
'And we will journey ever,' and round the mountain,
As they moved on like a shoal in the ravine bottom,
Winding as one, like a cloud across the sky,
Their distant singing swayed and ebbed with the wind
And I felt safe because these old men sought
The inland sea.

I remember a girl telling me
(Brown curly hair, fresh skin and open eyes
Sweet honest and innocent English abroad –
I don't think they are made like that any more –)
Of her meeting the man that she was now engaged to.
They had met and she dreamt that she was married to him
And the second time she saw him told him her dream.
She was not bold or fishing or plotting consequence
'Wasn't it strange' she'd said 'to have such a dream?'
And he asked her to marry him.

Why do I, a life time late, these years after
Talk of dreams, fabricating premises
When we both know it may be so or no
And not matter; when the direct truth
And the direct lie are mudded by convenience
And compromised;
When all is a game we would like to win, but know
The losing will shake us for only a little while
Before we slip back into our haze of self
Where all is slumber within wired-up walls?

Why? Listen. Come a little closer, near as you dare
To the edge of this spur. The soil's a little crumbly
But there are hawthorns, sloes and other bushes
Knitting the escarpment. Here is shade
And safety on the edge of danger. A place I found

By long trekking, retreating at times with care
Not to loosen rock, and going about
Another way until I found this nest.
Listen. Inch forward. What do you hear in the wind
That, freed from the bluffs, is meandering with the river?
Look up to the sky an instant, do you not see
Immense lakes of light lying within the clouds?
Part these grasses: spread out fair below
The hidden, ancient, still-fructifying source
Silent shines in sunlight.
Can you see? Come a bit nearer then. Now.
Look: we have come to the inland sea.

[1983]

Ant nest

As the establishment of an ant citadel under the top-soil makes desert a considerable area which yet shows a green surface, extending the sterility of the soil by the continuance of multifarious activity below, concentrated, unremitting, absorbing, unseen,

resulting in a lack of hold in such plants as go on attempting to grow on the soil, for they have to survive with a very curtailed rooting system – the honeycombed areas retain no moisture and have no nourishment –

So the death of his child years ago, unknown to most of his acquaintance, a wound covered over with courage, and determination to continue alive in this world, laid beneath layers of activity – the walking tours with his brother, the visits, in spring and autumn usually, to his wife's parents on the Welsh borders, the bringing of their skiff in off the river for the winter, the fruit-picking at the farm in the Vale of Evesham for his wife to make jam, the sending off for tickets for when the National Companies came to Worcester,

apparent coverage as bright and solid as a full herbaceous border,

So this grief chawing away made a place riddled with holes beneath all the associations, all his filling of his days. When he cracked up in the office over something that would not have worried a junior his colleagues emphasised their disbelief by repeating how perfectly well he had been and normal and competent, with no sign even in the previous day or two that anything was worrying him,

but anyone who knew about soil conditions and the ravages a colony of termites makes on substance if left undisturbed would have recognised the ashen skin and lethargy of the man as consequential. The unseeing stare, foredone; closure; concluded;

For there was no body to it, no nourishment to be had from it, all used up and made useless by the life of emasculation perpetually at work below the surface, taking all good from it, preventing conditions of soil recovery whatever was manfully done on the surface up in the air by a few tenacious plants.

[1997]

ROSEMARY TONKS
(*b*. 1932)

Rosemary Tonks is literally a poet who has fallen out of sight, her evangelical Christianity leading her to reject all aspects of her previous literary life. She published two collections of poetry in the 1960s, *Notes on Cafés and Bedrooms* (1963) and *Iliad of Broken Sentences* (1967), and was also a prolific novelist. Her poetic work is best characterised as a cross between Jean Rhys and Frank O'Hara in the setting of London Bohemia. She writes: 'What I write about must develop from my life and times... My concern...is with exact emotional proportions – proportions as they are now current for me. Ideally, whatever is heightened should be justified both by art and by life; while the poet remains vulnerable to those moments when a poem suddenly makes its own terms – and with an overwhelming force that is self-justifying... Telling the truth about feeling requires prodigious integrity... Some poets do manage to converge on their inner life by generating emotion from an inspired visual imagery; in this instance the images exist in their own right, but may be thought to be in a weaker position as the raw material of the emotion, in preference to a larger existence as illustration of it.' (Brown & Paterson, eds, *Don't Ask Me What I Mean*, pp.290-91)

Story of a Hotel Room

Thinking we were safe – insanity!
We went in to make love. All the same

171

Idiots to trust the little hotel bedroom.
Then in the gloom...
...And who does not know that pair of shutters
With the awkward hook on them
All screeching whispers? Very well then, in the gloom
We set about acquiring one another
Urgently! But on a temporary basis
Only as guests – just guests of one another's senses.

But idiots to feel so safe you hold back nothing
Because the bed of cold, electric linen
Happens to be illicit...
To make love as well as that is ruinous.
Londoner, Parisian, someone should have warned us
That without permanent intentions
You have absolutely no protection
– If the act is clean, authentic, sumptuous,
The concurring deep love of the heart
Follows the naked work, profoundly moved by it.

[1963]

The Sofas, Fogs and Cinemas

I have lived it, and lived it,
My nervous, luxury civilisation,
My sugar-loving nerves have battered me to pieces.

...Their idea of literature is hopeless.
Make them drink their own poetry!
Let them eat their gross novel, full of mud.

It's quiet; just the fresh, chilly weather... and he
Gets up from his dead bedroom, and comes in here
And digs himself into the sofa.
He stays there up to two hours in the hole – and talks
– Straight into the large subjects, he faces up to *everything*
It's...... damnably depressing.
(That great lavatory coat...the cigarillo burning
In the little dish... And when he calls out: 'Ha!'
Madness! – you no longer possess your own furniture.)

172

On my bad days (and I'm being broken
At this very moment) I speak of my ambitions...and he
Becomes intensely gloomy, with the look of something jugged, |
Morose, sour, mouldering away, with lockjaw...

I grow coarser; and more modern (*I*, who am driven mad
By my ideas; who go nowhere;
Who dare not leave my frontdoor, lest an idea...)
All right. I admit everything, everything!

Oh yes, the opera (Ah, but the cinema)
He particularly enjoys it, enjoys it *horribly*, when someone's ill
At the last minute; and they specially fly in
A new, gigantic, Dutch soprano. He wants to help her
With her arias.   Old goat! Blasphemer!
He wants to help her with her arias!

No, I...go to the cinema,
I particularly like it when the fog is thick, the street
Is like a hole in an old coat, and the light is brown as laudanum,
...the fogs! the fogs! The cinemas
Where the criminal shadow-literature flickers over our faces,
The screen is spread out like a thundercloud – that bangs
And splashes you with acid... or lies derelict,
                            with lighted waters in it,
And in the silence, drips and crackles – taciturn, luxurious.
...The drugged and battered Philistines
Are all around you in the auditorium...

And he...is somewhere else, in his dead bedroom clothes,
He wants to make me think his thoughts
And they will be *enormous*, dull – (just the sort
To keep away from).
...when I see that cigarillo, when I see it...smoking
And he wants to face the international situation...
Lunatic rages! Blackness! Suffocation!

– All this sitting about in cafes to calm down
Simply wears me out. And their idea of literature!
The idiotic cut of the stanzas; the novels, full up, gross.

I have lived it, and I know too much.
My café-nerves are breaking me
With black, exhausting information.

[1967]

Badly-Chosen Lover

Criminal, you took a great piece of my life,
And you took it under false pretences,
That piece of time
– In the clear muscles of my brain
I have the lens and jug of it!
Books, thoughts, meals, days, and houses,
Half Europe, spent like a coarse banknote,
You took it – leaving mud and cabbage stumps.

And, Criminal, I damn you for it (very softly).
My spirit broke her fast on you. And, Turk,
You fed her with the breath of your neck
– In my brain's clear retina
I have the stolen love-behaviour.
Your heart, greedy and tepid, brothel-meat,
Gulped it, like a flunkey with erotica.
And very softly, Criminal, I *damn* you for it.

[1967]

ANNE STEVENSON
(*b.* 1933)

Born in Cambridge, England, Stevenson, the daughter of philosopher Charles
L. Stevenson and Louise Destler, spent her first 12 years in Harvard before
moving to Yale in 1939, and then Ann Arbor where she attended the University
of Michigan, studying music, European literature and history. She married,
and immediately after graduation, returned to England in 1954, where she gave
birth to a daughter (later followed by two sons). Her first poem was published
in 1955. She returned to Michigan in 1961 where she was taught by Donald
Hall, who introduced her to the poetry of Elizabeth Bishop. Her first collec-
tion, *Living in America*, was published in 1965, followed by a critical book on
Bishop in 1966. Her poetry books include *Correspondences: A Family History
in Letters* (1974), *Travelling Behind Glass: Poems 1963-1973* (1974), *Enough of
Green* (1977), *Minute by Glass Minute* (1982), *The Fiction Makers* (1985), *The
Collected Poems 1955-1995* (1995), *Granny Scarecrow* (2000), *A Report from the
Border* (2002) and *Poems 1955-2005* (2005). Her biography of Sylvia Plath,
Bitter Fame, was published in 1989, and in 1998, two critical books, *Five Looks
at Elizabeth Bishop* and *Between the Iceberg and the Ship*. She received the
Northern Rock Foundation Writer's Award in 2002.

She wrote in 1993: 'Young American women of my generation...listened to Eliot, Leavis, and the fathers of the New Criticism because they taught us not only what was important to read but *how* to read; how, that is, to pay close attention to words, how to look for what was good or bad, convincing or weak in writing. It's that *how* that stays with me as the most valuable lesson of my college years, and not the *who* or *what* of anyone's prescriptive theory. I still believe that the readability of a book – outside of its time – secures it a place in tradition, and not the sex of its author or its moral value as "truth" – especially if you regard as "true" the sacred-sounding terminology of evangelical feminism... I don't say differences don't exist. As the 19th century wore on, women's writing engaged with a larger social spectrum; and in our own permissive time, women have as much access to public folly as men. As human beings, we are all flawed, wrong, sorry, tragic and comic, guided and influenced by each other, subject to the temptations of vanity, worldliness and all the assorted ills of nature. That is the human condition "traditional" writing engages with...' (*Where We Stand*, p.179).

from **Correspondences**

A daughter's difficulties as a wife: Mrs Reuben Chandler to her mother in New Orleans

SEPTEMBER 3, 1840   CINCINNATI, OHIO

Now that I've been married for almost four weeks, Mama,
        I'd better drop you and Papa dear a line.
            I guess I'm fine.

Ruby has promised to take me to the Lexington
        buggy races Tuesday, if the weather cools.
            So far we've not been out much.

Just stayed here stifling in hot Cincinnati.
        Clothes almost melt me, Mama, so I've not got out
            my lovely red velvet-and-silk pelisse yet,

or that sweet little lambskin coat with the fur hood.
        The sheets look elegant!
            I adore the pink monogram on the turnover

with exactly the same pattern on the pillowcases!
        Darlings!
            How I wish you could breeze in and admire them!

And the table linen,
    and the bone china,
        and the grand silver candlesticks,

and especially those
    long-stemmed Venetian wine glasses
      with the silver rims.

My, didn't your little daughter
    play the queen the other day
        serving dinner to a whole bevy of bachelors!

To tell the truth, Mama,
    Reuben was a silly to ask them,
      just imagine me, tiny wee me,

hostess to fourteen dragons
    and famished monsters,
        doing battle with fuming pipes and flying plugs.

Poor Rube!
    He doesn't chew and hardly ever smokes.
    He must have felt out of place.

I was frantic, naturally,
    for fear of wine stains and
      tobacco juice on the table cloth,

so I set Agatha to dart in and dab with a towel,
    and told Sue in the kitchen, to brew up some coffee
      quick, before they began speechmaking.

But it was no use.
    They would put me up on a chair after the ices,
      and one of them – Big Tom they call him –

(runs a sizable drygoods business here)
    well, this Tom pulled off my shoe,
      tried to drink wine out of it while

I was dying of laughter,
    and Tom was laughing too, when suddenly
      I slipped, and fell on the Flemish decanter!

It broke.
  Such a terrible pity.
    And so funny at the same time.

I must admit the boys were bricks,
    carrying the tablecloth out to the kitchen,
      holding it out while I

poured hot water from a height,
    just as you always said to.
      Everything would have been all right.

The party could have gone on.
    Then Reuben had to nose in and spoil things,
      sending me to bed!

So the boys went off, kind of sheepish.

Later Reuben said I had disgraced us
    and where was I brought up anyway,
      to behave like a bar maid!

But it wasn't my fault, Mama,
    They were his friends. He invited them.
      I like to give men a good time!

I'm writing this in bed because
    my head thumps and drums every time I move
      and I'm so dog tired!

The only time I sleep is in the morning
    when Reuben has left for the office.
      Which brings up a delicate subject, Mama.

I've been thinking and thinking,
    wondering whether I'll ever succeed in being
      the tender, devoted little wife you wanted me to be.

Because...oh, Mama,
    why didn't you tell me or warn me before I was married
      that a wife is expected to do it every night!

But how could we have guessed?
    Ruby came courting so cool and fine and polite,
      while beneath that gentlemanly, educated exterior...

well! I don't like to worry you, Mama.
You know what men are like!
I remember you said once the dears couldn't help it.

I try to be brave.
But if you did have a chance to speak to Papa,
mightn't you ask him to slip a word,

sort of man to man to Reuben...
about how delicate I am
and how sick I am every month,

not one of those cows
who can be used and used!
Someone's at the door.

I forgot,
I asked Fanny Daniels to come up this morning
to help fix a trim for my hat.

I'll have to hustle!
Give all my love to dear Spooky and Cookie.
How I miss them, the doggy darlings!

Oceans of hugs and kisses for you, too,
and for precious Papa,

From your suffering and loving daughter,

Marianne

[1974]

Making Poetry

'You have to inhabit poetry
if you want to make it.'

And what's 'to inhabit'?

To be in the habit of, to wear
words, sitting in the plainest light,

178

in the silk of morning, in the shoe of night;
a feeling bare and frondish in surprising air;
familiar... rare.

And what's 'to make'?

To be and to become words' passing
weather; to serve a girl on terrible
terms, embark on voyages over voices,
evade the ego-hill, the misery-well,
the siren hiss of *publish, success, publish,
success, success, success.*

And why inhabit, make, inherit poetry?

Oh, it's the shared comedy of the worst
blessed; the sound leading the hand;
a wordlife running from mind to mind
through the washed rooms of the simple senses;
one of those haunted, undefendable, unpoetic
crosses we have to find.

[1985]

A Marriage

When my mother knew why her treatment wasn't working,
She said to my father, trying not to detonate her news,
'Steve, you must marry again. When I'm gone, who's going
To tell you to put your trousers on before your shoes?'

My father opened his mouth to – couldn't – refuse.
Instead, he threw her a look; a man just shot
Gazing at the arm or leg he was about to lose.
His cigarette burned him, but he didn't stub it out.

Later, on the porch, alive in the dark together,
How solid the house must have felt, how sanely familiar
The night-lit leaves, their shadows patterning the street.
The house is still there. The elms and the people, not.

It was now, and it never was now. Like every experience
Of being entirely here, yet really not being.
They couldn't imagine the future that I am seeing,
For all his philosophy and all her common sense.

[1974]

Who's Joking with the Photographer?
(Photographs of myself approaching seventy)

(for Ernestine Ruben)

Not my final face, a map of how to get there.
Seven ages, seven irreversible layers, each
subtler and more supple than a snake's skin.
Nobody looks surprised when we slough off one
and begin to inhabit another.
Do we exchange them whole in our sleep, or
are they washed away in pieces, cheek by brow by chin,
in the steady abrasions of the solar shower?
Draw first breath, and time turns on its taps.
No wonder the newborn's tiny face crinkles and cries:
chill, then a sharp collision with light,
the mouth's desperation for the foreign nipple,
all the uses of eyes, ears, hands still to be learned
before the self pulls away in its skin-tight sphere
to endure on its own the tectonic geology of childhood.

Imagine in space-time irretrievable mothers viewing
the pensioners their babies have become.
'Well, that's life, nothing we can do about it now.'
They don't love us as much as they did, and
why should they? We have replaced them. Just as we're
being replaced by big sassy kids in school blazers.
Meanwhile, Federal Express has delivered my sixth face –
grandmother's, scraps of me grafted to her bones.
I don't believe it. Who made this mess,
this developer's sprawl of roads that can't be retaken,
high tension wires that run dangerously under the skin?
What is it the sceptical eyes are saying to the twisted lips:
ambition is a cliché, beauty a banality? In any case,
this face has given them up – old friends whose obituaries
it reads in the mirror with scarcely a regret.

So, who's joking with the photographer?
And what did she think she was doing,
taking pictures of the impossible? Was a radioscope
attached to her lens? Something teasing under the skull
has infiltrated the surface, something you can't see
until you look away, then it shoots out and tickles you.
You could call it soul or spirit, but that would be serious.
Look for a word that mixes affection with insurrection,
frivolity, child's play, rude curiosity,
a willingness to lift the seventh veil and welcome Yorick.
That's partly what the photo says. The rest is private,
guilt that rouses memory at four in the morning,
truths such as Hamlet used, torturing his mother,
all the dark half-tones of the sensuous unsayable
finding a whole woman there, in her one face.

[2002]

FLEUR ADCOCK

(*b*. 1934)

Born in Papakura in New Zealand, Kareen Fleur Adcock first lived in Britain
from 1939 to 1947. She read Classics at Victoria University, Wellington, and
married the poet Alistair Campbell in 1952. She had two sons and worked as a
lecturer and librarian. She married again briefly in 1961, and moved to Britain
with her younger son in 1963. *The Eye of the Hurricane* was published in New
Zealand in 1964. Her first book of poems to be published in Britain, *Tigers*,
appeared in 1967, including some poems from the earlier collection. It was
followed by *High Tide in the Garden* (1971), *The Scenic Route* (1974), *The Inner
Harbour* (1979), *Selected Poems* (1983), *The Virgin and the Nightingale: medieval
Latin lyrics* (1983), *The Incident Book* (1986), *Time Zones* (1991), *Looking Back*
(1997), and *Poems 1960-2000* (2000). Fleur Adcock is a freelance writer and
lives in London.

In 1985 she wrote: 'The question of my nationality has always seemed at
least as significant as the question of my gender...In my early poems there
were few women apart from fabularised or fictionalised versions of myself; the
men and the children were real, because I knew about men and children, but
I had to play most of the female roles myself.' (Couzyn, p.202). In the intro-
duction to her *Faber Book of 20th Century Women's Poetry* (1987) she writes:
'If I have a theory about the tradition informing [women's] poetry it is that
there is no particular tradition: there have been poets, and they have been
individuals, and a few of them have influenced a few others, but on the whole
there is no clear thread...What is different about poetry by women, of course,
is not in its nature but the fact that until recently it has been undervalued and

to some extent neglected...the reasons for it seem almost too well known to need rehearsing...They are: The publishing world was dominated by men. Editors, publishers and critics were usually male. Men tend not to take women seriously. Women as a result tended not to take themselves seriously enough, and were in any case usually too busy, too oppressed or too under-educated to write. "Poet" was a masculine word. The Muse was female, the poet was male. There was as deep-seated conviction that women couldn't do it.' (p.1).

Bogyman

Stepping down from the blackberry bushes
he stands in my path: Bogyman.
He is not as I had remembered him,
though he still wears the broad-brimmed hat,
the rubber-soled shoes and the woollen gloves.
No face; and that soft mooning voice
still spinning its endless distracting yarn.

But this is daylight, a misty autumn
Sunday, not unpopulated
by birds. I can see him in such colours
as he wears – fawn, grey, murky blue –
not all shadow-clothed, as he was that night
when I was ten; he seems less tall
(I have grown) and less muffled in silence.

I have no doubt at all, though, that he is
Bogyman. He is why children
do not sleep all night in their tree-houses.
He is why, when I had pleaded
to spend a night on the common, under
a cosy bush, and my mother
surprisingly said yes, she took no risk.

He was the risk I would not take; better
to make excuses, to lose face,
than to meet the really faceless, the one
whose name was too childish for us
to utter – 'murderers' we talked of, and
'lunatics escaped from Earlswood'.
But I met him, of course, as we all do.

Well, that was then; I survived; and later
survived meetings with his other
forms, bold or pathetic or disguised – the
slummocking figure in a dark
alley, or the lover turned suddenly
icy-faced; fingers at my throat
and ludicrous violence in kitchens.

I am older now, and (I tell myself,
circling carefully around him
at the far edge of the path, pretending
I am not in fact confronted)
can deal with such things. But what, Bogyman,
shall I be at twice my age? (At
your age?) Shall I be grandmotherly, fond

suddenly of gardening, chatty with
neighbours? Or strained, not giving in,
writing for *Ambit* and hitch-hiking to
Turkey? Or sipping Guinness in
the Bald-Faced Stag, in wrinkled stockings? Or
(and now I look for the first time
straight at you) something like you, Bogyman?

[1971]

A Surprise in the Peninsula

When I came in that night I found
the skin of a dog stretched flat and
nailed upon my wall between the
two windows. It seemed freshly killed –
there was blood at the edges. Not
my dog: I have never owned one,
I rather dislike them. (Perhaps
whoever did it knew that.) It
was a light brown dog, with smooth hair;
no head, but the tail still remained.
On the flat surface of the pelt
was branded the outline of the
peninsula, singed in thick black

183

strokes into the fur: a coarse map.
The position of the town was
marked by a bullet-hole; it went
right through the wall. I placed my eye
to it, and could see the dark trees
outside the house, flecked with moonlight.
I locked the door then, and sat up
all night, drinking small cups of the
bitter local coffee. A dog
would have been useful, I thought, for
protection. But perhaps the one
I had been given performed that
function; for no one came that night,
nor for three more. On the fourth day
it was time to leave. The dog-skin
still hung on the wall, stiff and dry
by now, the flies and the smell gone.
Could it, I wondered, have been meant
not as a warning, but a gift?
And, scarcely shuddering, I drew
the nails out and took it with me.

[1971]

Against Coupling

I write in praise of the solitary act:
of not feeling a trespassing tongue
forced into one's mouth, one's breath
smothered, nipples crushed against the
ribcage, and that metallic tingling
in the chin set off by a certain odd nerve:

unpleasure. Just to avoid those eyes would help –
such eyes as a young girl draws life from,
listening to the vegetal
rustle within her, as his gaze
stirs polypal fronds in the obscure
sea-bed of her body, and her own eyes blur.

There is much to be said for abandoning
this no longer novel exercise –
for not 'participating in
a total experience' – when
one feels like the lady in Leeds who
had seen *The Sound of Music* eighty-six times;

or more, perhaps, like the school drama mistress
producing *A Midsummer Night's Dream*
for the seventh year running, with
yet another cast from 5B.
Pyramus and Thisbe are dead, but
the hole in the wall can still be troublesome.

I advise you, then, to embrace it without
encumbrance. No need to set the scene,
dress up (or undress), make speeches.
Five minutes of solitude are
enough – in the bath, or to fill
that gap between the Sunday papers and lunch.

[1971]

A Way Out

The other option's to become a bird.
That's kindly done, to guess from how they sing,
decently independent of the word
as we are not; and how they use the air
to sail as we might soaring on a swing
higher and higher; but the rope's not there,

it's free fall upward, out into the sky;
or if the arc veer downward, then it's planned:
a bird can loiter, skimming just as high
as lets him supervise the hazel copse,
the turnip field, the orchard, and then land
on just the twig he's chosen. Down he drops

to feed, if so it be: a pretty killer,
a keen-eyed stomach weighted like a dart.
He feels no pity for the caterpillar,
that moistly munching hoop of innocent green.
It is such tender lapses twist the heart.
A bird's heart is a tight little red bean,

untwistable. His beak is made of bone,
his feet apparently of stainless wire;
his coat's impermeable; his nest's his own.
The clogging multiplicity of things
amongst which other creatures, battling, tire
can be evaded by a pair of wings.

The point is, most of it occurs below,
earthed at the levels of the grovelling wood
and gritty buildings. Up's the way to go.
If it's escapist, if it's like a dream
the dream's prolonged until it ends for good.
I see no disadvantage in the scheme.

[1979]

Prelude

Is it the long dry grass that is so erotic,
waving about us with hair-fine fronds of straw,
with feathery flourishes of seed, inviting us
to cling together, fall, roll into it
blind and gasping, smothered by stalks and hair,
pollen and each other's tongues on our hot faces?
Then imagine if the summer rain were to come,
heavy drops hissing through the warm air,
a sluice on our wet bodies, plastering us
with strands of delicious grass; a hum in our ears.

We walk a yard apart, talking
of literature and of botany.
We have known each other, remotely, for nineteen years.

[1979]

The Ex-Queen Among the Astronomers

They serve revolving saucer eyes,
dishes of stars; they wait upon
huge lenses hung aloft to frame
the slow procession of the skies.

They calculate, adjust, record,
watch transits, measure distances.
They carry pocket telescopes
to spy through when they walk abroad.

Spectra possess their eyes; they face
upwards, alert for meteorites,
cherishing little glassy worlds:
receptacles for outer space.

But she, exile, expelled, ex-queen,
swishes among the men of science
waiting for cloudy skies, for nights
when constellations can't be seen.

She wears the rings he let her keep;
she walks as she was taught to walk
for his approval, years ago.
His bitter features taunt her sleep.

And so when these have laid aside
their telescopes, when lids are closed
between machine and sky, she seeks
terrestrial bodies to bestride.

She plucks this one or that among
the astronomers, and is become
his canopy, his occultation;
she sucks at earlobe, penis, tongue

mouthing the tubes of flesh; her hair
crackles, her eyes are comet-sparks.
She brings the distant briefly close
above his dreamy abstract stare.

[1979]

187

AUDRE LORDE

(1934-92)

Born in Harlem, New York, Lorde was the third of three daughters. Her parents, Frederic Byron and Linda Belmar Lorde, had emigrated from the West Indies. Lorde attended Hunter College from 1954 to 1959 and later received a degree in library science from the University of Columbia in 1961. She married Edward Ashley Rollins and they had two children, divorcing in 1970. Lorde's first collection *The First Cities*, was published in 1968, followed by *Cables to Rage* (1970), *From a Land Where Other People Live* (1973), *New York Headshop and Museum* (1974), *Coal* (1976), *The Black Unicorn* (1978), *Chosen Poems: Old and New* (1982) and *Our Dead Behind Us* (1986). An updated edition of *Chosen Poems* entitled *Undersong: Chosen Poems Old and New* (1992) offers some new poems and revisions of others. *Sister Outsider: Essays and Speeches* was published in 1984. Her last collection, including poems written in the final stages of her illness, was the posthumously published *The Marvelous Arithmetics of Distance: Poems 1987-1992* (1993).

As a black lesbian woman, Lorde has been central to giving voice to women's experiences of oppression in North America, and to the exploration of sexuality and black experience. Her poems are frequently poems of testimony whether they are explicitly polemical or exploring the intimacy of lovers. She wrote, in 1977, of poetry as 'a revelatory distillation of experience...Poetry is not a luxury. It is a vital necessity of our existence...Poetry is the way we help give name to the nameless so it can be thought...Poetry is the skeleton architecture of our lives. It lays the foundation for a future of change, a bridge across our fears of what has never been before' (Herbert & Hollis, eds, *Strong Words*, p.138).

Coal

I   is the total black,
being spoken
from the earth's inside.

There are many kinds of open
how a diamond comes
into a knot of flame
how sound comes into a words
colored
by who pays what for speaking.

Some words are open
diamonds on a glass window
singing out within the crash

of passing sun
other words are stapled wagers
in a perforated book
buy and sign and tear apart
and come whatever wills all chances
the stub remains
an ill-pulled tooth
with a ragged edge.

Some words live in my throat
breeding like adders
others
know sun
seeking like gypsies
over my tongue
to explode through my lips
like young sparrows
bursting from shell.

Some words
bedevil me

Love is word, another kind of open.
As the diamond comes
into a knot of flame
I am Black
because I come from the earth's inside
take my word for jewel
in the open light.

1962 [1976]

The Women of Dan Dance with Swords in Their Hands to Mark the Time When They Were Warriors

I did not fall from the sky
I
nor descend like a plague of locusts
to drink color and strength from the earth
and I do not come like rain
as a tribute or symbol for earth's becoming

I come as a woman
dark and open
some times I fall like night
softly
and terrible
only when I must die
in order to rise again.
I do not come like a secret warrior
with an unsheathed sword in my mouth
hidden behind my tongue
slicing my throat to ribbons
of service with a smile
while the blood runs
down and out
through holes in the two sacred mounds
on my chest.

I come like a woman
who I am
spreading out through nights
laughter and promise
and dark heat
warming whatever I touch
that is living
consuming
only
what is already dead.

[1978]

GILLIAN CLARKE

(*b*. 1937)

Gillian Clarke was born in Cardiff and read English at University College, Cardiff. She went on to work for the BBC in London, returning to Wales in 1960. She was editor of the *Anglo-Welsh Review* from 1975 to 1984. The mother of three children, she now lives with her husband on a smallholding in Ceredigion. Her first collection was *Snow on the Mountain* (1971), followed by *The Sundial* (1978) and *Letter from a Far Country* (1982). Her first *Selected Poems* was published in 1985, followed by books including *Letting in the Rumour* (1989), *The King of Britain's Daughter* (1993), *Collected Poems* (1997), *Five Fields* (1998) and *Making the Beds for the Dead* (2004).

Clarke publishes only in English, but sometimes employs Welsh forms, or uses Welsh words in her poems. She writes 'Anne Stevenson says what she loves about Britain is that every bit of it has been born on, lived on, died on, and what she loves about America is that so much of it has never known a human footprint. I love the land for the former reason, sea sky, space…There's an extra loss for a Welsh poet writing in English, and that is the longing for Welsh, for the secret language, mother tongue of all the stories, of all the centuries of speech and song.' (2000)

Border

It crumbles
where the land forgets its name
and I'm foreign in my own country.
Fallow, pasture, ploughland
ripped from the hill
beside a broken farm.

The word's exactness
slips from children's tongues.
Saints fade in the parishes.
Fields blur between the scar
of hedgerow and new road.
History forgets itself.

At the garage they're polite.
'Sorry love, no Welsh.'
At the shop I am slapped
by her hard 'What!'
They came for the beauty
but could not hear it speak.

[1989]

Marged

I think of her sometimes when I lie in bed,
falling asleep in the room I have made in the roof-space
over the old dark parlŵr where she died
alone in winter, ill and penniless.

191

Lighting the lamps, November afternoons,
a reading book, whisky gold in my glass.
At my typewriter tapping under stars
at my new roof-window, radio tunes
and dog for company. Or parking the car
where through the mud she called her single cow
up from the field, under the sycamore.
Or looking at the hills she looked at too.
I find her broken crocks, digging her garden.
What else do we share, but being women?

[1989]

The Field-Mouse

Summer, and the long grass is a snare drum,
The air hums with jets.
Down at the end of the meadow,
far from the radio's terrible news,
we cut the hay. All afternoon
its wave breaks before the tractor blade.
Over the hedge our neighbour travels his field
in a cloud of lime, drifting our land
with a chance gift of sweetness.

The child comes running through the killed flowers,
his hands a nest of quivering mouse,
its black eyes two sparks burning.
We know it'll die, and ought to finish it off.
It curls in agony big as itself
and the star goes out in its eye.
Summer in Europe, the fields hurt,
and the children kneel in long grass
staring at what we have crushed.

Before day's done the field lies bleeding,
the dusk garden inhabited by the saved, voles,
frogs, a nest of mice. The wrong that woke
from a rumour of pain won't heal,
and we can't face the newspapers.

All night I dream the children dance in grass,
their bones brittle as mouse-ribs, the air
stammering with gunfire, my neighbour turned
stranger, wounding my land with stones.

[1998]

Women's Work

Their books come with me, women writers,
their verses borne through the rooms
out between the plum trees to the field,
as an animal will gather things,
a brush, a bone, a shoe,
for comfort against darkness.

August Sunday morning,
and I'm casting for words,
wandering the garden sipping their poems,
leaving cups of them here and there in the grass
where the washing steams in the silence
after the hay-days and the birdsong months.

I am sixteen again, and it's summer,
and the sisters are singing, their habits gathered,
sleeves rolled for kitchen work,
rosy hands hoisting cauldrons of greens.
The laundry hisses with steam-irons
glossing the collars of our summer blouses.

Then quietly they go along white gravel,
telling their beads in the walled garden
where *Albertine*'s heady rosaries spill
religious and erotic over the hot stones.
And there's restlessness in the summer air,
like this desire for poems,

our daily offices.

[1998]

193

Translation

after translating from Welsh, particularly a novel by Kate Roberts

Your hand on her hand – you've never been
this close to a woman since your mother's beauty
at the school gate took your breath away,
since you held hot sticky hands with your best friend,
since you, schoolgirl guest in a miner's house,
two up, two down, too small for guest rooms
or guest beds, shared with two sisters,
giggling in the dark, hearts hot with boy-talk.

You spread the script. She hands you a fruit.
You break it, eat, know exactly how
to hold its velvet weight, to bite, to taste it
to the last gold shred. But you're lost for words,
can't think of the English for *eirin* – it's on the tip of your –
But the cat ate your tongue, licking peach juice
from your palm with its rough *langue de chat*,
tafod cath, the rasp of loss.

[1998]

FRANCES HOROVITZ

(1938-83)

Frances Hooker was born in London. She read English and Drama at Bristol
University before training at RADA. She worked for a while as an actress but
became best-known as a broadcaster for the BBC, and a performer of poetry,
and she took part in the first staging of Ted Hughes' *Cave Birds*. In 1964 she
married the poet Michael Horovitz and their son was born in 1971. Much of
her early work was inspired by the Gloucestershire landscape. After several
early pamphlets her first full-length collection was *Water Over Stone* (1980).
In 1980 she moved to the North of England with the poet Roger Garfitt where
she worked on poems themed around Hadrian's Wall and became associated
with the LYC Gallery and painters including Winifred Nicholson. They moved
to Herefordshire in 1982, and she published a pamphlet, *Snow Light, Water
Light*, just before her death from cancer in 1983; her *Collected Poems*, edited
by Garfitt, followed in 1985. Her friend Anne Stevenson sees her work as
part of a continuation of the writing of Kathleen Raine and Frances Bellerby
but her spare imagist writing about the natural world also bears comparison
with the early work of Denise Levertov.

194

Visit to the British Museum

You take me to the room of clocks
to see some long-dead master's
sleight of mind and hand.
Time thickens here, revolves,
regards itself in mirrors;
almost, each minute holds its place.
You tell me why one second hand
moves forward and not back,
explain escapement or the dead-beat pendulum.
All stars and days are measured here –
I think of loving and the seepage of our lives.

The Assyrians next;
a king hunts lions in bas-relief,
has hunted now for near three thousand years.
Would we be lovers beneath such brazen skies?
We swelter in the blood and din.
Time traps and baits us like these lions;
our moment is as transient as theirs.

[1980]

Brigomaglos, a Christian, Speaks...

'Some say they saw the Bull,
stamping under the skyline
with the new sun rising between his horns.
They say the black blood flows like water...

I don't believe them.
It was only the officers,
never the men
(any god would do for us
till the White Christ came).
They'd see anything, anyway,
stumbling out of their caves
dizzy with darkness and the stink of blood.

195

Strange how they thought they brought the light to birth.

We pulled their temple down in the end,
opened it up to the proper light
– plenty of black birds flapping around
but never their Raven that flies to the sun.

We have the Sun,
our Christ is the Son who is brought to birth.
He is a white Dove
who walks in fields of light,
brighter than snow-light or water-light.
His light burns in us.
He has engraved our souls like glass
to hold his seeds of light.

Those old gods should keep their place
under the dark of stones
or in the deep wood.
They should fade like the last wood-ember
or the last sputtering flame of the lamp,
be echoed only in children's songs.

In sleep they crowd
riding the uneasy edge of dreams...'

*The Mithraic Temple at Carrawburgh is believed
to have been pulled down by Christians in A.D. 297.*

[1983]

CAROLE SATYAMURTI
(*b.* 1939)

Carole Satyamurti grew up in Kent, and has lived in North America, Singapore
and Uganda. Her first collection, *Broken Moon,* was published in 1987, followed
by *Changing the Subject* (1990), *Striking Distance* (1994), *Selected Poems* (1998),
Love and Variations (2000) and *Stitching the Dark: New & Selected Poems*
(2005). As well as being a poet, Satyamurti is a sociologist and teaches at the
University of East London and the Tavistock Clinic, and she co-edited *Acquainted
with the Night: psychoanalysis and the poetic imagination* (2003). She writes, in
a fascinating essay in which she makes a psychoanalytic exploration of her
creative process, of a revealing dream she had, soon after beginning to write:

'I climbed onto my desk in order to reach a door I had never noticed before, high up on the wall. I hauled myself in (a kind of reverse birth process) and found myself in a railway waiting room that looked as though it had been frozen in time. On the seats were a number of mummified old women, who had died waiting for a train which never came, and dried up where they sat... I passed through this room and into a light, large space beyond it, which was empty apart from a tapestry hanging on one wall...This tapestry represented not only me as I was, but also the colours and textures I had at my disposal from now on. The mood of that dream was one of joy, and of gratitude to these desiccated ancestors...There was a sense that I had arrived here at the expense of the dead women who had waited and never gone anywhere...' Later in the essay she goes on to reflect on the muse: 'The notion of the Muse, particularly when she doesn't take the form of a real person, owes something to the idea of the original mother who provided the facilitating environment. The poet is alone in her presence – ideally, she is there, but not breathing down the poet's neck, not prescribing the particular form the poem will take. The Muse is a benevolent and silent figure, and her presence gives the poet assurance that there will be a poem – that a poem is possible even though it doesn't exist yet. She represents a sort of permission.' ('First Time Ever', p.295; p.300)

Broken Moon
(for Emma)

Twelve, small as six,
strength, movement, hearing
all given in half measure,
my daughter,
child of genetic carelessness,
walks uphill, always.

I watch her morning face;
precocious patience as she hooks each sock,
creeps it up her foot,
aims her jersey like a quoit.
My fingers twitch;
her private frown deters.

Her jokes can sting:
'My life is like dressed crab –
lot of effort, rather little meat.'
Yet she delights in seedlings taking root,
finding a fossil,
a surprise dessert.

Chopin will not yield to her stiff touch;
I hear her cursing.
She paces Bach exactly,
firm rounding of perfect cadences.
Somewhere inside
she is dancing a courante.

In dreams she skims the sand,
curls toes into the ooze of pools,
leaps on to stanchions.
Awake, her cousins take her hands;
they lean into the waves,
stick-child between curved sturdiness.

She turns away from stares,
laughs at the boy who asks
if she will find a midget husband.
Ten years ago,
I showed her the slice of silver in the sky.
'Moon broken,' she said.

[1987]

Striking Distance

Was there one moment when the woman
who's always lived next door turned stranger
to you? In a time of fearful weather
did the way she laughed, or shook out her mats
make you suddenly feel as though
she'd been nursing a dark side to her difference
and bring that word, in a bitter rush
to the back of the throat – *Croat/Muslim/*
Serb – the name, barbed, ripping
its neat solution through common ground?

Or has she acquired an alien patina
day by uneasy day, unnoticed
as fallout from a remote explosion?
So you don't know quite when you came to think
the way she sits, or ties her scarf,

198

is just like a Muslim/Serb/Croat;
and she uses their word for water-melon
as usual, but now it's an irritant
you mimic to ugliness in your head,
surprising yourself in a savage pleasure.

Do you sometimes think, she could be you,
the woman who's trying to be invisible?
Do you have to betray those old complicities –
money worries, sick children, men?
Would an open door be too much pain
if the larger bravery is beyond you
(you can't afford the kind of recklessness
that would take, any more than she could);
while your husband is saying you don't understand
those people/Serbs/Muslims/Croats?

One morning, will you ignore her greeting
and think you see a strange twist to her smile –
for how could she not, then, be strange to herself
(this woman who lives nine inches away)
in the inner place where she'd felt she belonged,
which, now, she'll return to obsessively
as a tongue tries to limit a secret sore?
And as they drive her away, will her face
be unfamiliar, her voice, bearable:
a woman crying, from a long way off?

[1994]

Ourstory

Let us now praise women
with feet glass slippers wouldn't fit;

not the patient, nor even the embittered
ones who kept their place,

but awkward women, tenacious with truth,
whose elbows disposed of the impossible;

who split seams, who wouldn't wait,
take no, take sedatives;

who sang their own numbers, went uninsured,
knew best what they were missing.

Our misfit foremothers are joining forces
underground, their dusts mingling

breast-bone with scapula, forehead
with forehead. Their steady mass

bursts locks; lends a springing foot
to our vaulting into enormous rooms.

[1994]

PAULINE STAINER

(*b.* 1941)

Born in Stoke-on-Trent, Stainer read English at Oxford, and did not publish
her first collection until her late 40s. *The Honeycomb* (1989) was followed by
Sighting the Slave Ship (1992), *The Ice-Pilot Speaks* (1994), *The Wound-dresser's
Dream* (1996), *Parable Island* (1999) and *The Lady & the Hare: New & Selected
Poems* (2003).

Anne Stevenson has suggested that Stainer writes 'sacred poetry for the
scientific 21st century...She is deeply English and draws from a wealth of
sources: medieval lyrics, Eastern as well as Western art, Christian liturgy...
chemistry and optics.' Stainer writes in 1989: 'What absorbs me is incarnating
the image; finding the context where the scarlet particle jumps that free fall
between writer and reader, and the sparking chamber ignites. The immediacy
of paradise is things made whole' (*Don't Ask Me What I Mean*, p.277). More
recently she explains: 'I am wary of manifestos. I return instead to poets: Donne,
Emily Dickinson, David Jones, and never see a kestrel without invoking Hopkins.
But I am just as likely to be influenced by an article in a scientific magazine, a
detail in a painting, or the yellow gloom of driving between rape fields in the
rain. My touchstones are economy and immediacy of experience: Dante's *un
semplice lume* and that blue intake of breath before a drift of bluebells. Perhaps
most of all, it is the strange chemistry of juxtaposition which influences me: the
death of my daughter with the pressure of the sunlight, that zigzag between
breath and the moment as Mantegna's hares box beside the agony in the garden.
Even in the dark we are surprised by the white template of the swan on her
nest, the verve of forgotten things, hawthorn solid with moonlight.' (2005)

This Atomising of Things

In the dustless
centre of the lake
artisans sieve powdered
gold into lacquer

differing meshes,
spangled ground,
not so much fusion
as the smoke from it

ashore – beasts
of soft red sandstone
smouldering
along the spirit road

and the after-touch
of a girl warming
a pouch of silkworm eggs
between her breasts.

[1994]

Quanta

I

Reality happens
when you look at it –
the deer fawn
in the vertical light,
the crystal hunter
is killed by a single falling stone
on Annapurna.

But what perfects the casual –
Vermeer buried with three children
of unspecified sex,
the shaman in the glacier,
a crystalline disc pressed

to the strange blue tattoos
still intact on his breast?

II

Things happen
simultaneously
and in every direction
at once

hail drives
through the samphire
where the ammonites
show signs of healing

high-level
radioactive waste
is turned into molten glass
sealed in stainless steel

a pyx of white silver
is laid in a silken
compartment
in Christ's body

the limbs of mummies
crackle like chemical
glass-tubing
and give out great heat

the ovens work continuously;
no part of the prisoner is wasted;
dental gold is returned
to the Reichsbank

the city swings like a cradle –
the seven vials
spill their seven plagues
into the rubble

up above somewhere a fox crosses over
and the daughter of Jairus
is raised behind the geranium
on the windowsill.

III

What is for real
is the marvellous sufficiency
of the moment –
the automatic weapon on multiple lock –
electric plasmas
intransigent as angels.

Nothing is out of true:
purists whistle up
the bloodhounds,
those about to be executed
wear red blindfolds;

unhurried as lilies,
the disciples sit
at the holy supper
while the lovely boy
is hung *at a bough;*

no masking agent
for the heart
except insouciance –
the *mood indigo*
at the stroke of the green axe

willows breaking into F$^{\#}$ minor
for the flagellation
in a landscape,
the angel
at the inter-tidal funeral
announcing the end of time.

[1994]

The creatures preach to St Francis

They speak through my wounds
whether out of the body I cannot tell

the lion's eardrum flexing to the bees
in its own carcass

otters coupling in the burial boat

the stoat
who dances the questions put to him

reindeer sinews
lowering coffins through the ice

the mongoose tonguing the wind
from the feet of the dead

the muzzle of the snow-leopard
no more than after-image
in the extreme frost.

[1996]

EILÉAN NÍ CHUILLEANÁIN
(*b*. 1942)

Born in Cork, the daughter of the novelist and critic Eilís Dillon and Cormac
Ó Cuilleanáin, a professor of Irish at University College Cork, Eiléan Ní
Chuilleanáin studied for degrees in Literature and in History at University
College Cork, before attending Oxford, where she studied Elizabethan litera-
ture. Her books of poetry include *Acts and Monuments* (1972), *Site of Ambush*
(1975), *The Second Voyage* (1977/1986), *The Rose-Geranium* (1981), *The Magda-
lene Sermon* (1989), *The Brazen Serpent* (1994) and *The Girl Who Married the
Reindeer* (2001). With her husband Macdara Woods, Leland Bardwell, and
Pearse Hutchinson, she co-founded *Cyphers*, one of Ireland's longest running
literary magazines. She is a professor of English at Trinity College Dublin.
　　She has edited *Irish Women: Image and Achievement* (1985), *Maria Edge-
worth's Belinda* (1993), *Noble and Joyous Histories: English Romances 1375-1650*
(with J.D. Pheifer, 1993), *The Wilde Legacy* (2003) and *The Languages of Ireland*
(2003). She has also translated the work of Nuala Ní Dhomhnaill, sharing the
translations of *The Water Horse* (1999) with Medbh McGuckian, as well as that
of two Romanian poets, Denisa Comanescu and Ileana Malancioiu.

The House Remembered

The house persists, the permanent
Scaffolding while the stones move round.
Convolvulus winds the banisters, sucks them down;
We found an icicle under the stairs

Tall as a church candle;
It refused to answer questions
But proved its point by freezing hard.

The house changes, the stones
Choking in dry lichen stupidly spreading
Abusing the doorposts, frost on the glass.
Nothing stays still, the house is still the same
But the breast over the sink turned into a tap
And coming through the door all fathers look the same.

The stairs and windows waver but the house stands up;
Peeling away the walls another set shows through.
I can't remember, it all happened too recently.
But somebody was born in every room.

[1972]

The Real Thing

The Book of Exits, miraculously copied
Here in this convent by an angel's hand,
Stands open on a lectern, grooved
Like the breast of a martyred deacon.

The bishop has ordered the windows bricked up on this side
Facing the fields beyond the city.
Lit by the glow from the cloister yard at noon
On Palm Sunday, Sister Custos
Exposes her major relic, the longest
Known fragment of the Brazen Serpent.

True stories wind and hang like this
Shuddering loop wreathed on a lapis lazuli
Frame. She says, this is the real thing.
She veils it again and locks up.
On the shelves behind her the treasures are lined.
The episcopal seal repeats every coil,
Stamped on all closures of each reliquary
Where the labels read: *Bones
Of Different Saints. Unknown.*

Her history is a blank sheet,
Her vows a folded paper locked like a well.
The torn end of the serpent
Tilts the lace edge of the veil.
The real thing, the one free foot kicking
Under the white sheet of history.

[1994]

The Secret

Instead of burning the book or getting its value
They hid it and were silent, even at home,
So that the history of that lost year
Remained for each one her own delusion.
As the memory faded they had to live.
No one would buy their blood, but they sold
Their hair, the milk from their breasts,
Their signatures on slips of ravelled paper,
The grazing as far as the drawing-room window
And at last the fresh fine grass
That had started to grow under the first arch
Of the bridge beside the burnt-out paper-mill.

[1994]

SHARON OLDS

(*b.* 1942)

Born in San Francisco, Olds graduated from Stanford University, and wrote a
PhD on Emerson at Columbia. Her books include *Satan Says* (1980), *The Dead
and the Living* (1983), *The Gold Cell* (1987), *The Sign of Saturn: Poems 1980-
1987* (UK 1991), *The Father* (1992; UK 1993), *The Wellspring* (1996), *Blood,
Tin, Straw* (1999; UK 2000), *The Unswept Room* (2002; UK 2003) and *Strike
Sparks: Selected Poems 1980-2002* (USA 2004; *Selected Poems*, UK, 2005). She
teaches creative writing at New York University and at Goldwater Hospital,
New York, and was New York State Poet Laureate from 1998 to 2000.

Olds clearly has strong links with confessional poetry in her revelations of the
intimacies at the heart of a family. Yet she is clear in interview with Laurel
Blossom that she makes a distinction between her work and that of the con-
fessionals: 'I have an old-fashioned vision of the word confession. I believe that
a confession is a telling, publicly or privately, of a wrong that one has done,

which one regrets. And the confession is a way of trying to get to the other side and change one's nature. So I have written two or three confessional poems. I would use the phrase *apparently personal poetry* for the kind of poetry that I think people are referring to as "confessional". *Apparently* personal because how do we really know? We don't.' (*Poets & Writers Magazine*, 1993)

Ecstasy

As we made love for the third day,
cloudy and dark, as we did not stop
but went into it and into it and
did not hesitate and did not hold back we
rose through the air, until we were up above
timber line. The lake lay
icy and silver, the surface shirred,
reflecting nothing. The black rocks
lifted around it into the grainy
sepia air, the patches of snow
brilliant white, and even though we
did not know where we were, we could not
speak the language, we could hardly see, we
did not stop, rising with the black
rocks to the black hills, the black
mountains rising from the hills. Resting
on the crest of the mountains, one huge
cloud with scalloped edges of blazing
evening light, we did not turn back,
we stayed with it, even though we were
far beyond what we knew, we rose
into the grain of the cloud, even though we were
frightened, the air hollow, even though
nothing grew there, even though it is a
place from which no one has ever come back.

[1984]

I Go Back to May 1937

I see them standing at the formal gates of their colleges,
I see my father strolling out
under the ochre sandstone arch, the

red tiles glinting like bent
plates of blood behind his head,
I see my mother with a few light books at her hip
standing at the pillar made of tiny bricks with the
wrought-iron gate still open behind her, its
sword-tips black in the May air,
they are about to graduate, they are about to get married,
they are kids, they are dumb, all they know is they are
innocent, they would never hurt anybody.
I want to go up to them and say Stop,
don't do it – she's the wrong woman,
he's the wrong man, you are going to do things
you cannot imagine you would ever do,
you are going to do bad things to children,
you are going to suffer in ways you never heard of,
you are going to want to die. I want to go
up to them there in the late May sunlight and say it,
her hungry pretty blank face turning to me,
her pitiful beautiful untouched body,
his arrogant handsome blind face turning to me,
his pitiful beautiful untouched body,
but I don't do it. I want to live. I
take them up like the male and female
paper dolls and bang them together
at the hips like chips of flint as if to
strike sparks from them, I say
Do what you are going to do, and I will tell about it.

[1987]

It

Sometimes we fit together like the creamy
speckled three-section body of the fruit,
and sometimes it is like a blue comb of glass across my skin,
and sometimes I am bent over, as thick paper can be
folded, on the rug in the centre of the room
far from the soft bed, my knuckles
pressed against the grit in the grain of the rug's braiding where they
laid the rags tight and sewed them together,
my ass in the air like a lily with a wound on it

and I feel you going down into me as
if my own tongue is your cock sticking
out of my mouth like a stamen, the making and
breaking of the world at the same moment,
and sometimes it is sweet as the children we had
thought were dead being brought to the shore in the
long boats, boatload after boatload.
Always I am stunned to remember it,
as if I have been to Saturn or the bottom of a trench in the sea
      floor, I
sit on my bed the next day with my mouth open and think of it.

[1987]

The Lifting

Suddenly my father lifted up his nightie, I
turned my head away but he cried out
Shar!, my nickname, so I turned and looked.
He was sitting in the high cranked-up bed with the
gown up, around his neck,
to show me the weight he had lost. I looked
where his solid ruddy stomach had been
and I saw the skin fallen into loose
soft hairy rippled folds
lying in a pool of folds
down at the base of his abdomen,
the gaunt torso of a big man
who will die soon. Right away
I saw how much his hips are like mine,
the long, white angles, and then
how much his pelvis is shaped like my daughter's,
a chambered whelk-shell hollowed out,
I saw the folds of skin like something
poured, a thick batter, I saw
his rueful smile, the cast-up eyes as he
shows me his old body, he knows
I will be interested, he knows I will find him
appealing. If anyone had ever told me
I would sit by him and he would pull up his nightie
and I would look at him, at his naked body,

209

at the thick bud of his penis in all that
dark hair, look at him
in affection and uneasy wonder
I would not have believed it. But now I can still
see the tiny snowflakes, white and
night-blue, on the cotton of the gown as it
rises the way we were promised at death it would rise,
the veils would fall from our eyes, we would know everything.

[1992]

His Smell

In the last days of my father's life
I tried to name his smell – like yeast,
ochre catalyst feeding in liquid,
eating malt, excreting mash –
sour ferment, intoxicant, exaltant, the
strong drink of my father's sweat,
bent down over the hospital bed
and smelled it. It smelled like wet cement,
a sidewalk of crushed granite, quartz
and Jurassic shale, or the sour odour
of the hammered copper humidor
full of moist, bent, blackish
shreds of pipe tobacco; or the smelling-salts
tang of chlorine on the concrete floor of the
changing room at the pool in summer;
or the faint mould from the rug in his house
or the clouded pungence of the mouth and sputum
of a drinking man. And it was also the socket
of a man's leather shoe, acid with
polish and basic with stale socks –
always, in his smell, the sense
of stain and the attraction of the stain,
the harmony of oil and metal,
as if the life of manufacture and
industry were using his body
as a gland for their sweat. On the last day,
it rose on his forehead, a compound disc

of sweat, I brought it off on my lips.
After his last breath, he lay there
tilted on his side, not moving,
not breathing, making no sound,
but he smelled the same, that fresh tainted
industrial domestic male smell,
dark, reflecting points of light.
I had thought the last thing between us
would be a word, a look, a pressure
of touch, not that he would be dead
and I would be bending over him
smelling him, breathing him in
as you would breathe the air, deeply, before going into exile.

[1992]

LOUISE GLÜCK

(*b.* 1943)

Louise Glück was born in New York City. Her books of poetry include *First-born* (1968), *The House on Marshland* (1975), *Descending Figure* (1980), *The Triumph of Achilles* (1985), *Ararat* (1990), *The Wild Iris* (1996), *Meadowlands* (1998), *Vita Nova* (1999; UK 2000), *The Seven Ages* (2001) and *Averno* (2006). Her selection of critical essays *Proofs and Theories* was published in 1994. She won the Pulitzer Prize for *The Wild Iris*, and was U.S. Poet Laureate in 2003-04. Divorced, with one son, she teaches at Williams College, and lives in Cambridge, Massachusetts.

In her introduction to *The First Five Books of Poems* (1997), Glück charts her own development as a poet as she moves from finding herself after her first book 'trapped in fragments' to 'making poems as single sentences' and then trying 'to wean myself from conspicuous syntactical quirks and a recurring vocabulary'. She continues: 'After three books, I was tired of being taken for a tender lyricist, all quivering feeling and reactive nerves; I had been trying through the organisation of those short lyrics, to make something larger, a mosaic of intellectual as well as emotional dimension.' Such ambitions can be seen in the poems from *The Wild Iris* reproduced here (the last five poems in this selection). Like Sharon Olds, Louise Glück writes frequently about love and family life, exploring in particular relations between female family members, but Glück often places her explorations within a wider religious perspective, and a desire for spiritual transcendence. *The Wild Iris* is an attempt to work through psychological pain through a synergy of the Christian liturgy and a celebration of the natural world.

Poem

In the early evening, as now, a man is bending
over his writing table.
Slowly he lifts his head; a woman
appears, carrying roses.
Her face floats to the surface of the mirror,
marked with the green spokes of rose stems.

It is a form
of suffering: then always the transparent page
raised to the window until its veins emerge
as words finally filled with ink.

And I am meant to understand
what binds them together
or to the gray house held firmly in place by dusk

because I must enter their lives:
it is spring, the pear tree
filming with weak, white blossoms.

[1975]

Lullaby

My mother's an expert in one thing:
sending people she loves into the other world.
The little ones, the babies – these
she rocks, whispering or singing quietly. I can't say
what she did for my father;
whatever it was, I'm sure it was right.

It's the same thing, really, preparing a person
for sleep, for death. The lullabies — they all say
don't be afraid, that's how they paraphrase
the heartbeat of the mother.
So the living slowly grow calm; it's only
the dying who can't, who refuse.

The dying are like tops, like gyroscopes –
they spin so rapidly they seem to be still.
Then they fly apart: in my mother's arms,
my sister was a cloud of atoms, of particles – that's the difference.
When a child's asleep, it's still whole.

My mother's seen death; she doesn't talk about the soul's integrity.
She's held an infant, an old man, as by comparison the dark grew
solid around them, finally changing to earth.
The soul's like all matter:
why would it stay intact, stay faithful to its one form,
when it could be free?

[1990]

The Wild Iris

At the end of my suffering
there was a door.

Hear me out: that which you call death
I remember.

Overhead, noises, branches of the pine shifting.
Then nothing. The weak sun
flickered over the dry surface.

It is terrible to survive
as consciousness
buried in the dark earth.

Then it was over: that which you fear, being
a soul and unable
to speak, ending abruptly, the stiff earth
bending a little. And what I took to be
birds darting in low shrubs.

You who do not remember
passage from the other world
I tell you I could speak again: whatever
returns from oblivion returns
to find a voice:

from the center of my life came
a great fountain, deep blue
shadows on azure seawater.

[1996]

Matins

The sun shines; by the mailbox, leaves
of the divided birch tree folded, pleated like fins.
Underneath, hollow stems of the white daffodils,
    Ice Wings, Cantatrice; dark
leaves of the wild violet. Noah says
depressives hate the spring, imbalance
between the inner and the outer world. I make
another case – being depressed, yes, but in a sense passionately
attached to the living tree, my body
actually curled in the split trunk, almost at peace,
    in the evening rain
almost able to feel
sap frothing and rising: Noah says this is
an error of depressives, identifying
with a tree, whereas the happy heart
wanders the garden like a falling leaf, a figure for
the part, not the whole.

[1996]

Matins

Unreachable father, when we were first
exiled from heaven, you made
a replica, a place in one sense
different from heaven, being
designed to teach a lesson: otherwise
the same – beauty on either side, beauty
without alternative – Except
we didn't know what was the lesson. Left alone,
we exhausted each other. Years
of darkness followed; we took turns

working the garden, the first tears
filling our eyes as earth
misted with petals, some
dark red, some flesh colored –
We never thought of you
whom we were learning to worship.
We merely knew it wasn't human nature to love
only what returns love.

[1996]

Trillium

When I woke up I was in a forest. The dark
seemed natural, the sky through the pine trees
thick with many lights.

I knew nothing; I could do nothing but see.
And as I watched, all the lights of heaven
faded to make a single thing, a fire
burning through the cool firs.
Then it wasn't possible any longer
to stare at heaven and not be destroyed.

Are there souls that need
death's presence, as I require protection?
I think if I speak long enough
I will answer that question, I will see
whatever they see, a ladder
reaching through the firs, whatever
calls them to exchange their lives –

Think what I understand already.
I woke up ignorant in a forest;
only a moment ago, I didn't know my voice
if one were given me
would be so full of grief, my sentences
like cries strung together.
I didn't even know I felt grief
until that word came, until I felt
rain streaming from me.

[1996]

The Red Poppy

The great thing
is not having
a mind. Feelings:
oh, I have those; they
govern me. I have
a lord in heaven
called the sun, and open
for him, showing him
the fire of my own heart, fire
like his presence.
What could such glory be
if not a heart? Oh my brothers and sisters,
were you like me once, long ago,
before you were human? Did you
permit yourselves
to open once, who would never
open again? Because in truth
I am speaking now
the way you do. I speak
because I am shattered.

[1996]

VICKI FEAVER
(*b.* 1943)

Born in Nottingham, Feaver studied music at university, had a baby in her final
year, and became a music teacher before embarking on an English degree and
starting a PhD on the poetry of Stevie Smith. Her first book *Close Relatives*
was published in 1981; her second collection, *The Handless Maiden*, in 1994.
Influenced as a child by Blake and Dylan Thomas, Feaver cites Adrienne Rich's
essay 'When We Dead Awaken: Writing as Re-Vision' as an important factor
in her development as a writer. She has also spoken of the importance to her
of Sharon Olds, who gave her the courage to use the pronoun *I* rather than
the *she*, 'a device' she writes, 'I had used frequently in my first book as a way
of making poems appear less autobiographical. The effect was to split me off
from emotion that allowed in to the poem might have given them more energy
and conviction' (Curtis, ed, *How Poets Work*, p.140). Her exploration of mythic
(often murderous) women, is drawn in part from her sense that anger might
fruitfully fuel poems. Her most recent work is *The Book of Blood* (2006).

The River God

doesn't know why he's such a strong swimmer;
why he drinks nothing but frothy black Guinness;
why when he stands at the top
of a long flight of stairs
he has to struggle to stop himself
raising his arms, diving into a pool
of swaying air; why in his fantasies
the girls undress – uncovering white necks
and shoulders, brown and pink-nippled breasts,
the dark nests between their legs –
among reeds, under the grey-yellow light
of willows; why the women – in bars,
airports, at the Tennis and Squash Club –
he never spends more than a night with
seem flaky, juiceless; why he wants to smear
their mouths and ears and stomachs
with slime; why the water he shakes
from his hair, that twists
off his shoulders in the shower,
glitters with sticklebacks, snails,
minnows; why his wife follows
his wet footprints with a cloth;
makes him wear slippers.

[1994]

Women's Blood

Burn the soiled ones in the boiler,
my mother told me, showing me how to hook
the loops of gauze-covered wadding pads
onto an elastic belt, remembering
how my grandmother had given her
strips of rag she'd had to wash out
every month for herself: the grandmother
who had her chair by the boiler,
who I loved but was plotting to murder
before she murdered my mother, or my mother –

217

shaking, sobbing, hurling plates and cups,
screaming she wished she'd never been born,
screeching 'Devil!' and 'Witch!' –
murdered her. I piled up the pads
until the smell satisfied me
it was the smell of a corpse.
'How could you do such a thing?'
my mother asked, finding them
at the bottom of the wardrobe
where the year before she'd found
a cache of navy-blue knickers
stained with the black jelly clots
I thought were my wickedness
oozing out of me.

[1994]

Judith

Wondering how a good woman can murder
I enter the tent of Holofernes,
holding in one hand his long oiled hair
and in the other, raised above
his sleeping, wine-flushed face,
his falchion with its unsheathed
curved blade. And I feel a rush
of tenderness, a longing
to put down my weapon, to lie
sheltered and safe in a warrior's
fumy sweat, under the emerald stars
of his purple and gold canopy,
to melt like a sweet on his tongue
to nothing. And I remember the glare
of the barley field; my husband
pushing away the sponge I pressed
to his burning head; the stubble
puncturing my feet as I ran,
flinging myself on a body
that was already cooling
and stiffening; and the nights
when I lay on the roof – my emptiness

like the emptiness of a temple
with the doors kicked in; and the mornings
when I rolled in the ash of the fire
just to be touched and dirtied
by something. And I bring my blade
down on his neck – and it's easy,
like slicing through fish.
And I bring it down again,
cleaving the bone.

[1994]

Glow Worm

Talking about the chemical changes
that make a body in love shine,
or even, for months, immune to illness,
you pick a grub from the lawn
and let it lie on your palm – glowing
like the emerald-burning butt
of a cigarette. (We still haven't touched,
only lain side by side
the half stories of our half lives.)
You call them lightning bugs
from the way the males gather in clouds
and simultaneously flash.
This is the female, fat from a diet
of liquefied snails, at the stage in her cycle
when she hardly eats; when all her energy's
directed to drawing water and oxygen
to a layer of luciferin.
Wingless, wordless,
in a flagrant and luminous bid
to resist the narrative's pull to death,
she lifts her shining green abdomen
to signal *yes yes yes*.

1995 [2006]

Hemingway's Hat

Wearing a copy of the canvas
leather-peaked cap Hemingway wore
at the Finca Vigía – which your mother gave you
to make you look dashing, nerveless,

and which makes me feel
like a Shakespearean heroine
dressed as and played by a boy –
I wonder what I'd be like as a man:

not just brave but 'needing
to be seen to be brave' like Hem;
or like my father, gentle, nervous,
'not a man,' as my mother shrieked at him?

She'd wanted a son to replace her brother
lost in the last months of the war in Burma.
I tried – when I started to bleed,
getting my hair cut short as a boy's.

Then, while you raced stolen cars
for the thrill, I changed myself
into a girl – stilettos, stiff
nylon petticoats, a perm.

You travelled from war to war,
until you came here, where dark butterflies
reconnoitre the lawn, and the cats sleep
in the shade of your chair, and you heard –

among oaks and firs and birches –
a silence like the silence at Plei Me
when you saw the dead rising
above the field of battle.

In our games of changing hats,
we float free like those ghosts:
last night, me riding you,
our shared penis

a glistening pillar
sliding between us; this morning,
you washing me, soaping and rinsing
with a woman's tenderness.

1996 [2006]

EAVAN BOLAND

(*b*. 1944)

The daughter of a diplomat, Boland moved from Dublin at the age of six to
London. She returned to Ireland to complete her schooling and studied at
Trinity College Dublin, receiving her BA in 1966. Boland's first collection *New
Territory* was published in 1967 and followed by books including *The War
Horse* (1975), *Night Feed* (1982), *The Journey and other poems* (1987), *Outside
History* (1990), *In a Time of Violence* (1994), *Collected Poems* (1995), *The Lost
Land* (1998), *Code* (2001), *New Collected Poems* (2005) and *Domestic Violence*
(2006). Her other books include *Object Lessons: The Life of the Woman and the
Poet in Our Time* (1995) and *The Making of a Poem: A Norton Anthology of
Poetic Forms* (with Mark Strand, 2000). She is a professor of English at Stanford
University. She translated nine poems by German-speaking writers gathered
together in her anthology *After Every War: Twentieth-Century Women Poets* (2004).

Of her early experiences as a poet she writes: 'In a certain sense, I began in
a city and a poetic world where the choices and assumptions were near enough
to those of a 19th-century poet. The formal poem was respected. The wit of
the stanza was respected more than its drama...In my first collection, published
when I was 22 years of age... [I] struggled for skill and avoided risk...trying
to get cadences right and counting out stresses on a table. The poems are the
visible evidence. What is not visible is the growing confusion and anxiety I
felt...Above all I had no clear sense how my womanhood could connect with
my life as a poet, or what claims each would make on the other... I began to
realise that a subtle oppression could result from this fracture between the
instinctive but unexpressed life I lived every day and the expressive poetic
manners I had inherited which might easily – as manners often do – render
it merely as decorum.' (Preface to *Collected Poems*)

The Famine Road

'Idle as trout in light Colonel Jones
these Irish, give them no coins at all; their bones
need toil, their characters no less.' Trevelyan's
seal blooded the deal table. The Relief

Committee deliberated: 'Might it be safe,
Colonel, to give them roads, roads to force
from nowhere, going nowhere of course?'

> *'One out of every ten and then*
> *another third of those again*
> *women – in a case like yours.'*

Sick, directionless they worked; fork, stick
were iron years away; after all could
they not blood their knuckles on rock, suck
April hailstones for water and for food?
Why for that, cunning as housewives, each eyed –
as if at a corner butcher – the other's buttock.

> *'Anything may have caused it, spores,*
> *a childhood accident; one sees*
> *day after day these mysteries.'*

Dusk: they will work tomorrow without him.
They know it and walk clear. He has become
a typhoid pariah, his blood tainted, although
he shares it with some there. No more than snow
attends its own flakes where they settle
and melt, will they pray by his death rattle.

> *'You never will, never you know*
> *but take it well woman, grow*
> *your garden, keep house, goodbye.'*

'It has gone better than we expected, Lord
Trevelyan, sedition, idleness, cured
in one; from parish to parish, field to field,
the wretches work till they are quite worn,
then fester by their work; we march the corn
to the ships in peace; this Tuesday I saw bones
out of my carriage window, your servant Jones.'

> *'Barren, never to know the load*
> *of his child in you, what is your body*
> *now if not a famine road?'*

[1975]

The Women

This is the hour I love: the in-between,
neither here-nor-there hour of evening.
The air is tea-coloured in the garden.
The briar rose is spilled crepe-de-Chine.

This is the time I do my work best,
going up the stairs in two minds,
in two worlds, carrying cloth or glass,
leaving something behind, bringing
something with me I should have left behind.

The hour of change, of metamorphosis,
of shape-shifting instabilities.
My time of sixth sense and second sight
when in the words I choose, the lines I write,
they rise like visions and appear to me:

women of work, of leisure, of the night,
in stove-coloured silks, in lace, in nothing,
with crewel needles, with books, with wide open legs

who fled the hot breath of the god pursuing,
who ran from the split hoof and the thick lips
and fell and grieved and healed into myth,

into me in the evening at my desk
testing the water with a sweet quartet,
the physical force of a dissonance –

the fission of music into syllabic heat –
and getting sick of it and standing up
and going downstairs in the last brightness

into a landscape without emphasis,
light, linear, precisely planned,
a hemisphere of tiered, aired cotton,

a hot terrain of linen from the iron,
folded in and over, stacked high,
neatened flat, storing heat and white.

[1983]

223

The Emigrant Irish

Like oil lamps we put them out the back,

of our houses, of our minds. We had lights
better than, newer than and then

a time came, this time and now
we need them. Their dread, makeshift example.

They would have thrived on our necessities.
What they survived we could not even live.
By their lights now it is time to
imagine how they stood there, what they stood with,
that their possessions may become our power.

Cardboard. Iron. Their hardships parcelled in them.
Patience. Fortitude. Long-suffering
in the bruise-coloured dusk of the New World.

And all the old songs. And nothing to lose.

[1983]

The Black Lace Fan My Mother Gave Me

It was the first gift he ever gave her,
buying it for five francs in the Galeries
in pre-war Paris. It was stifling.
A starless drought made the nights stormy.

They stayed in the city for the summer.
They met in cafés. She was always early.
He was late. That evening he was later.
They wrapped the fan. He looked at his watch.

She looked down the Boulevard des Capucines.
She ordered more coffee. She stood up.
The streets were emptying. The heat was killing.
She thought the distance smelled of rain and lightning.

These are wild roses, appliqued on silk by hand,
darkly picked, stitched boldly, quickly.
The rest is tortoiseshell and has the reticent,
clear patience of its element. It is

a worn-out, underwater bullion and it keeps,
even now, an inference of its violation.
The lace is overcast as if the weather
it opened for and offset had entered it.

The past is an empty café terrace.
An airless dusk before thunder. A man running.
And no way now to know what happened then –
none at all – unless, of course, you improvise:

The blackbird on this first sultry morning,
in summer, finding buds, worms, fruit,
feels the heat. Suddenly she puts out her wing –
the whole, full, flirtatious span of it.

[1990]

CAROL RUMENS

(*b*. 1944)

Carol Rumens was born in Forest Hill, South London and began but did not
complete a degree in Philosophy at the University of London. She married in
1964 and has two daughters. Her first poetry collection, *A Strange Girl in Bright
Colours*, was published in 1973 and followed by books including *Unplayed Music*
(1981), *Star Whisper* (1983), *Direct Dialling* (1985), *Selected Poems* (1987), *The
Greening of the Snow Beach* (1988), *From Berlin to Heaven* (1989), *Thinking of
Skins: New & Selected Poems* (1993), *Best China Sky* (1995), *Holding Pattern*
(1998), *Hex* (2002) and *Poems 1968-2004* (2004). She is a freelance writer, has
held many residencies in Britain and Ireland, and is now Chair of Creative
Writing at Hull University. She has also translated several Russian poets,
including Evgeny Rein, and edited Elizabeth Bartlett's *Two Women Dancing*.

The editor of *Making for the Open: The Chatto Book of Post-Feminist Poetry*
(1985), she writes in her revised introduction of 1987: 'A poetry which fails to
make full use of all the linguistic resources open to it is in danger of ceasing
to be poetry. The prevalent notion that women writers are required in some
way to invent literary language has its attractions...However, it seems to me
that the "man-made language" theory grossly underestimates women's articulate-

ness and their powers of communication, powers which go back far beyond the written word. Is it not rather more likely that those people who throughout history have spent much of their lives talking to children, singing them songs and repeating rhymes to them have played the greater part in the evolution of language, particularly literary language?' (pxvii). More recently she has written of the importance to her of Edith Sitwell: 'The first woman poet I cared about was Edith Sitwell. This was mainly because my mother didn't like her. She was on TV a lot in the 50s. But I read her poems in Palgrave's *Golden Treasury*, and wrote a verse, when I was about 10, which was dedicated to her. As I remember, it went: "Creative as the stars' seraphic host / Words of great feeling from thy lips fall free. / Poet of the age, I love thee most / – Mortal, with thoughts of immortality"' (Phillips, 2004).

Marriage

Mondays, he trails burr-like fragments
of the weekend to London –
a bag of soft, yellow apples from his trees –
a sense of being loved and laundered.

He shows me a picture of marriage
as a small civilisation,
its parks, rosewood and broadloom;
its religion, the love of children

whose anger it survived
long ago, and who now return like lambs,
disarmed, adoring.
His wife sits by the window,

one hand planting tapestry daisies.
She smiles as he offers her the perfect apple.
On its polished, scented skin
falls a Renaissance gilding.

These two have kept their places,
trusting the old rules
of decorous counterpoint.
Now their lives are rich with echoes.

Tomorrow, she'll carry a boxful
of apples to school. Her six-year-olds
will weigh, then eat them, thrilling
to a flavour sharp as tears.

I listen while he tells me about her sewing,
as if I were the square of dull cloth
and his voice the leaping needle
chasing its tail in a dazzle of wonderment.

He places an apple in my hand;
then, for a moment, I must become his child.
To look at him as a woman
would turn me cold with shame.

[1981]

Geography Lesson

Here we have the sea of children; here
A tiny piece of Europe with dark hair.
She's crying. I am sitting next to her.

Thirty yellow suns blobbed on cheap paper,
Thirty skies blue as a Smith's Salt-wrapper
Are fading in the darkness of this weeper.

She's Czechoslovakia. And all the desks
Are shaking now. The classroom window cracks
And melts. I've caught her sobs like chicken-pox.

Czechoslovakia, though I've never seen
Your cities, I have somehow touched your skin.
You're all the hurt geography I own.

[1983]

Two Women

Daily to a profession – paid thinking
and clean hands – she rises,
unquestioning. It's second nature now.
The hours, though they're all of daylight, suit her.
The desk, typewriter, carpets, pleasantries
are a kind of civilisation, built on money,
of course, but money, now she sees, is human.
She has learned giving from her first chequebook,
intimacy from absence. Coming home
long after dark to the jugular torrent
of family life, her smile
cool as the skin of supermarket apples,
she's half the story. There's another woman
who bears her name, a silent, background face
that's always flushed with effort.
The true wife, she picks up scattered laundry,
and sets the table with warmed plates to feed
the clean-handed woman. They've not met.
If they were made to touch, they'd scald each other.

[1987]

A Memo About the Green Oranges

They sat like a disarmament proposal
On our table in the hotel dining-room,
Looking less and less negotiable.
Even the vegetarians flinched from them.

The Talks beside the lake weren't going well.
Neither was the turnover in these
Miniature ballistic atrocities –
Which now began to occur at every meal.

Oranges Are Orange. Grass Is Green –
Like policemen's greatcoats. Never Trust A Red.
(It's better to be dead than dyed that shade.)
You Can't Tell A *Sosiska* By Its Skin...

But what about an orange? Feeling less
Hopeful than thirsty on Sadóvaya Street
One day, I bought a mossy half-a-kilo.

The Geneva Talks stand just as still, or stiller,
And this is simply a memo, a PS,
To say those green-skinned oranges are sweet.

[1988]

Stealing the Genre

It was the shortest night of the year. I'd been drinking
But I was quite lucid and calm. So, having seen her
The other side of the bar, shedding her light
On no one who specially deserved it, I got to my feet
And simply went over and asked her, in a low voice,
If she'd come to my bed. She raised her eyebrows strangely
But didn't say 'no'. I went out. I felt her follow.

My mind was a storm as we silently crossed the courtyard
In the moist white chill of the dawn. Dear God, I loved her.
I'd loved her in books, I'd adored her at the first sighting.
But no, I'm a woman, English, not young. How could I?
She'd vanished for years. And now she was walking beside me.
Oh what am I going to do, what are *we* going to do?
Perhaps she'll know. She's probably an old hand –
But this sudden thought was the most disturbing of all.

As soon as we reached my room, though, it was plain
She hadn't a clue. We stood like window-displays
In our dawn-damp suits with the short, straight, hip-hugging skirts
(Our styles are strangely alike, I suppose it's because
Even she has to fight her corner in a man's world)
And discussed the rain, which was coming down, and the view,
Which was nothing much, a fuchsia hedge and some trees,
And we watched each other, as women do watch each other,
And tried not to yawn. Why don't you lie down for a bit?
I whispered, inspired. She gratefully kicked off her shoes.

229

She was onto the bed in no time, and lay as if dumped
On the furthest edge, her face – dear God – to the wall.
I watched for a while, and, thinking she might be in tears,
Caressed the foam-padded viscose that passed for her shoulder,
And begged her not to feel guilty. Then I discovered
That all she was doing was breathing, dead to the world.

It wasn't an insult, exactly, but it was a let-down –
And yet I admired her. Sleep. If only I could.
I rested my hand at an uncontroversial location
South of her breasts, maybe North, I don't remember,
And ached with desire and regret and rationalisation.
I'd asked her to bed. And she'd come to bed. End of story.
Only it wasn't the story I'd wanted to tell.
Roll on, tomorrow, I urged, but tomorrow retorted:
I'm here already, and nothing ever gets better.

But then, unexpectedly, I began to feel pleased.
To think she was here, at my side, so condensed, so weighty!
In my humble position (a woman, English, not young,
Et cetera) what more could I ask of an Irish dawn
Than this vision, alive, though dead to the world, on my duvet?
What have I done to deserve her? Oh, never mind,
Don't think about words like 'deserve'. So we lay in grace.
The light. Her hair. My hand. Her breath. And the fuchsias.
I thought of the poem I'd write, and fell asleep, smiling.

I woke in a daze of sublime self-congratulation
And saw she was gone. My meadow, my cloud, my aisling!
I could hardly believe my own memory. I wanted to scream
All over the courtyard, come back, come to bed, but how could I?
She might be anywhere, people were thick in the day
Already, and things were normal. Why are things normal?

I keened her name to the walls, I swam bitterest rivers,
I buried my face in the cloth where her blushes had slipped
And left a miraculous print that would baffle the laundry:
Oh let me die now. And the dark was all flame as I drank
The heart-breaking odour of Muguets des Bois and red wine –
Hers, though I have to admit, it could have been mine.

[1993]

230

MIMI KHALVATI

(b. 1944)

Born in Tehran, Khalvati was sent to boarding school in England at the age
of six, speaking only her first language, Farsi, and grew up on the Isle of Wight.
She was later educated in Switzerland at the University of Neuchâtel, and in
London at the Drama Centre and the School of African and Oriental Studies.
She has worked as an actor and director and was the founder of Matrix, a
women's experimental theatre group, and the co-founder of Theatre in Exile.
She currently runs The Poetry School, tutoring creative writing workshops
in London.

I Know a Place, a children's book, was published in 1985, and her first
collection of poems, *In White Ink* appeared in 1991, followed by *Mirrorwork*
(1995), *Entries on Light* (1997), *Selected Poems* (2000) and *The Chine* (2002).
She writes: 'For much of my adult life I worked in theatre and left poetry
behind, or so I thought. Now I see how close to poetry theatre is, not least
in Shakespeare, but more particularly in my directing work, where again you
read the spaces around and between the script as much as the print. These
are dreaming spaces, left for the reader to travel in, make connections, a way
of "owning" the poem or script. I've never been drawn to the overtly dramatic,
but rather to the fluidity of connections, the fragility of boundaries and how
we affect or are affected by the smallest things' (Sprackland, 2001).

Amanuensis

Mirza, scribe me a circle beneath
the grid that drew Columbus
from isle to isle, tipped the scale,
measured a plus and minus

in our round lives. Amanuensis,
do you hear me? Look at the tree
holding the sky in its arms, the earth
in its bowels. Oh, draw me

the rings in its bark, a beaded spiral
where I may walk on Persian
carpets woven in hues from sandbanks
where goats graze and the melon

cools in the stream. Have you seen the dome
of the mosque? Our signatures are there,
among galaxies, infinities: an incredulity
that leads even infidels to prayer!

The pool in the square is green with twine.
The tiles in the arch are floods
of blue brocade. And those painted stars
in the vault, this hive of hoods

and white arcades, are the stars and the sky
I saw on a night in Spain:
coves of milk and stalactites; the very same.
So leave your sacks of grain

my Mirza, your ledgers and your abacus. Turn back
to brighter skills than these:
your mirrors and mosaics. From each trapezium,
polygon, each small isosceles

face, extract me, entwine me. Be my double
helix! My polestar! My asterisks!
Nestle in my silences. But spell me out
and rhyme me in your lunes and arabesques!

[1991]

A Persian Miniature

(Shirin committing suicide over Khusraw's coffin)

She told us: take a picture, an art postcard
– I took this Persian miniature – then take
the top right-hand corner and describe it.
Well... it looks like a face; two of the arches
that march across the background look like eyebrows
– not Persian eyebrows meeting in the middle –
but intersected by a nose, a pillar.
The nose has peeled and left a patch that looks
rather like a map of The British Isles.

The top left-hand corner she said to use
for the second verse – here I am on cue –
is also a face, only this one's nose,
believe it or not, sports a large pink map
of America, or at least, the West Coast.
As if to banish doubts, a sea of stars
beneath it waves the flag. You see how hard
it is, how far away one gets from art,
and sixteenth-century Persian art at that.

Well, the third and final stanza – although
I can't imagine how I'll ever get it
all in one – is to take the two-inch square
at the bottom centre of the picture,
describe it, wrap it up and there you are,
you've got your poem. O.K. Three lines left:
Shirin and Khusraw (Romeo and Juliet)
are dying: he's in agony but she,
though spraying blood on him, seems quite at peace.

So. That's hardly the place to end a poem.
It's interesting, though, to think: here is England
on the right, America on the left
and caught between the two, like earth itself
twin-cornered by the eyes of gods, Iran's
most famous lovers lie, watched and dying.
How could a painter in Shiraz have known,
four hundred years ago, of this? Has time
rewritten him? Or was it always so?

Has power always called for sacrifice,
the dream of love on earth to trade itself
for paradise, the 'Rose that never blows
so red as where some buried Caesar bled'?
And still the fountain flows from bowl to bowl,
from lips of stone to fields, from mines to graves;
and there, in Zahra's Paradise for martyrs,
still bears the 'Hyacinth the Garden wears
Dropt in her Lap from some once lovely Head'.

[1991]

Zahra's Paradise: Tehran's largest cemetery.

JANE DURAN

(*b*. 1944)

Born in Cuba to a Spanish father and an American mother, Jane Duran was brought up in the USA and Chile. She was educated at Cornell University and has lived in Britain since 1966. She has published three collections of poetry. *Breathe Now Breathe* (1995) is very much concerned with the intimacies of family relationships and women's experiences. She writes: 'As my father was Spanish, I grew up...alongside other Spanish refugees in New York. Not living in or near the places of my childhood, or even in the culture of my father, is there in my work as an undercurrent. Through the poems, I am also able to rescue moments and places from loss. Many of the images in my poems spring from childhood in the United States. These early connections to particular land, sea, trees and weather can be powerful and enduring. They often find their way into my poems, even as a way of expressing or understanding something that is happening to me in the present, far from my roots. Being carried along by a first line that has occurred to me spontaneously (but which doubtless has its own long genesis) and that may have in it the "code" for the whole poem; then, hardly navigating as the poem progresses, I come to a resolution which surprises me, but which seems inevitable in the terms of the poem. Surprise, discovery, go with an openness to allow images and memories to connect – however disparate they may appear on the surface; and language to present itself – however unusual the words or syntax may seem.' (2005) A long poem sequence, *Silences from the Spanish Civil War* (2002), takes as its starting point her father's silence concerning his experiences fighting in Spain with the Republican army. Her third collection is *Coastal* (2006). She names as influences Lorca, Vallejo, Neruda, Seferis, Cavafy, Rilke, William Carlos Williams, Sylvia Plath, Elizabeth Bishop and Galway Kinnell.

Conversations with Lois

I like the fact that our most important conversations are held in
       the sea,
that I wear an electric blue swimsuit and you a yellow sarong
so we can identify each other between revelations and relatives.
Whole families pass between us up to their waists in foam, pink
boogie boards and neon. We discuss childlessness.
Our shoulders are hidden, our faces become memories for minutes.
You tell me about your new lover. A wave grows up behind us
and beautifies into a mist, universal and funny. Your listening –
and the whole sea is aware. *Illnesses, what he said to her,
regretted*...unintelligible. We use words like *forever*
and *searing*. Our stories pass into salt, crystallise.

We're distracted by goosebumps, seaweed, undertow, nylon
cradle-tents on the edge of collapse, cliffs. Aunts, cousins
wade in intelligently. How we know of no book readable
at this moment but this one, engaged in our meanings.
How there is nothing we say that is not water and air.

[1995]

Great Grandfathers
(for Henry Crompton)

Sometimes you glimpse one –
a great grandfather –
among the trees
with his white hair blown forward
seated and secret,
glad to see you there
only just higher than his knees,
the checkered blanket,
sugar-line of the rivermouth
on his mouth.

You can hardly remember, later.
You were only four when he died
and neither of you in full faculties
when you met, so your greeting
was really a goodbye:
a blanket, leaves, a scrap of beard,
a river happening to a beach,
your heaven against his.

Still, when you think of him
he is tall, he is broad
as if he were set about with himself,
as if all the forests of Lancashire
had been used to build him.
He lones in his age.

His age is becoming fabulous.
Your mother says if he were alive now
he would be 102.

And there is that bundle of letters
he left behind
which you are only allowed to touch
with the delicacy of a ladybird alighting –
so brittle, so see-through.

Great, he is greater than your father,
grandfather, less great than his.
You think of going backward
like the sandpiper chasing the lost wave
wrestling with the tide
adept and forlorn
or how the balloon breath rushes back into
your mouth when you are trying
very hard to blow it up
to take to the park,
how it could blow you all the way back
right against his heart.

[1995]

SELIMA HILL

(*b.* 1945)

The daughter of two painters, Hill went to Cambridge to study Moral Sciences
before switching to English, and has lived in Dorset for many years. Her
adoption of surrealist techniques of shock, bizarre, juxtaposition and defamil-
iarisation work to subvert conventional notions of self and the feminine. Her
first collection, *Saying Hello at the Station*, 'edited and shaped' by the now
Poet Laureate, Andrew Motion, was published in 1984. Hill's early use of
Egyptian imagery deliberately estranged her from the logic and proportion of
the classical world, setting it up (as had the Egyptian surrealist Joyce Mansour
and H.D.) as a trope for femininity, as well as using it as a device to give
distance from autobiographical experience. By her second book *My Darling
Camel* (1988), Hill was experimenting with narratives, and her third book,
The Accumulation of Small Acts of Kindness (1989), was a book-length poem
charting the mental breakdown and return to health of a young woman, a theme
revisited from a different perspective in *Lou-Lou* (2004). Hill returns repeatedly
to fragmented narratives, charting extreme experience with a dazzling excess,
as in *A Little Book of Meat* (1993), *Violet* (1997), *Bunny* (2001), *Portrait of My
Lover as a Horse* (2002) and *Red Roses* (2006). She has also published *Trembling
Hearts in the Bodies of Dogs: New & Selected Poems* (1994), combining her first
three books with a new collection, *Aeroplanes of the World*.

Questioning Mr Bonnet

Mr Bonnet, the helpful Egyptologist,
explains the strange cosmology
in his *Reallexikon der ägypschen
Religionsgeschichte* that he wrote
when he was dying in Berlin:
Horus, the god of light, hid his semen
in a dish of chopped lettuce leaves,
and greedy Seth, the god of darkness,
pig-headed, metal-boned, swallowed it,
and so, by trickery, the moon was born:
Thoth, on a lotus flower, the blue baboon!

He crosses the celestial ocean
as helmsman of the world,
called Aah, the vizier of Ra, the sun.
He loads the gleaming boat
with palm leaves which record
the days and nights in notches,
for he is the measurer of time,
and he invented writing.
He carries an ivory writing palette
in his long black fingers, to instruct
the scribes who squat before him on the sand.

And he helps them on their later journey
through the Night Of A Million Years
as Thoth, the protector of the dead:
he takes them kindly by the hand
and guides them through the underworld;
his nine baboon musicians line
the long bank where the travellers
pass on their way to Osiris,
dreaming of playing draughts
with the gods and dancing with them
in the Field of Reeds.

Mr Bonnet, did you meet him, and will I,
when I step on board the silver barque?
Will he be saying *Pleased to meet you,*

Mrs Hill, and how's the writing going?
as we descend the corridors of night
into the Judgment Hall. Will he pat me
on the shoulder with his cracked
avuncular hand and, tucking my book
inside his sky-blue cape, will he wink
before he picks his tail up and climbs
onto his special perch above the scales?

[1984]

Elegy for the Bee-god

Stingless bees
were bred in tree hollows
for beeswax and honey.
Every year, in the month
called Tzec, the bee-keepers
played their raspadores
and danced across the fields
with bells and ribbons
round their feet, to honour
the fat bee-god, who buzzed
in the heated air
to their music.
He lived in a gold house
in the hotlands, and drank
cocoa sweetened with honey.

All's quiet now, it's June,
and he's not here, the late,
the long-forgotten bee-god,
who sped on zigzag wings
across the sky to the faithful.
Cross-eyed, bejewelled
and tattooed, drumming
his fluffy yellow feet
on the tree hollows,
he gave the bees new hope,
and cocoa sweetened with honey.

If ever I find him – thin,
justly offended, dead
in the dry chaparral –
I will put jade beads
and honey on his tongue,
and wrap him in a shroud
of wings, and loop his neck
with pearls from Guatemala;
I will light him candles
of beeswax, bringing sleep,
and he will rest in the shade
of the First Tree,
and wait for me there –
humming a tune, and drinking
cocoa sweetened with honey.

[1984]

Parrots

I am surrounded by parrots.
They leave their chopped tomatoes on my head.
They pile at my feet like dying socks.

Their lettuce-coloured shoulders are so heavenly
the people at the zoo go mad about them.
One of them is looking in my eyes,

and saying, *What's the matter, Billy?* (meaning me).
Catch them, someone, take them back to Paradise,
they're giving me a terrible disease.

[1989]

from The Accumulation of Small Acts of Kindness

Masters

I step across the white dust of the runway
towards a man with pistols for a face.

He's tall and thin with one hand in a bandage.
I hear a faint *pow-pow* of disgrace.

'Departing for womanhood.' Crap. Green velvet cushions.
The baker's sons are being introduced.
The canteen of the airport smells of pepper.
I follow him towards the setting sun.
The avenue of cacti like an elephant
shelter silent groups of staring men.
We go upstairs. His buckle scrapes the brick-work.
Lust and grief. Unusual cakes. He's kind.
I'm menstruating on a stranger's blankets.
Sorrow like a silver spool unwinds.

The sun is hot. My head is full of silence
attracting hordes of angry bees like bells.
A swallow-tail, an amber necklace, henna.
I want to be so calm. 'Devotion frees.'

People, horizontal, lit, ascending,
now declare their everlasting love
by open windows, where the tepid evening
is tempting them to cast aside their clothes.

See me see me see me in the garden.
I'm made of ants.
Whose voice is that?
It's hers.
Feel between my legs two lips like lollies,
or like a blood-hound on the verge of tears.

Talking to him in a voice as distant
as unborn daughters kneeling by my bed.

Turkish delight, brazil nuts, sweetened yoghourt.
I treasure every word I think he said.

The only men were doctors. We were dollies
put to sleep in resonating halls.

The bell is ringing like an English cherry.
Picasso in his villa touches girls.

The boots that crush the roses hear me whisper
You mustn't kiss me now. He takes my hand.
Ecstasy, which makes him feel nearer,
has made me ill. I never talk. I'm banned.

The offices are empty, only you:
a violet light, a pleated skirt, a prayer
rising in the dark then drifting downward
to join the other voices of the air;
while in the muted villa, calmed by sorrow,
someone feels a lightening of snow.
We'll move you to another bed tomorrow,
we'll move you to a place where good girls go.

[1989]

Prawns de Jo

Because she was wrong,
because it was all her fault right from the beginning,
because she was ashamed of even thinking about it,
and should never have been his daughter in the first place;
because she was ugly
and he was magnificent
and she was the scum of the earth,
it must never be mentioned:
the unforgettable smell of the singeing baby,
the unforgettable sight of billowing curtains like brides,
the cot,
the charred muslin,
the endless procession of leggy inquisitive flies,
the orange buzz of the electric fire,
and how she'd sit for hours squeezing oranges,
and how she'd sit and fan the flies away,
and hurry down the streets with aching breasts
to part the veil of flies to please the doctors,
the orange ash, the orange carrot-juice,
are never to be mentioned. In that case
what is she to do with the head
that has to be oiled and covered and never mentioned,

241

as crisp as the colour of violets sprinkled with salt
that grow in the dark
to within half an inch of her brain,
as the colour of prawns sprinkled with salt and pepper
and served to the rats at a diner named PRAWNS DE JO;
that somebody feels beside herself with guilt about
and wheels her off to the sun-tanned arms of a specialist
and all she wants is for him to unpeel it off
and patch it up with a patch from the lawn of her leg,
but he's kitting her out with a rat-sized wig instead
that she keeps in a box
like pet pubic hair
she's secretly proud of because she is horrified by
but never wears because what's the use of a head
with a tuft of hair like a hat from a cracker on top
that's always about to come skew and slither off;
and what's the use of a scar if it's not to be mentioned,
and the milling of flies
and the sight of the flame-proof fireman
with a baby slung over his shoulder as if she's a pig?
And what's the use of the hand-knitted matinee jacket
the surgeon had to pick out with a pair of tweezers?

[2001]

WENDY COPE

(*b*. 1945)

Born in Erith, Kent, Cope read History as St Hilda's College, Oxford. She
was a primary school teacher from 1967 to 1981 and 1984 to 1986. In 1986,
with the publication of her first collection, *Making Cocoa for Kinglsey Amis*
(1986), she became a freelance writer. She received a Cholmondeley Award
in 1987, and was a television critic for *The Spectator* until 1990. Her second
collection, *Serious Concerns*, appeared in 1992, and *If I Don't Know* (2001)
was shortlisted for the Whitbread Poetry Award. She was given the Michael
Braude Award for Light Verse (American Academy of Arts and Letters) in
1995. Cope is also the editor of *The Orchard Book of Funny Poems* (1993), *Is
That The New Moon?* (1989), *The Funny Side: 101 Humorous Poems* (1998),
The Faber Book of Bedtime Stories (1999) and *Heaven on Earth: 101 Happy
Poems* (2001). She has written two children's books: *Twiddling Your Thumbs*
(1988) and *The River Girl* (1991). She lives in Winchester.

My Lover

For I will consider my lover, who shall remain nameless.

For at the age of 49 he can make the noise of five different kinds
of lorry changing gear on a hill.

For he sometimes does this on the stairs at his place of work.

For he is embarrassed when people overhear him.

For he can also imitate at least three different kinds of train.

For these include the London tube train, the steam engine, and
the Southern Rail electric.

For he supports Tottenham Hotspur with joyful and unswerving
devotion.

For he abhors Arsenal, whose supporters are uncivilised and rough.

For he explains that Spurs are magic, whereas Arsenal are boring
and defensive.

For I knew nothing of this six months ago, nor did I want to.

For now it all enchants me.

For this he performs in ten degrees.

For first he presents himself as a nice, serious, liberated person.

For secondly he sits through many lunches, discussing life and
love and never mentioning football.

For thirdly he is careful not to reveal how much he dislikes losing
an argument.

For fourthly he talks about the women in his past, acknowledging
that some of it must have been his fault.

For fifthly he is so obviously reasonable that you are inclined to
doubt this.

For sixthly he invites himself round for a drink one evening.

For seventhly you consume two bottles of wine between you.

For eighthly he stays the night.

For ninthly you cannot wait to see him again.

For tenthly this does not happen for several days.

For having achieved his object he turns again to his other interests.

For he will not miss his evening class or his choir practice for a
woman.

For he is out nearly all the time.

For you cannot even get him on the telephone.

For he is the kind of man who has been driving women round the
bend for generations.

For, sad to say, this thought does not bring you to your senses.

For he is charming.

For he is good with animals and children.

For his voice is both reassuring and sexy.

For he drives an A-registration Vauxhall Astra estate.

For he goes at 80 miles per hour on the motorways.

For when I plead with him he says, 'I'm not going any slower than *this*.'

For he is convinced he knows his way around better than anyone else on earth.

For he does not encourage suggestions from his passengers.

For if he ever got lost there would be hell to pay.

For he sometimes makes me sleep on the wrong side of my own bed.

For he cannot be bossed around.

For he has this grace, that he is happy to eat fish fingers or Chinese takeaway or to cook the supper himself.

For he knows about my cooking and is realistic.

For he makes me smooth cocoa with bubbles on the top.

For he drinks and smokes at least as much as I do.

For he is obsessed with sex.

For he would never say it is overrated.

For he grew up before the permissive society and remembers his adolescence.

For he does not insist it is healthy and natural, nor does he ask me what I would like him to do.

For he has a few ideas of his own.

For he has never been able to sleep much and talks with me late into the night.

For we wear each other out with our wakefulness.

For he makes me feel like a light-bulb that cannot switch itself off.

For he inspires poem after poem.

For he is clean and tidy but not too concerned with his appearance.

For he lets the barber cut his hair too short and goes round looking like a convict for a fortnight.

For when I ask if this necklace is all right he replies, 'Yes, if no means looking at three others.'

For he was shocked when younger team-mates began using talcum powder in the changing-room.

For his old-fashioned masculinity is the cause of continual merriment on my part.

For this puzzles him.

[1986]

244

The Lavatory Attendant

I counted two and seventy stenches
All well defined and several stinks!
COLERIDGE

Slumped on a chair, his body is an S
That wants to be a minus sign.

His face is overripe Wensleydale
Going blue at the edges.

In overalls of sacerdotal white
He guards a row of fonts

With lids like eye-patches. Snapped shut
They are castanets. All day he hears

Short-lived Niagaras, the clank
And gurgle of canescent cisterns.

When evening comes he sluices a thin tide
Across sand-coloured lino,

Turns Medusa on her head
And wipes the floor with her.

[1986]

VERONICA FORREST-THOMSON
(1947-75)

Born in Malaya and brought up in Glasgow, Veronica Forrest-Thomson was educated at the Universities of Liverpool and Cambridge; at Cambridge she studied with the poet J.H. Prynne. Her first collection, *Identi-Kit*, was published in 1967 under the name Veronica Forrest, and was followed by *twelve academic questions* (1970) and *Language Games* (1971). As can be seen from the titles of these latter collections, Forrest-Thomson was interested in the work of the philosopher Ludwig Wittgenstein. A critic as well as a poet, Forrest-Thomson wrote her doctoral thesis on 'Poetry as Knowledge: A Theory of Twentieth Century Poetry' (1971). Her critical work, *Poetic Artifice*, was published posthumously in 1978. In this book she expounds her theory of poetic artifice, suggesting that as readers we must learn to suspend what she calls 'naturalisation', 'an attempt to reduce the strangeness of poetic language and poetic organisation by making it intelligible, by translating it into a statement about the non-verbal external world' (cited by Alison Mark in *Veronica Forrest-Thomson and Language Poetry*, p.6). Forrest-Thomson is, for example, keen to redeem the work of Sylvia Plath from the purely biographical, urging the reader rather to reflect on, as Alison Mark has pointed out, 'the linguistic and formal innovation which characterises [her] later poems' (Mark, p.97). Two further collections of poetry were published, *Cordelia or 'A poem should not Mean but Be'* (1974) and the posthumous *On the Periphery* (1976). Her *Collected Poems and Translations*, edited by Anthony Barnett, was published in 1990, and *Selected Poems: Language Games, On the Periphery and Other Writings* in 1999.

The Garden of Proserpine

Th'expense of spirit in a waste of shame
Is lust in action and, till action, lust
Until my last lost taper's end be spent
My sick taper does begin to wink
And, O, many-toned, immortal Aphrodite,
Lend me thy girdle.
You can spare it for an hour or so
Until Zeus has got back his erection.

Here where all trouble seems
Dead winds' and spent waves' riot
In doubtful dreams of dreams.
The moon is sinking, and the Pleiades,
Mid Night; and time runs on she said.
I lie alone. I am aweary, aweary,
I would that I were dead.
Be my partner and you'll never regret it.
Gods and poets ought to stick together;
They make a strong combination.
So just make him love me again,
You good old triple goddess of tight corners.
And leave me to deal with gloomy Dis.

Death never seems a particularly informative topic for poets
Though that doesn't stop them dilating at length upon it.

But then they would dilate on anything.
Love, on the other hand, however trite, is always interesting
At least to those in its clutches
And usually also to their readers.
For, even if the readers be not in its clutches
They think they would like to be
Because they think it is a pleasant experience.
I, however, know better.
And so do Sappho, Shakespeare, Swinburne, Tennyson and Eliot.
Not to mention the Greek dramatists:
Sophocles, Euripedes, Aeschylos, and Eliot.
We all know better.
Love is hellish.
Which is why Aphrodite is also Persephone,
Queen of love and death.
Love kills people and the police can't do anything to stop it.
Love will:

> ravage your beauty
> disrupt your career
> break up your friendships
> squander your energy
> spend every last drop of your self-possession

Even supposing you had such qualities to start with.
The god knows why we bother with it.
It is because it bothers with us.
It won't leave us alone for a minute.
For without us it wouldn't exist.
And that is the secret of all human preoccupation
(As others have said before me)
Love, death, time, beauty, the whole bag of tricks.
All our own work including, of course, the gods.
And we let them ride us like the fools we are.
Of all follies that is the penultimate:
To let our own inventions destroy us,
The ultimate folly, of course, is not to let them destroy us.
To pretend a stoic indifference, mask merely of stupidity.
To become ascetic, superior to the pure pleasures of the senses,
Arrogant and imbecile senecans, unconscious
Of what is going on even in their own bodies
Old whatsisname stuck up on his pillar,
A laughing stock, the ultimate in insensitivity.

The only thing, contrarily, to do with the problem of love –
As with all other problems –
Is to try to solve it.
You won't succeed but you won't make a fool of yourself, trying
Or, at least, not so much of a fool as those who refuse to try.
So here we go for another trip and hold onto your seat-belt, Persephone.

> I loved you and you loved me
> And then we made a mess.
> We still loved each other but
> We loved each other less.

> I got a job, I wrote a book,
> I turned again to play.
> However I found out by then
> That you had gone away.

> My dignity dictated
> A restrained farewell.
> But I love you so much
> Dignity can go to hell.

> I went to hell with dignity,
> For by then, we were three.
> And whatever I feel about you,
> I certainly hate she.

> The god knows what will be the end
> And he will never tell.
> For I love you and you love me
> Although we are in hell.

> And what death has to do with it
> Is always simply this:
> If it isn't your arms I'm heading for
> It's the arms of gloomy Dis.

[1976]

Sonnet

My love, if I write a song for you
To that extent you are gone
For, as everyone says, and I know it's true:
We are all always alone.

Never so separate trying to be two
And the busy old fool is right.
To try and finger myself from you
Distinguishes day from night.

If I say 'I love you' we can't but laugh
Since irony knows what we'll say.
If I try to free myself by my craft
You vary as night from day.

So, accept the wish for the deed my dear.
Words were made to prevent us near.

[1976]

LIZ LOCHHEAD

(*b*. 1947)

Liz Lochhead was born in Motherwell, Lanarkshire, and studied at Glasgow
School of Art. Also a dramatist, she has published numerous books of poetry,
including *Memo for Spring* (1972), *The Grimm Sisters* (1981), *Dreaming Franken-
stein and Collected Poems* (1984), *Bagpipe Muzak* (1991) and *The Colour of
Black and White: Poems 1984-2003* (2003), as well as *True Confessions and
New Clichés* (1985), a collection of raps, songs, sketches and monologues.
Performing in revues and drawing on music hall traditions Liz Lochhead has
been a key figure in the revitalising of the dramatic monologue. With her
emphasis on voice, and in making lively and humorous use of the demotic,
she has brought a feminist consciousness to both myth and history, and to
the exploration of female and Scottish identities. Her versions of Grimm
compare interestingly with Anne Sexton's *Transformations* (1972) but also
with Angela Carter's fiction and her friend Carol Ann Duffy's later Grimm-
inspired volume *The World's Wife* (1999).

The Grim Sisters

And for special things
(weddings, school-
concerts) the grown up girls next door
would do my hair.

Luxembourg announced Amami night.

I sat at peace passing bobbipins
from a marshmallow pink cosmetic purse
embossed with jazzmen,
girls with pony tails and a November
topaz lucky birthstone.
They doused my cow's-lick, rollered
and skewered tightly.
I expected that to be lovely
would be worth the hurt.

They read my Stars,
tied chiffon scarves to doorhandles, tried
to teach me tight dancesteps
you'd no guarantee
any partner you might find would ever be able to
keep up with as far as I could see.

There were always things to burn
before the men came in.

For each disaster
you were meant to know the handy hint.
Soap at a pinch
but better nailvarnish (clear) for ladders.
For kisscurls, spit.
Those days womanhood was quite a sticky thing
and that was what these grim sisters came to mean.

'You'll know all about it soon enough.'
But when the clock struck they
stood still, stopped dead.
And they were left there
out in the cold with the wrong skirt-length

and bouffant hair,
dressed to kill,

who'd been
all the rage in fifty-eight,
a swish of Persianelle,
a slosh of perfume.
In those big black mantrap handbags
they snapped shut at any hint of *that*
were hedgehog hairbrushes,
cottonwool mice and barbed combs to tease.
Their heels spiked bubblegum, dead leaves.

Wasp waist and cone breast, I see them yet.
I hope, I hope
there's been a change of more than silhouette.

[1981]

Rapunzstiltskin

& just when our maiden had got
good & used to her isolation,
stopped daily expecting to be rescued,
had come to almost love her tower,
along comes This Prince
with absolutely
all the wrong answers.
Of course she had not been brought up to look for
originality or gingerbread
so at first she was quite undaunted
by his tendency to talk in strung-together cliché.
'Just hang on and we'll get you out of there,'
he hollered like a fireman in some soap opera
when she confided her plight (the old
hag inside etc & how trapped she was);
well, it was corny but
he did look sort of gorgeous
axe and all.
So there she was, humming & pulling
all the pins out of her chignon,

throwing him all the usual lifelines
till, soon, he was shimmying in & out
every other day as though
he owned the place, bringing her
the sex manuals & skeins of silk
from which she was meant, eventually,
to weave the means of her own escape.
'All very well & good,' she prompted,
'but when exactly?'
She gave him till
well past the bell on the timeclock.
She mouthed at him, hinted,
she was keener than a TV quizmaster
that he should get it right.
'I'll do everything in my power,' he intoned, 'but
the impossible (she groaned) might
take a little longer.' He grinned.
She pulled her glasses off.
'All the better
to see you with my dear?' he hazarded.
She screamed, cut off her hair.
'Why, you're beautiful?' he guessed tentatively.
'No, No, No!' she
shrieked & stamped her foot so
hard it sank six cubits through the floorboards.
'I love you?' he came up with
as she finally tore herself in two.

[1981]

The Hickie

I mouth
sorry in the mirror when I see
the mark I must have made just now
loving you.
Easy to say it's all right
adultery
like blasphemy is for believers but
even in our
situation simple etiquette says

252

love should leave us both unmarked.
You are on loan to me like a library book
and we both know it.
Fine if you love both of us
but neither of us must too much show it.

In my misted mirror
you trace two toothprints
on the skin of your shoulder and sure
you're almost quick enough
to smile out bright and clear for me
as if it was OK.

Friends again, together in this bathroom
we finish washing love away.

[1981]

Dreaming Frankenstein
(for Lys Hansen, Jacki Parry and June Redfern)

She said she
woke up with him in
her head, in her bed.
Her mother-tongue clung to her mouth's roof
in terror, dumbing her, and he came with a name
that was none of her making.

No maidservant ever
in her narrow attic, combing
out her hair in the midnight mirror
on Hallowe'en (having eaten
that egg with its yolk hollowed out
then filled with salt)
– oh never one had such success as this
she had not courted.
The amazed flesh of her
neck and shoulders nettled
at his apparition.

Later, stark staring awake to everything
(the room, the dark parquet, the white high Alps beyond)
all normal in the moonlight

and him gone, save a ton-weight sensation,
the marks fading visibly where
his buttons had bit into her and
the rough serge of his suiting had chafed her sex,
she knew – oh that was not how –
but he'd entered her utterly.

This was the penetration
of seven swallowed apple pips.
Or else he'd slipped like a silver dagger
between her ribs and healed her up secretly
again. Anyway
he was inside her
and getting him out again
would be agony fit to quarter her,
unstitching everything.

Eyes on those high peaks
in the reasonable sun of the morning,
she dressed in damped muslin
and sat down to quill and ink
and icy paper.

[1984]

PENELOPE SHUTTLE
(*b*. 1947)

Penelope Shuttle was born in Middlesex. First published as a novelist, her
fiction includes *All the Usual Hours of Sleeping* (1969), *Wailing Monkey
Embracing a Tree* (1973) and *Rainsplitter in the Zodiac Garden* (1977). Her
first collection of poetry, *The Orchard Upstairs*, was published in 1980, and
followed by *The Child Stealer* (1983), *The Lion from Rio* (1986), *Adventures
with My Horse* (1988), *Taxing the Rain* (1992), *Selected Poems 1980–1996* (1997),
A Leaf out of His Book (1999) and *Redgrove's Wife* (2006). Shuttle was married
to the writer Peter Redgrove who died in 2003. Together they wrote a col-
lection of poems, *The Hermaphrodite Album* (1973), two novels, *The Terrors of
Dr Treviles: A Romance* (1974) and *The Glass Cottage: A Nautical Romance*
(1976), and a study, *The Wise Wound: Menstruation and Everywoman* (1978).

On *Adventures with My Horse* she writes: 'Women have a huge dynamo of
energy that is focussed on our physical ability to conceive and bear children,
but how many of us will want to have a great many children? We have one,
or two, or three, and then what? Because the energy goes on, cycle after cycle.

254

What's it for?...For me it engendered a son of poetry. That force shoving us on and on to create more persons, confusing inner and outer needs, had to be channelled; this inward son.. grew, became companion and prophet...If feminist writing must exist, and if this is it, then it travels in my own poems from and to a further place that is non-nihilist, non sadistic, non-disposable.' (*Don't Ask Me What I Mean*, pp.262-63).

Taxing the Rain

When I wake the rain's falling
and I think, as always, it's for the best,

I remember how much I love rain,
the weakest and strongest of us all;

as I listen to its yesses and no's,
I think how many men and women

would, if they could,
against all sense and nature,

tax the rain for its privileges;

make it pay for soaking our earth
and splashing all over our leaves;

pay for muddying our grass
and amusing itself with our roots.

Let rain be taxed, they say,
for riding on our rivers
and drenching our sleeves;

for loitering in our lakes
and reservoirs. Make rain pay its way.

Make it pay for lying full length
in the long straight sedate green waters

of our city canals,
and for working its way through processes

of dreamy complexity
until this too-long untaxed rain comes indoors

and touches our lips,
bringing assuagement – for rain comes

to slake all our thirsts, spurting
brusque and thrilling in hot needles,

showering on to anyone naked;
or balming our skins in the shape of scented baths.

Yes, there are many who'd like to tax the rain;
even now they whisper, it can be done, it must be done.

[1992]

Angel

The angel is coming down,
white-hot, feet-first,
abseiling down the sky.

Wingspan? At least the width
of two young men lying head to head,
James and Gary, their bare feet
modestly defiant, pointing north,
south.

The angel has ten thousand smiles,
he is coming down
smooth as a sucking of thumbs,

he is coming down on a dangle of breath,
in blazing bloodsilk robes.
See the size and dignity of his great toes!

He comes down in a steam of feathers,
a dander of plumes,
healthy as a spa,
air crackling round him.

Yes, he comes down
douce and sure-winged,
shouting sweetly through the smoke,
'J'arrive!'

Hovering on fiery foppish wings,
he gazes down at me
with crane-neck delicacy.

I turn my head from his furnace,
his drastic beauty...
he is overcoming me.

On my crouched back his breath's
a solid scorching fleece.
In my hidden eyes, the peep of him hurts.

He waits,
he will not wait long.

Flames flicker along my sleeve
of reverence as I thrust my hand
into the kiln of the seraph.

Howling, I shoulder my pain,
and tug out one feather,
tall as my daughter.

When I look up,
he's gone on headlong wings,
in a billow of smoulders,
sparks wheeling, molten heels

slouching the side wind. 'Adieu!'

Goodbye, I wave,
my arm spangled with blisters
that heal as I stare at the empty sky.

And the feather?
                    Is made of gold.
Vane and rachis, calamus
and down. For gold like an angel
joyeth in the fire.

[1992]

Delicious Babies

Because of spring there are babies everywhere,
sweet or sulky, irascible or full of the milk of human kindness.
Yum, yum! Delicious babies!
Babies with the soft skins of babies, cheeks
of such tit-bit pinkness, tickle-able babies, tasty babies,
mouth-watering babies.

The pads of their hands! The rounds
of their knees! Their good smells of bathtime
and new clothes and gobbled rusks!
Even their discarded nappies are worthy of them, reveal their powers.
Legions and hosts of babies! Babies bold as lions, sighing babies,
tricksy babies, omniscient babies, babies using a plain language

of reasonable demands and courteous acceptance.
Others have the habit of loud contradiction,
can empty a railway carriage (though their displeasing howls
cheer up childless women).
Look at this baby, sitting bolt upright in his buggy!
Consider his lofty unsmiling acknowledgement of our adulation,

look at the elfin golfer's hat flattering his fluffy hair!
Look next at this very smallest of babies
tightly wrapped in a foppery of blankets.
In his high promenading pram he sleeps sumptuously,
only a nose, his father's, a white bonnet and a wink
of eyelid showing.

All babies are manic-serene, all babies are mine,
all babies are edible, the boys taste best.
I feed on them, nectareous are my babies,
manna, confiture, my sweet groceries.

I smack my lips,
deep in my belly the egg ripens,
makes the windows shake,
another ovum-quake
moves earth, sky and me...

Bring me more babies! Let me have them for breakfast,
lunch and tea! Let me feast, let my honey-banquet babies
go on forever, fresh deliveries night and day!

[1992]

RUTH PADEL
(*b*. 1947)

Born in London, the great-great-granddaughter of Charles Darwin, Padel
studied classics at Oxford, where she wrote a DPhil on Greek tragedy and was
the first woman fellow of Wadham College, Oxford. She has published two
critical books, *In and Out of the Mind: Greek Images of the Tragic Self* (1992)
and *Whom Gods Destroy: Elements of Greek and Tragic Madness* (1995), as well
as *I'm a Man: Sex Gods and Rock 'n' Roll* (2000) and *52 Ways of Looking at
a Poem* (2002). Padel is a freelance writer. In her most recent book, *Tigers in
Red Weather* (2005), she travels the world in search of tigers, documenting
her experiences.

Padel's first collection *Summer Snow* was published in 1990 and followed
by *Angel* (1993), *Fuse Wire* (1996), *Rembrandt Would Have Loved You* (1998),
Voodoo Shop (2002) and *The Soho Leopard* (2004). Writing about *Rembrandt
Would Have Loved You*, she says 'Listening to a lot of women's rock, and the
ways at going at things I've been finding in P.J. Harvey, Tori Amos, Sinéad
O'Connor, Liz Phair, Michelle Shocked, Carole King, Laurie Anderson, has
been a revelation. They have the same problems women poets have, but in a
far more violent form: how the bulk of what's gone before has been made by
the boys, you value the work but have to find yourself reacting to it.' (*Don't
Ask Me What I Mean*, pp.212-13)

Icicles Round a Tree in Dumfriesshire

We're talking different kinds of vulnerability here.
    These icicles aren't going to last for ever
Suspended in the ultraviolet rays of a Dumfries sun.
    But here they hang, a frozen whirligig of lightning,
And the famous American sculptor
    Who scrambles the world with his tripod
For strangeness *au naturel*, got sunset to fill them.
    It's not comfortable, a double helix of opalescent fire

259

Wrapping round you, swishing your bark
    Down cotton you can't see,
On which a sculptor planned his icicles,
    Working all day for that Mesopotamian magic
Of last light before the dark
    In a suspended helter-skelter, lit
By almost horizontal rays
    Making a mist-carousel from the House of Diamond,

A spiral of Pepsodent darkening to the shadowfrost
    Of cedars at the Great Gate of Kiev.
Why it makes me think of opening the door to you
    I can't imagine. No one could be less
Of an icicle. But there it is –
    Having put me down in felt-tip
In the mystical appointment book,
    You shoot that quick

Inquiry-glance, head tilted, when I open up,
    Like coming in's another country,
A country you want but have to get used to, hot
    From your *bal masqué*, making sure
That what you found before's
    Still here: a spiral of touch and go,
Lightning licking a tree
    Imagining itself Aretha Franklin

Singing 'You make me feel like a natural woman'
    In *basso profondo*,
Firing the bark with its otherworld ice
    The way you fire, lifting me
Off my own floor, legs furled
    Round your trunk as that tree goes up
At an angle inside the lightning, roots in
    The orange and silver of Dumfries.

Now I'm the lightning now you, you are,
    As you pour yourself round me
Entirely. No who's doing what and to who,
    Just a tangle of spiral and tree.
You might wonder about sculptors who come all this way
    To make a mad thing that won't last.
You know how it is: you spend a day, a whole life.
    Then the light's gone, you walk away

To the Galloway Paradise Hotel. Pine-logs,
    Cutlery, champagne – OK,
But the important thing was making it.
    Hours, and you don't know how it'll be.
Then something like light
    Arrives last moment, at speed reckoned
Only by horizons: completing, surprising
    With its three hundred thousand

Kilometres per second.
    Still, even lightning has its moments of panic.
You don't get icicles catching the midwinter sun
    In a perfect double helix in Dumfriesshire every day.
And can they be good for each other,
    Lightning and tree? It'd make anyone,
Wouldn't it, afraid? That rowan would adore
    To sleep and wake up in your arms

But's scared of getting burnt.
    And the lightning might ask, touching wood,
'What do you want of me, now we're in the same
    Atomic chain?' What can the tree say?
'Being the centre of all that you are to yourself –
    That'd be OK. Being my own body's fine
But it needs yours to stay that way.'
    No one could live for ever in

A suspended gleam-on-the-edge,
    As if sky might tear any minute.
Or not for ever for long. Those icicles
    Won't be surprise any more. The little snapped threads
Blew away. Glamour left that hill in Dumfries.
    The sculptor went off with his black equipment.
Adzes, twine, leather gloves.

What's left is a photo of
    A completely solitary sight
In a book anyone might open.
    But whether our touch at the door gets forgotten
Or turned into other sights, light, form,
    I hope you'll be truthful
To me. At least as truthful as lightning,
    Skinning a tree.

[1998]

SUSAN WICKS

(*b*. 1947)

Susan Wicks grew up in Kent and read French at Hull before writing a PhD on André Gide at Sussex. *Singing Underwater*, her first collection, was published in 1992, followed by *Open Diagnosis* (1994), *The Clever Daughter* (1996) and *Night Toad: New & Selected Poems* (2003). Her other books include a memoir, *Driving My Father* (1995), and two novels *The Key* (1997) and *Little Thing* (1998). She teaches at the University of Kent.

She writes: 'I've been more influenced by novelists than I have by poets. I often find myself more interested in criteria of tone, distance and reliability than I am in language for its own sake. I hope that in my best poems "language" almost disappears. What I would like to achieve is a language that could make the reader read more slowly and attentively almost without his or her knowledge, and allow the connections in a poem to surface gradually' (Forbes, p.31). Sharon Olds has been an important poet to her: 'If we aren't prepared to take emotional and aesthetic risks...how can we expect our readers to be fully human and vulnerable as they read?'

Rain Dance

This is how they make rain, the raw
repeated drumbeat of two pulses, this green gauze
that settles on their skin and gleams
like light on water. This is how he creates her,
fluid as green drops fusing
on new growth, bent to this holy posture
of damage, her raised green satin instep
stroking her own right cheek, as he still turns her,
twists her as if through creepers,
this green sediment of branches
layered on air, as his taut body
dances on hers. They will reach the light soon. He bends her
this way and that, her head flips backwards
into his darkness, her neck surely broken.
Her two legs split perfectly open
like roots. There is moisture
between them now as he drags her, wood
rasping her inside thighs. The rapt watchers
gasp with her pain, if she could only
feel it. Curved for his blessing,
her skin glistens as he still strokes her

like a green pot into being
on this wheel of rhythms
where they are gods, unmindful now of bodies,
our single-jointed history
of breakage, and the sweat runs off them.

[1996]

Persephone

Wanting someone who looked natural,
they cast you as Persephone, not thinking
how at regular intervals you were taken
to visit your own mother
under a flaking sky of cream paint
down the echoing corridor
to the long-stay ward, where trees
froze in the black glass
of winter – how you were no stranger
to the clockwork rhythms of figures
moaning and swaying, the mechanical
hands that moved across faces
or scattered things in odd corners,
the hungry hands that flapped after
with their wings of ragged knitting.
Each time you would leave her and return
to birdsong, the urgent green
through frost, the melting grass, the world
you would give her if she would only
recognise you through the heavy doors
your father closed between you. Each week
you rehearsed your flower-steps
with a basket of paper petals
as your teachers smiled down on you, exclaiming
at your sweet face,
at the way you seemed never to see him coming –
as if each last dance were the first dance,
and every mother won over by so little.

[1996]

263

My Father's Caul

Is this my father's skin
or my grandmother's,
twice folded
in its blue envelope,
like a promise of wings?

I tease it open,
see the intimate creases
whitened and flaking,
see my own fingers
shine through it,
as if my father
floated clear of us,
his skin perfect
and impermeable,
his life melting to wax.

Now this dry moon rises
in cold currents.
The attic shadows
play over it.
I see it falling
through air,
its stretch of membrane
slick with grease,
the purple features
flattened to a gasp,
the new-born
mouth, nose, eyes, fingers
sealed in a bag of skin
and sent back to her,
slippery, anonymous.

[1996]

Night Toad

You can hardly see him –
his outline, his cold skin
almost a dead leaf,
blotched brown, dull green,
khaki. He sits so quietly
pumping his quick breath
just at the edge of water
between ruts in the path.

And suddenly he is the centre
of a cone of light
falling from the night sky –
ruts running with liquid fire,
cobwebs imprinted on black,
each grass-blade clear
and separate – until the hiss
of human life removes itself,
the air no longer creaks,
the shaking stops
and he can crawl back
to where he came from.

But what *was* this,
if it was not death?

[2003]

DENISE RILEY
(*b.* 1948)

Denise Riley was born in Carlisle. A poet and critic, her critical works include:
War in the Nursery: Theories of the Child and Mother (1983), *'Am I That Name?':*
Feminism and the Category of 'Women' in History (1988), *The Words of Selves:*
Identification, Solidarity, Irony (2000), *The Flesh of Words* (with Jean-Jacques
Lecercle, 2004) and *Impersonal Passion: Language as Affect* (2005). She has
also edited *Poets on Writing: Britain 1970-1991* (1992). Her books of poetry
include *Dry Air* (1985), *Mop Mop Georgette: New and Selected Poems 1986-*
1993 (1993) and *Selected Poems* (2000). Her work was also included in *Penguin*
Modern Poets 10.

Riley is sometimes grouped with poets associated with the Cambridge School (Andrew Crozier, Veronica Forrest-Thomson, J.H. Prynne) and the American Language poetry "movement" which began in the 1970s. Of the women poets associated with radical experimentation, Riley is the most warmly received by the mainstream. Like the Cambridge and Language poets, Riley is concerned to disrupt syntax, defamiliarise and thus attempt to decommodify poetic language. Her work is also involved with feminist issues: her creative and her critical work both address what it means to assume an "identity". She is currently a professor of Literature at the University of East Anglia.

Affections must not

This is an old fiction of reliability

is a weather presence, is a righteousness
is arms in cotton

this is what stands up in kitchens
is a true storm shelter
& is taken straight out of colonial history, master & slave

arms that I will not love folded nor admire for their "strength"
linen that I will not love folded but will see flop open
tables that will rise heavily in the new wind & lift away,
                    bearing their precious burdens

of mothers who never were, nor white nor black
mothers who were always a set of equipment & a fragile balance
mothers who looked over a gulf through the cloud of an act &
                    at times speechlessly saw it

inside a designation there are people permanently startled to
                    bear it, the not-me against sociology
inside the kitchens there is realising of tightropes
milk, if I do not continue to love you as deeply and truly as
                    you want and need
that is us in the mythical streets again

support, support.

the houses are murmuring with many small pockets of emotion
on which spongy ground adults' lives are being erected & paid
                    for daily

while their feet and their children's feet are tangled around
                              like those of fen larks
in the fine steely wires which run to & fro between love &
                    economics

affections must not support the rent

I.   neglect.   the.   house

[1985]

Shantung

It's true that anyone can fall
in love with anyone at all.
Later, they can't. Ouf, ouf.

How much mascara washes away each day
and internationally, making the blue one black.
Come on everybody. Especially you girls.

Each day I think of something about dying.
Does everybody? do they think too, I mean.
My friends! some answers. Gently
unstrap my wristwatch. Lay it face down.

[1992]

Lyric

Stammering it fights to get
held and to never get held
as whatever motors it swells
to hammer itself out on me

then it can call out high
and rounded as a night
bird's cry falling clean
down out of a black tree.

I take on its rage at the cost
of sleep. If I love it I sink
attracting its hatred. If I
don't love it I steal its music.

Take up a pleat in this awful
process and then fold me flat
inside it so that I don't see
where I was already knotted in.

It is my burden and subject
to listen for sweetness in hope
to hold it in weeping ears though
each hurt each never so much.

[1992]

Cruelty Without Beauty

Go on working around my hairline with a blade
and all you'll come to is a white sheen of bone
and all that would tell you is that I'm, what else,
human. I can tell you that now. Don't make
yourself into such a fine instrument of knowledge
that you slice uselessly back into your own hand
shocking yourself. There is a body, or soul, under
your skin too, but you won't assuage your doubts
about it by unpeeling me; no, that will uncover nothing
but your worse original anxiety. If I speak with formal
heaviness, that's the weight of stiff grief bending down
leaves, and the mild rain spotting their dust into rings.
No I don't much like this bland authoritative tone either
but it is what I took from years of reworded loss.
So if my skin slid downwards to the ground
you would see only a standing pillar of blood.
Believe that this would be true also of you.
– Such distanced care for self, rendered as knowing,
makes anybody ill: I'll drop this clinic voice to say
that this hot scowl on songs marks rage for
closeness just not found in a true human love –
burn, work, burn blue, since one clean word on

someone's blank makes salt well under any tongue,
am I to go unswollen, arm across my shoulders
good, that's who off the end of a wrist? so tired of
howling more more grand babe yet if there's angel too
this thick extent of longing's ugly as it's true. Heavy
water. Show your wound: Ah yes mine's deeper:
Is that my shaming subject after all. Best get this
done on paper no one hears so I'll stay still in life
where I hear water speaking, may stand where light
falls as the plain light will – no that lot skims on wire
rhetoric, totters from tightly civic pause to weeping
open cut and back but can't get balanced; its figure
sways with outflung arms, I do, to hold the deadly
wish to be white eye stripped out of human motion
as if sight crashed to clearness, clean of me:
Brown rock and leaden sea. Crows in the wood
faced to the wind, pinned on high branches. Dark
blobs. Clacks on the wind. The drumming light.
Yet no one should say to me, Nothing's enough
for you, ever. But I do want to kill and die.

[1992]

GILLIAN ALLNUTT

(b. 1949)

Allnutt was born in London, spending half of her childhood there and half in
Newcastle upon Tyne. She read English and Philosophy at Newnham College,
Cambridge, and also studied at the University of Sussex. She has worked as
a teacher, performer, journalist and editor. She was a member of the feminist
collective publishing house, Sheba, from 1981 to 1983, and poetry editor of
City Limits from 1983 to 1988. She returned to the North East in 1988, and
lives in Esh Winning, Co. Durham. In 2005 she won the Northern Rock
Foundation Writer's Award.

Her first collection was *Spitting the Pips Out* (1981), which was followed
by *Beginning the Avocado* (1987), *Blackthorn* (1994), *Nantucket and the Angel*
(1997), *Lintel* (2001) and *Sojourner* (2004). She co-edited *The New British
Poetry* (1988) and is the author of *Berthing: A Poetry Workbook* (1991). She
writes: 'I think that people are looking for spirituality. They seem lost in this
overly material world. I certainly feel out of place here. If there is one thing
which I'd like readers to take away with them from my work it is reassurance
that they are not alone.'

Bringing the Geranium in for Winter

Almost dark, the rain begins
again. I steal into my own
October garden

with a small black bucketful of
compost and a trowel.
I kneel

as if you, beautiful
before time with your small pale flowers still
opening, were my soul

and God,
in spite of groundfrost
and the book of rules for growing,

could
exist, incomprehensible, companion of
the overcoming darkness in the grass and apple garden.

I return among the small grave stones
I made your borders with
to kneel, to feel

about, to, probing, put my trowel in, pull you from
your unmade bed,
your mad

dishevelled garden: lifted out of,
orphaned bit of
truth

your petals wet with
rain. It's rain I somehow am
no longer stiff with

now my hands
the barest hands I have
are briefly of this earth and have begun
to learn the part of
root and leaf
to live

with
potting and repotting.
So I set

you, lastly, in the dry
companionable kitchen
on a plate,

my table
laid with cloth of quiet
October light.

[1994]

Sarah's Laughter

Sarah's laughter's sudden, like a hurdle, like an old loud crow
that comes out of the blue.

The graceful men at the makeshift table –
there, in the shade of the tree, in the heat of the day, in Bethel –

look up from the all too tender veal,
the buttermilk, the three small

cakes of meal she's made them. For her husband
Abraham, she's sifted, shaped them in her old dry hand.

Good Lord, no. Laugh? Not I. For Sarah's suddenly afraid.
She did what she could

when she sent him in to that Hagar, handmaid, then,
yes, then dealt hardly with her, only then

let her bide with the lad
Ishmael. A sturdy lad.

It's hidden, the hurt, like a hard little bird in the tent
of her heart. She's tended it.

[2001]

MEDBH McGUCKIAN

(*b.* 1950)

Maeve McCaughan was born in Belfast, one of three sisters, and was educated at Dominican Convent, Fortwilliam Park. She read English at Queen's University, Belfast, where she was a contemporary of Paul Muldoon, and wrote a Masters dissertation 'Gothic Influence on 19th-century Anglo-Irish Fiction'. Her first published poem appeared in 1975. In 1977 she married John McGuckian, changing her name to Medbh McGuckian, an act she saw as 'repudiating the Anglicisation of myself'. Her collections include *The Flower Master* (1982; revised 1993), *Venus and the Rain* (1984; revised 1994), *On Ballycastle Beach* (1988; revised 1995), *Marconi's Cottage* (1991), *Captain Lavender* (1994), *Selected Poems 1978-1994* (1997), *Shelmalier* (1998), *Drawing Ballerinas* (2001), *The Face of the Earth* (2002), *Had I a Thousand Lives* (2003) and *The Book of the Angel* (2004).

McGuckian's work has often been associated with that of the French feminist philosophers Hélène Cixous and Luce Irigaray, in particular with the idea of an *écriture féminine*, a woman's writing which arises from the particular economies of the female body. McGuckian writes in a way which plays syntax off against meaning, but must also be read through her interest in Irish gothic. Many of her poems work as responses to 'ur' texts, often opening up a dialogue with a male writer. In 'Slips', for example, she "steals" the footnotes from Freud's *Psychopathology of Everyday Life* to construct a poem; 'Vanessa's Bower' makes comment, through recourse to their letters, on the relations between Swift and Esther Van Homreigh, whom he called Vanessa.

Slips

The studied poverty of a moon roof,
The earthenware of dairies cooled by apple trees,
The apple tree that makes the whitest wash...

But I forget names, remembering them wrongly
Where they touch upon another name,
A town in France like a woman's Christian name.

My childhood is preserved as a nation's history,
My favourite fairytales the shells
Leased by the hermit crab.

I see my grandmother's death as a piece of ice,
My mother's slimness restored to her,
My own key slotted in your door –

272

Tricks you might guess from this unfastened button,
A pen mislaid, a word misread,
My hair coming down in the middle of a conversation.

[1982]

Vanessa's Bower

I will tell you words which you will
Probably soon afterwards throw out of
Your head, where everything is in order,
And in bloom, like the bird-cherry reading
In a frostless climate, or the cheerfulness
Of ships being wooed by the sea away from
My possessive arm. Dear owner, you write,
Don't put me into your pocket, I am not
A willow in your folly-studded garden
Which you hope will weep the right way.
And there are three trains leaving, none
Of which connects me to your E-shaped
Cottage. Alas, I have still the feeling,
Half-fatherly, half-different, we are
Travelling together in the train with this letter,
Though my strange hand will never be your sin.

[1984]

From the Dressing-room

Left to itself, they say, every foetus
Would turn female, staving in, nature
Siding then with the enemy that
Delicately mixes up genders. This
Is an absence I have passionately sought,
Brightening nevertheless my poet's attic
With my steady hands, calling him my blue
Lizard till his moans might be heard
At the far end of the garden. For I like

His ways, he's light on his feet and does
Not break anything, puts his entire soul
Into bringing me a glass of water.

I can take anything now, even his being
Away, for it always seems to me his
Writing is for me, as I walk springless
From the dressing-room in a sisterly
Length of flesh-coloured silk. Oh there
Are moments when you think you can
Give notice in a jolly, wifely tone,
Tossing off a very last and sunsetty
Letter of farewell, with strict injunctions
To be careful to procure his own lodgings,
That my good little room is lockable,
But shivery, I recover at the mere
Sight of him propping up my pillow.

[1984]

Aviary

Well may you question the degree of falsehood
In my round-the-house men's clothes, when I seem
Cloaked for a journey, after just relearning to walk,
Or turning a swarthy aspect like a cache-
Enfant against all men. Some patterns have
A very long repeat, and this includes a rose
Which has much in common with the rose
In your drawing, where you somehow put the garden
To rights. You call me aspen, tree of the woman's
Tongue, but if my longer and longer sentences
Prove me wholly female, I'd be persimmon,
And good kindling, to us both.
Remember
The overexcitement of mirrors, with their archways
Lending depth, until my compact selvedge
Frisks into a picot-edged valance, some
Swiss-fronted little shop? All this is as it
Should be, the disguise until those clear red
Bands of summerwood accommodate next
Winter's tardy ghost, your difficult daughter.

274

I can hear already in my chambered pith
The hammers of pianos, their fastigiate notes
Arranging a fine sightscreen for my nectary,
My trustful mop. And if you feel uncertain
Whether pendent foliage mitigates the damage
Done by snow, yet any wild bird would envy you
This aviary, whenever you free all the birds in me.

[1984]

Coleridge
(for Michael Longley)

In a dream he fled the house
At the Y of three streets
To where a roof of bloom lay hidden
In the affectation of the night,
As only the future can be. Very tightly,
Like a seam, she nursed the gradients
Of his poetry in her head;
She got used to its movements like
A glass bell being struck
With a padded hammer.
It was her own fogs and fragrances
That crawled into the verse, the
Impression of cold braids finding
Radiant escape, as if each stanza
Were a lamp that burned between
Their beds, or they were writing
The poems in a place of birth together.
Quietened by drought, his breathing
Just became audible where a little
Silk-mill emptied impetuously into it
Some word that grew with him as a child's
Arm or leg. If she stood up (easy,
Easy) it was the warmth that finally
Leaves the golden pippin for the
Cider, or the sunshine of fallen trees.

[1988]

275

The Dream-Language of Fergus

1

Your tongue has spent the night
In its dim sack as the shape of your foot
In its cave. Not the rudiment
Of half a vanquished sound,
The excommunicated shadow of a name,
Has rumpled the sheets of your mouth.

2

So Latin sleeps, they say, in Russian speech,
So one river inserted into another
Becomes a leaping, glistening, splashed
And scattered alphabet
Jutting out from the voice,
Till what began as a dog's bark
Ends with bronze, what began
With honey ends with ice;
As if an aeroplane in full flight
Launched a second plane,
The sky is stabbed by their exits
And the mistaken meaning of each.

3

Conversation is as necessary
Among these familiar campus trees
As the apartness of torches;
And if I am a threader
Of double-stranded words, whose
Quando has grown into now,
No text can return the honey
In its path of light from a jar,
Only a seed-fund, a pendulum,
Pressing out the diasporic snow.

[1988]

GRACE NICHOLS

(*b*. 1950)

Born in Georgetown, Guyana, Nichols worked as a teacher and journalist before moving to Britain in 1977. Her first book *i is a long memoried woman* was published in 1983 and won the Commonwealth Poetry Prize. It was followed by *The Fat Black Woman's Poems* (1984). Her first novel, *Whole of a Morning Sky*, set in 1960s Guyana, was published in 1986. Further collections of poetry include *Lazy Thoughts of a Lazy Woman* (1989) and *Sunris* (1996). Her children's books, influenced by Guyanese folklore and Amerindian legends, include *Come on into My Tropical Garden* (1988) and *Give Yourself a Hug* (1994). In *The Fat Black Woman's Poems*, Nichols plays with stereotypes of femininity and blackness, offering, often with great humour, the Fat Black Woman's body as a site of resistance to colonialism and patriarchy. Nichols's most recent book for children is *The Poet Cat* (2000). She lives with her partner the poet John Agard in Lewes, East Sussex.

Invitation

1

If my fat
was too much for me
I would have told you
I would have lost a stone
or two

I would have gone jogging
even when it was fogging
I would have weighed in
sitting the bathroom scale
with my tail tucked in

I would have dieted
more care a diabetic

But as it is
I'm feeling fine
feel no need
to change my lines
when I move I'm target light

Come up and see me sometime

2

Come up and see me sometime
Come up and see me sometime

My breasts are huge exciting
amnions of water melon
                    your hands can't cup
my thighs are twin seals
                    fat as slick pups
there's a purple cherry
below the blues
                    of my black seabelly
there's a mole that gets a ride
each time I shift the heritage
of my behind

Come up and see me sometime

[1984]

Thoughts drifting through the fat black woman's head while having a full bubble bath

Steatopygous sky
Steatopygous sea
Steatopygous waves
Steatopygous me

O how I long to place my foot
on the head of anthropology

to swig my breasts
in the face of history

to scrub my back
with the dogma of theology

to put my soap
in the slimming industry's
profitsome spoke

Steatopygous sky
Steatopygous sea
Steatopygous waves
Steatopygous me

[1984]

The Fat Black Woman Versus Politics

The fat black woman
could see through politicians
like snake sees through rat
she knows the oil
that ease the tongue
she knows the soup-mouth tact
she knows the game
the lame race for fame
she knows the slippery hammer
wearing down upon the brain

In dreams she's seen them
stalking the corridors of power
faces behind a ballot-box cover
the fat black woman won't be their lover

But if you were to ask her
What's your greatest political ambition?
she'll be sure to answer

    To feed powercrazy politicians a manifesto of lard
    To place my X against a bowl of custard

[1984]

Out of Africa

Out of Africa of the suckling
Out of Africa of the tired woman in earrings
Out of Africa of the black-foot leap

Out of Africa of the baobab, the suck-teeth
Out of Africa of the dry maw of hunger
Out of Africa of the first rains, the first mother.

Into the Caribbean of the staggeringly blue sea-eye
Into the Caribbean of the baleful tourist glare
Into the Caribbean of the hurricane
Into the Caribbean of the flame tree, the palm tree,
the ackee, the high smelling saltfish
and the happy creole so-called mentality.

Into England of the frost and the tea
Into England of the budgie and the strawberry
Into England of the trampled autumn tongues
Into England of the meagre funerals
Into England of the hand of the old woman
And the gent running behind someone
who's forgotten their umbrella, crying out,
'I say... I say-ay.'

[1989]

ANNE CARSON

(b. 1950)

Born in Toronto, Anne Carson grew up in Ontario, and studied Greek and
Latin at the University of Toronto, where she completed a PhD on Sappho
in 1981. Her first UK publication, *Glass and God* (1998), reprints her chap-
book *Short Talks* (1992) with most of her first full-length collection, *Glass,
Irony and God* (1995). These were followed by *Plainwater: Essays and Poetry*
(1995), *Autobiography of Red: A Novel in Verse* (1998), *Men in the Off Hours*
(2000), and *The Beauty of the Husband: a fictional essay in 29 tangos* (2001),
for which she won the 2002 T.S. Eliot Prize. Her other honours include a
Lannan Award, Pushcart Prize, Griffin Poetry Prize, and Guggenheim and
MacArthur Fellowships.

She is also the author of *Eros the Bittersweet* (1996), *Economy of the Unlost:
Reading Simonides of Keos with Paul Celan* (1999) and *If Not, Winter: fragments
of Sappho* (translated with commentary, 2002). She has described her primary
interests as the 'cross between languages (English, Greek, Latin, German) and
genres (poetry, fiction, classical scholarship, literary criticism, translation) to
imagine new forms of writing'. Carson divides her time between Montreal,
where she is McNaughton Chair of Classical Studies at McGill University,
and the USA, where she has taught at several universities.

from **The Beauty of the Husband**

> *Otho calls me his lion, – should I blush*
> *To be so tamed? so –*
>   JOHN KEATS,
>   Otho the Great: A Tragedy in Five Acts, 4.2.42-43

XXII *Homo Ludens*

Omens are for example hearing someone say victory as they pass
        you in the street
or to be staring
at the little sulfur lamps in the grass
all around the edge of the hotel garden
just as they come on. They come on at dusk.

What was he thinking to bring her here?
Athens. Hotel Eremia.
He knew very well. Détente and reconciliation, let's start again,
thinking oysters and glacé fruits, it needs a light touch,
narrow keys
not very deep.
Hotel gardens at dusk are a place where the laws governing matter
get pulled inside out,
like the black keys and the white keys on Mozart's piano.
It cheered him to remember Mozart
borrowing money every night
and smiling his tilted smile.
Necessity is not real! after all.
The husband swallows his ouzo and waits for its slow hot snow
        inside him.
Mozart
(so his wife told him at lunch)
scored his Horn Concerto

in four different colors of ink: a man at play.
A husband whose wife knows just enough history to keep him going.
Cheer is rampant in the husband now.
Infinite evening ahead.
Its shoals appear to him and he navigates them one by one
slipping the dark blue keel ropes this way and that
on a bosom of inconceivable silver – ah here she is.

The husband can be seen to rise as his wife crosses the garden.
Why so sad.
No I'm not sad.
Why in your eyes –
What are you drinking.
Ouzo.
Can you get me a tea.
Of course.

He goes out.
She waits.
Waiting, thoughts come, go. Flow. This flowing.

Why sadness? This flowing the world to its end. Why in your eyes –

It is a line of verse. Where has it stepped from. She searches
       herself, waiting.
Waiting is searching.
And the odd thing is, waiting, searching, the wife suddenly knows
a fact about her husband.
This fact for which she had not searched
jerks itself into the light
like a child from a closet.
She knows why he is taking so long at the bar.

Over and over in later years when she told this story she marvelled
at her husband's ability to place the world within brackets.
A bracket's worth of mirage! all he ever needed.

A man who after three years of separation would take his wife to
       Athens –
for adoration, for peace,
then telephone New York every night from the bar
and speak to a woman
who thought he was over on 4th Street
working late.
And upstairs that night, which proved a long night, as he was dragging
his wounded honor about the hotel room like a damaged queen of
       moths
because she mentioned Houyhnhnms and he objected
to being 'written off as an object of satire,' they moved
several times through a cycle of remarks like –

What is this, what future is there
I thought
You said
We never
When exactly day year name anything who I was who I am who
        did you
Did you or did you not
Do you or do you not
This excuse that excuse pleasure pain truth
What truth is that
All those kilometers
Faith
Letters
You're right
Never oh all right once –

which, like the chain of Parmenides' well-rounded Truth you can
        follow
around in a circle and always end up where you began, for
'it is all one to me where I start – I arrive there again soon enough'

as Parmenides says. So the wife
was thinking (about Parmenides)
with part of her mind while throwing Ever Never Liar at her husband
and he was holding Yes and No together with one hand
while parrying the words of his wife when –

they stopped. Silence came. They stood aligned,
he at the door with his back to it
she at the bed with her back to it,
in that posture which experts of conflict resolution tell us ensures
        impasse,
and they looked at one another
and there was nothing more to say.

Kissing her, I love you, joys and leaves of earlier times flowed
        through the husband
and disappeared.

Presence and absence twisted out of sight of one another inside
        the wife.

They stood.
Sounds reach them, a truck, a snore, poor shrubs ticking on a tin wall.

His nose begins to bleed.

Then blood runs down over his upper lip, lower lip, chin.
To his throat.
Appears on the whiteness of his shirt.

Dyes a mother-of-pearl button for good.
Blacker than a mulberry.
Don't think his heart had burst. He was no Tristan
(though he would love to point out that in the common version
Tristan is not false, it is the sail that kills)
yet neither of them had a handkerchief
and that is how she ends up staining her robe with his blood,
his head in her lap and his virtue coursing through her

as if they were one flesh.
Husband and wife may erase a boundary.
Creating a white page.

But now the blood seems to be the only thing in the room.

If only one's whole life could consist in certain moments.
There is no possibility of coming back from such a moment
to simple hatred,
black ink.

If a husband throws the dice of his beauty one last time, who is to
      blame?

Rich proposition, drastic economy, hours, beds, pronouns, no one.
No one is to blame.
Change the question.
We are mortal, balanced on a day, now and then
it makes sense to say Save what you can.

Wasn't it you who told me civilisation is impossible in the absence
      of a spirit of play.

Anyway what would you have done –
torn the phone off the wall? smothered him with a pillow?
emptied his wallet and run?
But you overlook
an important cultural function of games.
To test the will of the gods.
Huizinga reminds us that war itself is a form of divination.

Husband and wife did not therefore engage in murder
but continued their tour of the Peloponnese,
spending eight more wary days
in temples and buses and vine-covered tavernas,
eight days which had the internal texture of πετραδάκι
    (ancient πέτρος)
– that is 'broken crushed stone, roadstone, gravel' –
but which served a purpose within the mode of justice that was
    their marriage.
Waiting for the future and for the gods,

husband and wife rested,

as players may rest against the rules of the game,
if it is a game, if they know the rules,
and it was and they did.

[2001]

MENNA ELFYN

(*b.* 1951)

Menna Elfyn writes exclusively in Welsh, and has published many Welsh-language collections, including *Mwyara* (1976), *'Stafelloedd Aros* (1977), *Tro'r Haul Arno (1982), Mynd Lawr i'r Nefoedd (1986), Aderyn Bach mewn Llaw: Detholiad o gerddi: 1976-1990* (1990), *Dal Clêr* (1993), *Madfall ar y Mur* (1993) and *Perffaith Nam* (2005). Her bilingual collections are *Eucalyptus: Selected Poems 1978-1994* (1995), *Cell Angel* (1996) and *Cusan Dyn Dall / Blind Man's Kiss* (2001). She has also written stage plays, libretti and novels for teenagers. In 2002 she was appointed Poet Laureate for the Children of Wales. The English translations of the two poems here are by Gillian Clarke.

In an interview with Janice Moore Fuller in 2002, Elfyn has explained: 'When people ask me why I write in this tiny language of Welsh, I want to say that my worldview and vocabulary aren't any smaller than anybody else's. It could be they are enlarged because I am aware of all the different tiny villages, tiny communities all over the world. But, my reply to people who say, "Why don't you write in English?" is that I have to be true to myself...If I'm writing in English, it will not be me because the whole way I see life is through my Welsh language. So it's not so much about choosing a language. I think a language chooses you...' Discussing her relationship to traditional Welsh forms, such as *cynghannedd*, she elaborates: 'I found myself in conflict, writing in a language that was in awe of that tradition yet wanting to write in the conversational tone of an Auden, Yeats, Frost, or Bishop. I was going against the grain of what Welsh poetry was all about. In the last five to ten years, there has been a more radical shift toward revolutionising these old forms and making them pertinent as they resonate in the world literature arena.'

Cell Angel

Mae'r celloedd llwyd o bob tu iddo
yn ei ddal mewn esgyrn sy'n cuddio
am eiliad bwysau'r briwiau yno

ac eto onid dynol oedd yr angylion
ar dir Groeg a Phersia'n llonni dial
nid araf yn y Llyfr Mawr i ymrafael?

aeth ef â mi o'i gell, ef, angel, i'r neuadd fawr,
myfi, efe ac un piano grande,
allweddi'n aflonyddu wrth ddal fy llaw,

dan glo, dechreuodd ei gyngerdd i'r noddreg,
twinkle, twinkle, yn un donc ddyfal –
cyn methu'r esgyniad – at y llethrau duon.

Angel penffordd, heb bentan na mynegbyst
a'r nen wedi colli yn mherfedd y berdoneg
How I wonder what you are.

Daw'r seibiau a'r solo i ben. Allweddi'n cloi,
cau dwrn du y piano, yn grop. Disgordiau,
yn offeryn segur ar ei wyneb. Disgyniad

angel a'i angerdd i greu concerto
yn troi'n lled-fyw rhyw nodau o gryndod –
er byd mor ansoniarus. Canfod un tant persain.

* * *

Pes gallwn mi rown gwotâu ar angylion,
gwahardd sopranos, rhai seraphimaidd
o fan uchel eglwysig lle mae'r sêr yn seinio

eu pibau rhy rhwydd wrth euro'r corau,
yn fechgyn angylaidd, yn lleisiau gwydr mirain,
o'r marmor i'r eco. Rhy lân yw. Ni all duw fod yno,

yn fwy nag yma, yng nghell yr angel,
lle mae cordiau heb ddesgant,
eto rwyf ar fy nhraed o glai yn cymeradwyo

Cell Angel

Grey cells either side of him
keep safe the bones that hide
for a second their weight of pain

yet weren't the angels mortal,
Greek and Persian soil joyous with vengeance,
the Bible quick with quarrels?

He led me from his cell, this angel, to the hall,
him and me and a grand piano,
the door-keys restless in my hand.

Locked, he began a concert for his patron –
twinkle, twinkle, then one violent tone –
before failing to ascend the black slopes

an angel on the road, homeless, lost
and the sky drowned in the piano's depths.
How I wonder what you are.

The pause ends the solo. Keys locked sharp
in the black fist of the piano. Discord
an unplayed instrument in his face. Descending

angel and his passionate concerto
turn suddenly to notes reverberating
through this musicless place. To reach for one fine string.

      *   *   *

I would give quotas on angels,
ban seraphic sopranos
from high-church places where stars play

their easy flutes in gilded choirs
of angelic boys, their voices clean as glass
between the marble and the echoes. God's no more there

than here, in the angel cell
where chords ring without descant
where I rise to my feet of clay to applaud.

encôr, i ddyhead un cell angel
fel y gall ehedeg yn ansylweddol
drwy furiau, heb gysgod, yn ysgafn,

adeiniog at gôr dwyfol y Gadeirlan –
Ond tu hwnt i'r drws mae criw yn paffio
chwerthin yn y cnewyllyn talcen gwydr,

Ac i bob Mihangel, Gabriel, Raphael,
mae cell sy'n eu cadw yn angylion cwymp,
a thry'r meidrolyn sy'n dal yr allwedd
yn ddim ond alaw cariad. Yn dduw heb agoriad.

[1996]

Cusan Hances

Mae cerdd mewn cyfieithiad fel cusan drwy hances.
R.S. THOMAS

Anwes yn y gwyll?
Rhyw bobl lywaeth oeddem

yn cwato'r gusan ddoe.
Ond heddiw, ffordd yw i gyfarch

ac ar y sgrin fach, gwelwn
arweinwyr y byd yn trafod,

hulio hedd ac anwes las;
ambell un bwbach. A'r delyneg

o'i throsi nid yw ond cusan
drwy gadach poced, medd ein prifardd.

Minnau, sy'n ymaflyd cerdd ar ddalen
gan ddwyn i gôl gariadon-geiriau.

A mynnaf hyn. A fo cerdd bid hances
ac ar fy ngwefus

sws dan len.

[2001]

Encore to the dream of a cell angel
that he might fly bodiless
through walls, without shadow, light

winged to the great cathedral.
But behind this door the boy-gangs box
laughing through a chink in the brow of glass.

And for every Michael, Gabriel, Raphael,
there's a cell to keep him fallen
and the keeper of the keys
is only a love song. A god without power to unlock.

[1996]

Handkerchief Kiss

A poem in translation is like kissing through a handkerchief.
R.S. THOMAS

A caress in the dark.
What a tame lot we were,

with our secretive yesterday's kisses.
Today, it's a common greeting,

and we watch on the small screen
world leaders deal peace

with a cold embrace,
or an adder's kiss. The lyric

translated is like kissing
through a hanky, said the bard.

As for me, I hug those poems between pages
that bring back the word-lovers.

Let the poem carry a handkerchief
and leave on my lip

its veiled kiss.

[2001]

JORIE GRAHAM

(*b*. 1951)

Jorie Graham was born in New York and spent much of her childhood in Italy. She attended New York University, received an MFA from the University of Iowa, where she later taught for many years, and is currently the Boylston Professor of Rhetoric and Oratory at Harvard University. Her collections include *Hybrids of Plants and of Ghosts* (1980), *Erosion* (1983), *The End of Beauty* (1987), *Region of Unlikeness* (1991), *Materialism* (1993), *The Dream of the Unified Field: Poems 1974-1994* (1995), *The Errancy* (1997), *Swarm* (2000), *Never* (2002) and *Overlord* (2005).

In an interview in 1987, Graham discusses the importance of the abstract expressionist painter Jackson Pollock '[W]hat Pollock was trying to do was open up...the gap between the end of his gesture and the beginning of the painting. I love to imagine that one-inch gap between the end of the brush and the beginning of the canvas on the floor...in our Western, most noble and wonderful ambitions, we have typically interfered to limit the kinds of activities of which the moment of process is actually capable. The methods the Surrealist way of proceeding has come up with, for example, seem to me somewhat limited...I feel like I'm writing as part of a group of poets – historically who are potentially looking at the end of the medium itself as a vital part of their culture – unless they do something to help it reconnect itself to mystery and power. However great their enterprise, we have been handed by much of the generation after the modernists – by their strictly secular sense of reality (secular, confessional), as well as their unquestioned relationship to the act of representation – an almost untenably narrow notion of what that in-between space is capable of...Issues being raised by other art forms...by critical theory, philosophy, and the science of our day...are often more ambitious than the issues raised by our poetry' (Gardner, p.215).

The Geese

Today as I hang out the wash I see them again, a code
as urgent as elegant,
tapering with goals.
For days they have been crossing. We live beneath these geese

as if beneath the passage of time, or a most perfect heading.
Sometimes I fear their relevance.
Closest at hand,
between the lines,

the spiders imitate the paths the geese won't stray from,
imitate them endlessly to no avail:

things will not remain connected,
will not heal,

and the world thickens with texture instead of history,
texture instead of place.
Yet the small fear of the spiders
binds and binds

the pins to the lines, the lines to the eaves, to the pincushion bush,
as if, at any time, things could fall further apart
and nothing could help them
recover their meaning. And if these spiders had their way,

chainlink over the visible world,
would we be in or out? I turn to go back in.
There is a feeling the body gives the mind
of having missed something, a bedrock poverty, like falling

without the sense that you are passing through one world,
that you could reach another
anytime. Instead the real
is crossing you,

your body an arrival
you know is false but can't outrun. And somewhere in between
these geese forever entering and
these spiders turning back,

this astonishing delay, the everyday, takes place.

[1980]

San Sepolcro

In this blue light
        I can take you there,
snow having made me
        a world of bone
seen through to. This
        is my house,

my section of Etruscan
        wall, my neighbor's

lemontrees, and, just below
        the lower church,
the airplane factory.
        A rooster

crows all day from mist
        outside the walls.
There's milk on the air,
        ice on the oily
lemonskins. How clean
        the mind is,

holy grave. It is this girl
        by Piero
della Francesca, unbuttoning
        her blue dress,
her mantle of weather,
        to go into

labor. Come, we can go in.
        It is before
the birth of god. No one
        has risen yet
to the museums, to the assembly
        line – bodies

and wings – to the open air
        market. This is
what the living do: go in.
        It's a long way.
And the dress keeps opening
        from eternity

to privacy, quickening.
        Inside, at the heart,
is tragedy, the present moment
        forever stillborn,
but going in, each breath
        is a button

coming undone, something terribly
        nimble-fingered
finding all of the stops.

[1983]

292

The Guardian Angel of Self-Knowledge

How razor-clean was it supposed to become,
the zero at the core of each of these
mingling with leaves as they fork up in wind – bright yellow
      distillations of –
uprising evidence of this one world's gigantic
curvature – how clean, how denuded of *their* foliage,
these desperate, ain-dess ones in twos along the built-up paths,
in ones in corridors, these ones so skillfully grouped up
in liquid clutches of impermanence,
now taking the long way back along the lake,
now in the auditorium beaten upon by wind and then a little
rain. They look in their envelopes.
They look on their paper calendars, under their tongues,
stare at the shadows their bodies cast, stare at the shadows their
      folding-chairs cast,
with each glance something like a leaflet loose,
I watch it float, each eyelashed lurching forward, each hoarse
and giddy self-appraisal, I watch them
let it go, each owner standing so stilly now behind his words as they
      are given up,
on lunch-break, beside the phone-booth where one's crying softly now
into the glistening receiver, beside the bookseller, the fruitseller
where one comes right to the warm brink
of a yellow pear – oh from here
it looks so like a dream of shelter –
the way that reaching hand mimics the eye, romancing,
the way it quickens at its root, desiring,
the other one now rooting in a pocket for some change,
and other ones now touching a chin, a lip, an index-finger rough
on a cheek, as if to wipe away a glance – down there – oh how much must
      I see – how clean
did they want to become,
shedding each possibility with gusts of self-exposure,
bubbling-up into gesture their quaint notions of perfection,
then letting each thought, each resting-place, get swept away –
because that was *not what I meant – was not at all –*
and since the future isn't real, is just an alarmclock,
where the last domino can finally drop,
wearing a street-address around its medicated neck –
oh that – of course – the wound we cannot medicate –

you know – the room of icons so preserved we move them round to fit
the furniture, opinions nestling in them, down in the folds, the inlays,
opinions and calculations and bits of stardom
right down in there in the grain of the icons,
some truth in there too now, maybe in the form, who can tell,
maybe even some ecstasy, some little monstrosity,
though it doesn't matter,
since we can't tell the difference,
since it's all pre-recorded, or something like that –
who will they be when they get to the bottom of it,
when they've stripped away the retrospect, when they've peeled away the
orphanhood, the shimmering merriments of consolation?
How will they feel the erasures erase them?
Who will they resemble when they're done with resemblance?

[1997]

KERRY HARDIE

(*b*. 1951)

Kerry Hardie was born in Singapore, grew up in Co. Down, and now lives
in Co. Kilkenny. She has published three collections: *A Furious Place* (1996),
Cry for the Hot Belly (2000) and *The Sky Didn't Fall* (2003). She has also
written two novels, *A Winter Marriage* (2000) and *The Bird Woman* (forth-
coming). She was joint winner of the Hennessey Award for Poetry in 1995,
and in 1996 won the Friends Provident/National Poetry Prize. In 2005 she
was joint winner with Sinéad Morrissey of the Michael Hartnett Poetry Award.

She writes: 'I mostly grew up in Northern Ireland. In the 70s – when I was
in my 20s – I was a researcher and radio interviewer for the BBC in Belfast
and Derry. This period coincided with the most violent years of the Troubles,
and through my job I had access to situations and people I might not other-
wise have known. I became fascinated with people who found themselves in a
hard place and with how they reacted to this place. Some people adapted
astonishingly fast to their new realities, but others spent their energies resist-
ing and could only change to meet them when they had in some way been
broken by them. Later, after I'd married and left Northern Ireland, I too
found myself, through sickness, in a hard place. I spent more than five years
in bed and many more when I was only well enough to be up for a few hours
a day. I too resisted and was broken by the experience, and it was only very
gradually that I began to realise that acceptance was my only option. I am
much better now, but exhaustion and pain are still fairly constant compan-
ions. Being chronically sick puts you in touch with failure and with the dark
underside of life. It also makes you an observer rather than a participant.'
(2003)

Stranger

He thinks that bearded iris
is female, nineteenth century.
He doesn't know why.
I think he is thinking of systems of mourning:
of women in black for years, then in full purple,
of fringes and beadwork and brooches displaying
coils of gold hair looped into fleurs-de-lis.

I don't see it like that, unless it's Wilde –
the same exotic and ungainly body –
I see it eighteenth century, androgynous,
its stiff buds and bearded lip,
its mauve crown-petals open to receive.

The way I see it, the way he sees it –
neither able to handle
its odd and stately presence in the long bed,
this sense of something complex and evolved
inhabiting our green untidy acre,
while all the fields beyond
are high with grasses flowering into hay.

[2000]

Things That Are Lost

My mother teaches me the fading skills:
how to clean fish, plait garlic, draw pheasants;
how to distinguish wading birds,
how to make linen lace.

I know her ache because it is in me.
I try to teach to anyone who'll listen
wild flowers: their legends, properties, names.
I do this in full love of the fresh world.

But a voice says,
Lose things, forget them, let them go.
See all things always the first time.
Unnamed. In wonder.

[2000]

Sheep Fair Day

The real aim is not to see God in all things, it is that God,
through us, should see the things that we see.
SIMONE WEIL

I took God with me to the sheep fair. I said, 'Look
there's Liv, sitting on the wall, waiting;
these are pens, these are sheep,
this is their shit we are walking in, this is their fear.
See that man over there, stepping along the low walls
between pens, eyes always watching,
mouth always talking, he is the auctioneer.
That is wind in the ash trees above, that is sun
splashing us with running light and dark.
Those men over there, the ones with their faces sealed,
are buying or selling. Beyond in the ring
where the beasts pour in, huddle and rush,
the hoggets are auctioned in lots.
And that woman with the ruddy face and the home-cut hair
and a new child on her arm, that is how it is to be woman
with the milk running, sitting on wooden boards
in this shit-milky place of animals and birth and death
as the bidding rises and falls.'

Then I went back outside and found Fintan.
I showed God his hand as he sat on the rails,
how he let it trail down and his fingers played
in the curly back of a ewe. Fintan's a sheep-man
he's deep into sheep, though it's cattle he keeps now,
for sound commercial reasons.
                              'Feel that,' I said,
'feel with my heart the force in that hand
that's twining her wool as he talks.'
Then I went with Fintan and Liv to Refreshments,
I let God sip tea, boiling hot, from a cup,
and I lent God my fingers to feel how they burned
when I tripped on a stone and it slopped.
'This is hurt,' I said, 'there'll be more.'
And the morning wore on and the sun climbed
and God felt how it is when I stand too long,
how the sickness rises, how the muscles burn.

Later, at the back end of the afternoon,
I went down to swim in the green slide of river,

I worked my way under the bridge, against the current,
then I showed how it is to turn onto your back
with, above you and a long way up, two gossiping pigeons,
and a clump of valerian, holding itself to the sky.
I remarked on the stone arch as I drifted through it,
how it dapples with sunlight from the water,
how the bridge hunkers down, crouching low in its track
and roars when a lorry drives over.

And later again, in the kitchen,
wrung out, at day's ending, and empty,
I showed how it feels
to undo yourself,
to dissolve, and grow age-old, nameless:

woman sweeping a floor, darkness growing.

[2003]

NUALA NÍ DHOMHNAILL

(*b*. 1952)

Born in Lancashire, Nuala Ní Dhomhnaill grew up in the Irish-speaking areas
of West Kerry and in Tipperary. She studied English and Irish at University
College Cork, and after living in Turkey and Holland, returned to Ireland in
1980. She teaches at University College Dublin, and was Ireland Professor of
Poetry in 2002-04. Her poetry draws on Irish folklore and mythology, com-
bined with contemporary themes of femininity, sexuality and culture. She
chooses to write only in Irish and believes that 'perhaps, at some very deep level'
the language of her childhood had chosen her: 'Irish is a language of enormous
elasticity and emotional sensitivity; of quick and hilarious banter and a welter
of references both historical and mythological; it is an instrument of imagina-
tive depth and scope, which has been tempered by the community for gener-
ations until it can pick up and sing out every hint of emotional modulation that
can occur between people. Many international scholars rhapsodise that this
speech of ragged peasants seems always on the point of bursting into poetry.'
(*New York Times*, 8 January 1995)

Ní Dhomhnaill's Irish-language collections include *An Dealg Droigh* (1981),
Féar Suaithinseach (1984), *Feis* (1991) and *Cead Aighnis* (1998). Michael Hart-
nett translated a *Selected Poems* in 1986, and she has since published three
bilingual selections: *Pharoah's Daughter*, with 13 poet-translators (1990), *The
Astrakhan Cloak*, translated by Paul Muldoon (1992), and *The Water Horse*,
with translations by Medbh McGuckian and Eiléan Ní Chuilleanáin (1999).
Her *Selected Essays* was published in 2005. The English translations of the
three poems here are by Paul Muldoon.

An Crann

Do tháinig bean an leasa
le *Black & Decker*,
do ghearr sí anuas mo chrann.
D'fhanas im óinseach ag féachaint uirthi
faid a bhearraigh sí na brainsí
ceann ar cheann.

Tháinig m'fhear céile abhaile tráthnóna.
Chonaic sé an crann.
Bhí an gomh dearg air,
ní nach ionadh. Dúirt sé
'Canathaobh nár stopais í?
Nó cad is dóigh léi?
Cad a cheapfadh sí
dá bhfaighinnse *Black & Decker*
is dul chun a tí
agus crann ansúd a bhaineas léi,
a ghearradh anuas sa ghairdín?'

Tháinig bean an leasa thar n-ais ar maidin.
Bhíos fós ag ithe mo bhricfeasta.
D'iarr sí orm cad dúirt m'fhear céile.
Dúrtsa léi cad dúirt sé,
go ndúirt sé cad is dóigh léi,
is cad a cheap fadh sí
dá bhfaigheadh sé siúd *Black & Decker*
is dul chun a tí
is crann ansúd a bhaineas léi
a ghearradh anuas sa ghairdín.

'Ó,' ar sise, '*that's very interesting.*'
Bhí béim ar an *very*.
Bhí cling leis an *-ing*.
Do labhair sí ana-chiúin.

Bhuel, b'shin mo lá-sa,
pé ar bith sa tsaol é,
iontaithe bunoscionn.
Thit an tóin as mo bholg
is faoi mar a gheobhainn lascadh cic

As for the Quince

There came this bright young thing
with a Black & Decker
and cut down my quince tree.
I stood with my mouth hanging open
while one by one
she trimmed off the branches.

When my husband got home that evening
and saw what had happened
he lost the rag,
as you might imagine.
'Why didn't you stop her?
What would she think
if I took the Black & Decker
round to her place
and cut down a quince tree
belonging to her?
What would she make of that?'

Her ladyship came back next morning
while I was at breakfast.
She enquired about his reaction.
I told her straight
that he was wondering how she'd feel
if he took a Black & Decker
round to her house
and cut down a quince tree of hers,
et cetera et cetera.

'O,' says she, 'that's very interesting.'
There was a stress on the 'very'.
She lingered over the 'ing'.
She was remarkably calm and collected.

These are the times that are in it, so,
all a bit topsy-turvy.
The bottom falling out of my belly
as if I had got a kick up the arse
or a punch in the kidneys.

nó leacadar sna baotháin
líon taom anbhainne isteach orm
a dhein chomh lag san mé
gurb ar éigin a bhí ardú na méire ionam
as san go ceann trí lá.

Murab ionann is an crann
a dh'fhan ann, slán.

[1984]

Ceist na Teangan

Cuirim mo dhóchas ar snámh
i mbáidín teangan
faoi mar a leagfá naíonán
i gcliabhán
a bheadh fite fuaite
de dhuilleoga feileastraim
is bitiúman agus pic
bheith cuimilte lena thóin

ansan é leagadh síos
i measc na ngiolcach
is coigeal na mban sí
le taobh na habhann,
féachaint n'fheadaraís
cá dtabharfaidh an sruth é,
féachaint, dála Mhaoise,
an bhfóirfidh iníon Fharoinn?

[1990]

A fainting-fit coming over me
that took the legs from under me
and left me so zonked
I could barely lift a finger
till Wednesday.

As for the quince, it was safe and sound
and still somehow holding its ground.

[1990]

The Language Issue

I place my hope on the water
in this little boat
of the language, the way a body might put
an infant

in a basket of intertwined
iris leaves,
its underside proofed
with bitumen and pitch,

then set the whole thing down amidst
the sedge
and bulrushes by the edge
of a river

only to have it borne hither and thither,
not knowing where it might end up;
in the lap, perhaps,
of some Pharaoh's daughter.

[1990]

Dípfríos

Cornucopia na haoise, an cóifrín draíochta
as a dtógaimid nua gacha bia agus sean gacha dí –
oiread sólaistí agus d'iarrfadh do bhéal
is gan aon dá ghreim acu ar aon bhlaiseadh.

Bolg soláthair gach teaghlaigh, tobar slánaithe
ár n-ocrais oidhreachtúil ná méadaíonn
is ná téann i ndísc. Adhraimid a chairn
ollmhaitheasa. Níl aon teora lena shlaodaibh oigheartha

de mhil is uachtar, de phéitseoga is úlla,
de strúisíní Gaelacha, sceallóga,
ceathrúna mairteola ina fheoil mhionaithe,
iarphroinnte, cístí milse, dhá chaora.

Tá cúig bhollóg aráin ann is dhá iasc
faoi choinne sluaite comharsan (má thagann siad).
Is cé chuir an cat marbh seo i measc an spionáiste?
– A Jimín Mháire Thaidhg, gearánfad tú led Mham!

Suite go buacach i gcroílár gach cisteanach
feidhmíonn mar mheafar bunaidh ár sibhialtachta.
Is iad ceolta sí na cruinne seo a chluinimid
ná a mhiam sástachta, cáithníní áthais srutha leictrise.

Momento mori, par excellence, ná feaca
riamh ceann, samhlaoid uafar ar an díog
dar di sinn is gur chuici atáimid;
íomhánna greanta gach a gcúblálaimid inti:

marbh agus cruaidh is chomh fuar leis an uaigh.

[1992]

Deep-Freeze

A modern Horn of Plenty, a magic coffer
from which we take the best of food and drink –
every comestible we might savour
and no two tasting the same. A trunk

of household odds and ends, a healing well
that staves off our deepest hungers, it ne'er o'erbrims
nor gangs dry. We adore its monumental
wealth, its illimitable, icy streams

of milk and honey, apples and peaches,
Irish stews, crinkle-cut chips,
pre-ground legs of beef, batches
of dessert, sweet cakes, a couple of whole sheep.

Here are the five loaves and two Spanish
mackerel to feed the multitude, if ever they come –
Who put the dead cat in with the spinach? –
Jimín Mháire Thadhg! Wait till I tell your mum!

In the dead centre of every kitchen
it holds its own, it glumly stands its ground:
these are the strains of no Otherworldly musicians
but the hum of its alternating current.

From here, if ever I saw one, is a fit
emblem of the ditch or long barrow
from which we derive and wherein lies our fate:
it chills me to the marrow

that we should most truly find ourselves
among its fatted and its golden calves.

[1992]

303

HELEN DUNMORE

(*b.* 1952)

Helen Dunmore was born in Yorkshire, and read English at the University of York. *The Apple Fall* was published in 1983, and followed by *The Sea Skater* (1986), *The Raw Garden* (1988), *Short Days, Long Nights: New and Selected Poems* (1991), *Recovering a Body* (1994), *Bestiary* (1997) and *Out of the Blue: Poems 1975-2001* (2001).

The winner of the Orange Prize for Fiction, she has published several novels, including *Zennor in Darkness* (1993), *Burning Bright* (1994), *A Spell of Winter* (1995), *Talking to the Dead* (1996), *The Siege* (2001) and *Mourning Ruby* (2004), as well as books of short stories, fiction and poetry for teenagers. She writes: 'Over the years I kept finding parallels between this branch of research science [protein crystallography]...and some aspects of creativity. There's the same craft apprenticeship, the accumulation, conscious and unconscious, of a mass of data and a solid base of technique, and then, overlying this, a play of intuition and experimentation which struggles to apprehend patterns while at the same time it tries to break through them...If writing fiction has affected my poetry, it has probably done so in a paradoxical way, by making my poems shorter and more lyrical.' (*Don't Ask Me What I Mean*, pp.66-68)

Domestic poem

So, how decisive a house is:
quilted, a net of blood and green
droops on repeated actions at nightfall.

A bath run through the wall
comforts the older boy sleeping
meshed in the odours of breath and Calpol

while in the maternity hospital
ancillaries rinse out the blood bottles;

the feel and the spore
of babies' sleep stays here.

Later, some flat-packed plastic
swells to a parachute of oxygen
holding the sick through their downspin,

now I am well enough, I
iron, and place the folded sheets in bags

from which I shall take them, identical,
after the birth of my child.

And now the house closes us,
                              close on us,
like fruit we rest in its warm branches

and though it's time for the child to come
nobody knows it, the night passes

while I sleepwalk the summer heat.

Months shunt me and I bring you
like an old engine hauling the blue
spaces that flash between track and train time.

Mist rises, smelling of petrol's
burnt offerings, new born,

oily and huge, the lorries drum
on Stokes' Croft,

out of the bathroom mirror the sky
is blue and pale as a Chinese mountain.

and I breathe in.

It's time to go now. I take nothing
but breath, thinned.
A blown-out dandelion globe
might choose my laundered body to grow in.

[1983]

Three Ways of Recovering a Body

By chance I was alone in my bed the morning
I woke to find my body had gone.
It had been coming. I'd cut off my hair in sections
so each of you would have something to remember,

then my nails worked loose from their beds
of oystery flesh. Who was it got them?
One night I slipped out of my skin. It lolloped
hooked to my heels, hurting. I had to spray on
more scent so you could find me in the dark,
I was going so fast. One of you begged for my ears
because you could hear the sea in them.

First I planned to steal myself back. I was a mist
on thighs, belly and hips. I'd slept with so many men.
I was with you in the ash-haunted stations of Poland,
I was with you on that grey plaza in Berlin
while you wolfed three doughnuts without stopping,
thinking yourself alone. Soon I recovered my lips
by waiting behind the mirror while you shaved.
You pouted. I peeled away kisses like wax
no longer warm to the touch. Then I flew off.

Next I decided to become a virgin. Without a body
it was easy to make up a new story. In seven years
every invisible cell would be renewed
and none of them would have touched any of you.
I went to a cold lake, to a grey-lichened island,
I was gold in the wallet of the water.
I was known to the inhabitants, who were in love
with the coveted whisper of my virginity:
all too soon they were bringing me coffee and perfume,
cash under stones. I could really do something for them.

Thirdly I tried marriage to a good husband
who knew my past but forgave it. I believed in the power
of his penis to smoke out all those men
so that bit by bit my body service would resume,
although for a while I'd be the one woman in the world
who was only present in the smile of her vagina.
He stroked the air where I might have been.
I turned to the mirror and saw mist gather
as if someone lived in the glass. Recovering
I breathed to myself, *'Hold on! I'm coming.'*

[1994]

306

JO SHAPCOTT

(*b.* 1953)

Born in London, Jo Shapcott was educated at Trinity College Dublin, Dublin College of Music, Oxford and Harvard. Her first collection, *Electroplating the Baby* (1988), combines a Bishopesque interrogation of the object with – to use Bishop's phrase – an interest in 'the always-more-successful surrealism of everyday life'. Her brilliant sequence of Robert and Elizabeth poems charts the dynamic of male/female creativity between characters who are overlays of Robert Lowell and Elizabeth Hardwick, and Robert Browning and Elizabeth Barrett Browning. Shapcott has more recently become interested in what constitutes her 'Englishness' and the title poem of her second collection *Phrase Book* (1992) looks at the fragmentation of the body in the face of remote warfare as she draws together military jargon with the language learner's phrasebook phrases. Her third collection *My Life Asleep* (1998) was followed by *Her Book: Poems 1988-1998* (2000).

Most of *Tender Taxes* (2001) consists of "versions" of Rilke's French poems, which see her engaged in a creative dialogue with a male writer, which she describes in her preface as 'responses, arguments, even dramatisations'. She writes: 'I began to see that...Rilke's roses were women. And more than that – petal – space – petal – these poems were versions of female genitalia. Once this perception had taken hold I couldn't follow Rilke's pattern of addressing the roses: he speaks to them, tells them what they are like, what makes them up, where their essence is to be found. My roses are given their own voice. They speak. And if you put my poems alongside Rilke's, more often than not you'll find my roses addressing his, saying, in effect: "It's not like that, it's like this." And, for me, this parachuted the whole notion of gender relations into the business of translation. Who's doing what to whom? And, more importantly, how does a woman poet relate to the poets who have gone before.' She is co-editor, with Matthew Sweeney of *Emergency Kit: Poems for Strange Times* (1996), and with Linda Anderson, of *Elizabeth Bishop: Poet of the Periphery* (2002).

Elizabeth Looks at Robert

> *For a woman to hang down her head like a lily through life, and*
> *'die of a rose in aromatic pain' at her death, – to sit or lounge as in*
> *a Book of Beauty, and be 'defended' by the strong and mighty*
> *thinkers on all sides of her – this he thinks, is her destiny and glory.*
>
> ELIZABETH BARRETT
> Letter to Miss Mitford, February 1845

Terminology was a science she wasn't at all sure of.
She suspected that Robert, more political animal,
proudly bristling his resilient epidermis
would have moved with confidence

at the court of Terminus, rare god of boundaries.
She eyed him cautiously on the other sofa:
yes – cantankerous, but certainly comfortable.
He could parse anything and was a fiend
with crosswords. She sucked her pen thoughtfully
surprising the ailing clockwork in her chest
into another cough. Her lungs
felt like a pair of rotting bellows
in a smithy where the strange conjunction
of heat, flesh, metal, moisture and noise
had made the leather crack unbearably
where the air pressed on the seams.

[1988]

Robert Watches Elizabeth Knitting

> *It will be found that DNA mentions nothing but relations...*
> *The relata, the end components of the relationships in the*
> *corporeal world, are perhaps never mentioned.*
>
> GREGORY BATESON,
> Mind and Nature

Knitting is a bore but Elizabeth
nods and smiles and clicks to herself
as though it were more than just useful.
She goes happily about the task,
moving in and out of it without haste,
perfecting tension, cabling, ribs.
She looks forward to the sewing-up
but not too much, knowing how to mesh
the pleasure of the final thing,
all sensuality and wholeness,
with the independent life of every stitch.

Where does it come from, this compulsion
to call her a whole list of things
other than what she is? The string-winder,
the long-fingered, the sitting clock,
the fur-maker and on and on and on.
From shanks by sharp shears to Shape Shoulders
she is what she is, my hank-shifter,
the one who weaves and stitches up wool.

The needles click in a rhythm I can't get at:
part and whole, part and whole;
two heartbeats, a breath, two heartbeats.
Her lips silently move to mark
the four or five last stitches in the line.

Elizabeth's pattern is cut small
and pasted in her diary: a book of days,
a book of stitches; lunch-dates and meetings,
Right Border and Neckband, Left Front.
There is no picture, only the long strings
of phonemes – purls and plains
made unpronounceable by the feminine science
of the knitting pattern. She bows
her head to translate the printed page
into this odd manipulation of sticks and string.

I can't get my mind round knitting.
It starts to have everything
when you come down to it – rhythm,
colour and slow but perceptible change.
The meaning is all in the gaps:
a pattern of holes marked out by woolly colour,
a jumper made of space, division and relations.

Strange to see these youngish hands,
with no puffiness or obvious veins,
repeat the banal and tiny motions
over days over weeks over months.
I ask too much and am too hasty;
this knitting is an exercise in trust.

[1988]

Phrase Book

I'm standing here inside my skin,
which will do for a Human Remains Pouch
for the moment. Look down there (up here).
Quickly. Slowly. This is my own front room

where I'm lost in the action, live from a war,
on screen. I am an Englishwoman, I don't understand you.
What's the matter? You are right. You are wrong.
Things are going well (badly). Am I disturbing you?

TV is showing bliss as taught to pilots:
Blend, Low silhouette, Irregular shape, Small,
Secluded. (Please write it down. Please speak slowly.)
Bliss is how it was in this very room

when I raised my body to his mouth,
when he even balanced me in the air,
or at least I thought so and yes the pilots say
yes they have caught it through the Side-Looking

Airborne Radar, and through the J-Stars.
I am expecting a gentleman (a young gentleman,
two gentlemen, some gentlemen). Please send him
(them) up at once. This is really beautiful.

Yes they have seen us, the pilots, in the Kill Box
on their screens, and played the routine for
getting us Stealthed, that is, Cleansed, to you and me,
Taken Out. They know how to move into a single room

like that, to send in with Pinpoint Accuracy, a hundred Harms.
I have two cases and a cardboard box. There is another
bag there. I cannot open my case – look out,
the lock is broken. Have I done enough?

Bliss, the pilots say, is for evasion
and escape. What's love in all this debris?
Just one person pounding another into dust,
into dust. I do not know the word for it yet.

Where is the British Consulate? Please explain.
What does it mean? What must I do? Where
can I find? What have I done? I have done
nothing. Let me pass please. I am an Englishwoman.

[1992]

In the Bath

She was interested in prehistory.
It didn't seem so long ago and offered
pleasant notions of a time before civic duty,
when disease was accepted and fought through,
or not. Hers wasn't a museum interest:
it was as tight, neat and uncomplicated
as a reef knot. 'If I came here as a visitor
from Mars, I would be impressed by the water,
the relative health of the inhabitants, the indecent
urge of atoms for complexity – they don't just split
once, think they're clever, and then stop.' She imagined
her body cells spreading like a film to cover the earth,
coating every frond in the tropical rain forest,
every blade of grass on the pampas. Herself
spread thin and making the surface of the world
sparkle. It was a stunning vision of the future.
She lay in the bath with the water touching
her all over, and remembered that not even
the most tender lover could do that. She wondered
if every molecule on the surface of her skin
was wet and what wet meant to such very
tiny matter. To make things worse, or at least
more difficult for the water, she raised her body
slightly, building an island chain of hip bones,
belly, breasts all of which began to dry at once.
She loved the water trails over her body curves,
the classical lines between wet and dry
making graph patterns which she thought might follow
the activity in her brain – all she wanted
was to be a good atlas, a bright school map
to shine up the world for everyone to see.

[1992]

The Mad Cow Tries to Write the Good Poem

The police came once when I was doing my death dance
to the amazing circular music which had entered a gap
near my cortex and acted as powerfully as a screwdriver

on my soul. I wove in and out of the green trees. I used
my hooves as gentle weapons in the air. A bit of newspaper
fame came my way that day, but shit, it was a performance,
ephemeral, and certainly not the good poem. Lasting.
How can I last when I live in a shed and even
the postman doesn't know how to find me?
It's dark in here. Light would echo the gaps
in my brain coils and set off a fizzing reaction,
not so much pounding, more an explosion
followed by a flowing moment when the taboo
people arrive. They're dressed in red and
stand formally around my skull as though staged
for an opera. And when they sing – sometimes as many
as seven at once – then, friend, please, the good
poem is sounding all round this hut, my head, the world,
I hear it written in the streaky emulsion on the walls,
in my own messing on the floor, in the nation's smeary dailies,
in lovely people's ears, their breath, your breath:
it's new every time, always wanted and easy to spot
because I know what it looks like with my eyes closed.

[1992]

Motherland
(after Tsvetayeva)

Language is impossible
in a country like this. Even
the dictionary laughs when I look up
'England', 'Motherland', 'Home'.

It insists on falling open instead
three times out of the nine I try it
at the word 'Distance' –
degree of remoteness, interval of space –

the word is ingrained like pain.
So much for England and so much
for my future to walk into the horizon
carrying distance in a broken suitcase.

312

The dictionary is the only one
who talks to me now. Says laughing,
'Come back HOME!' but takes me
further and further away into the cold stars.

I am blue, bluer than water
I am nothing, for all I do
is pour syllables over aching brows.

England. It hurts my lips to shape
the word. This country makes me say
too many things I can't say, home
of my rotting pride, my motherland.

[1998]

from The Roses
(after Rilke)

Rosa sancta

Now you've made
a saint out of me,
Saint Rose, open-handed,
she who smells of God naked.

But, for myself, I've learned
to love the whiff of mildew
because though not Eve, exactly,
yes, I stink of the Fall.

Rosa odorata

I can't turn a smell
into a single word;
you've no right
to ask. Warmth
coaxes rose fragrance
from the underside of petals.

The oils meet air:
rhodinol is old rose;
geraniol, like geranium;
nerol is my essence
of magnolia; eugenol,
a touch of cloves.

[2001]

PASCALE PETIT
(*b.* 1953)

Born in Paris, Pascale Petit grew up in France and Wales. Her books include
Heart of the Deer (1998), *The Zoo Father* (2001) and *The Huntress* (2005).
Trained originally as a sculptor, Petit has travelled extensively and her poetry
reflects this, not least in her explorations of the Amazon jungle. Her most
recent work examines fraught family relationships, with her estranged father
in *The Zoo Father* (making her work somewhat reminiscent of Sharon Olds),
and a mentally ill mother in *The Huntress*. Her examination of extreme
experience can also be compared with that of Selima Hill. Petit says in inter-
view with Lidia Vianu: 'I don't have British roots, nor any firm roots, I'm an
outsider; I don't try to vie with the male tradition – I just do my own thing'
(2003). Elsewhere, she writes: 'When I was at art school, there were a few
poetry books circulating around the sculpture studios – Ted Hughes, Peter
Redgrove and Sylvia Plath were revered by a number of us for the vivid and
entire visual worlds they created with words. Here was image-making on a
par with sculpting. If this was contemporary poetry, then we art students had
better catch up! Plath's work was direct and emotional. I'd not encountered
that before. She had her own way with language a dramatic and idiomatic
address. Most novel of all was the fact that she was a woman and wrote in a
devil-may-care fashion about things male poets wouldn't touch. Her style,
however, was frustrating to emulate – it was just impossible to write like her.
So I'd say her influence on me then was more as a role model – her boldness
and originality something to aim for, when I wrote my first "book" of poems
as part of my fine art degree.' (Phillips, 2004).

The Fish Daughter

You tell me you loved fishing.
So I flop across your bed
like a giant pirarucú
and show you my armour-plated body

314

and my bony tongue.
You could make a rasp
from the teeth on my tongue,
with the things I'm saying,
and grate the past with it.
I open my cavernous mouth
so you can see how everything
is toothed: my jaws,
palate, pharynx – how you've caught
the biggest prize in the Amazon.

But when I go into the kitchen
and come back too quickly
and catch you peeing into a bottle
I know just what I've to do:
shrink myself to a tiny candiru,
the most feared fish in the river,
swim up your stream of urine
into your urethra. Father,
and wedge my backward-pointing barbs
deep inside your penis.

[2001]

The Snake Dress

In the old olivewood box
you'll find a dress sewn
from the skins of grass snakes,
the ones that left their ghosts
on our vineyard walls.
Open the moss-lined lid,
shake out the folds
from their beds of brown leaves.
Unwrap my gift long
as our dry stream
and sheer as moonlight.
See how I've stitched the seams
with spider silk
stronger than steel,
so that each silver stripe

315

and diamond scale
is intact, your hands
soft as the southern breeze.
Let me clean the earth
from your face, my mother,
with this vial of walnut water.
And as you slip the dress
over your head – remember
how the snakes' eyes
go milky just before sloughing,
then clear, as the skin
loosens around their lips,
how they rub their sides
against stones before
turning themselves inside out.

[2001]

IMTIAZ DHARKER

(*b*. 1954)

Imtiaz Dharker was born in Lahore, but spent her childhood in Glasgow before going to live in India. Her first collection, *Purdah and Other Poems* was published in India in 1989, and in Britain in the double volume *Postcards from god* (1994). Her later books are *I Speak for the Devil* (UK 2001 / India 2003) and *The Terrorist at My Table* (2006). Dharker is also an artist (her poetry books incorporate her drawings) and a documentary film-maker, and divides her time between London and Bombay.

She writes: 'The image of purdah for me was on the dangerous edge of being almost seductive: the hidden body, the highlighted eyes, the suggestion of forbidden places. But of course it is also one of the instruments of power used to bring women to heel in the name of religion. God has been hijacked by power-brokers to justify all kinds of acts of violence. The speaker in the first *Postcards from god* poem is a somewhat bewildered god. This god looks out at a fractured landscape: Bombay, where I live, is a city of grandiose dreams and structures held together with sellotape and string... Sectarian violence (such as Bombay has known) suddenly forces people who had not thought of themselves as religious to take a stand, define themselves in terms of the religion they were born into, confine themselves within smaller borderlines. There is a moment when the neighbours' children become the sinister enemy, and the name of god takes on a dangerous sound. I enjoy the benefits of being an outcast in most societies I know. I don't want to have to define myself in terms of location or religion. In a world that seems to be splitting itself into narrower national and religious groups, sects, castes, subcastes, we can go on excluding others until we come down to a minority of one.' (Astley, ed, *New Blood*, p.41)

Blessing

The skin cracks like a pod.
There never is enough water.

Imagine the drip of it,
the small splash, echo
in a tin mug,
the voice of a kindly god.

Sometimes, the sudden rush
of fortune. The municipal pipe bursts,
silver crashes to the ground
and the flow has found
a roar of tongues. From the huts,
a congregation: every man woman
child for streets around
butts in, with pots,
brass, copper, aluminium,
plastic buckets,
frantic hands,

and naked children
screaming in the liquid sun,
their highlights polished to perfection,
flashing light,
as the blessing sings
over their small bones.

[1989]

Grace

It is not often
that you come across a place
where you are sure to find
some kind of peace.
The masjid at least, you think.
The grace of light through marble,
a space where fear is filtered out.
Perhaps a patch of ground

where you can at last lay down
your own name, and take another on
a bright mantle
that will fold itself around you:
God the Compassionate, the Merciful.

A wash of marble at your feet.
The man at the door turns
to speak. You look for wisdom,
thinking that is what old men are for.

He does not look at you.
Instead, 'A woman comes
with her eyes concealed.
She trails the month behind her.
We are defiled.'

He rolls his reason on his tongue
and spits it out.
You know again the drought
the blazing eye of faith
can bring about.

'Allah-u-Akbar.'
You say the words to reassure yourself.
Your mouth clears.
God the Compassionate, the Merciful,
created man from clots of blood.

'Bismillah.'
You taste it on your tongue.
Salt, sweet.

A clearing the heart.

[1989]

MONIZA ALVI

(*b.* 1954)

Born in Lahore, Pakistan, Moniza Alvi grew up in Hertfordshire, only return-
ing to Pakistan as an adult in the mid-90s. Her first collection *The Country at
My Shoulder* (1993), shortlisted for the T.S. Eliot and Whitbread poetry prizes,
was followed by *A Bowl of Warm Air* (1996), *Carrying My Wife* (2000), *Souls*

(2002) and *How the Stone Found Its Voice* (2005). She writes: 'The points where East and West converge are as crucial as they were in my earlier work, but in a less directly autobiographical sense' (Forbes, p.87). And: 'When I first started writing seriously I was reading Angela Carter, Italo Calvino and J.G. Ballard's science fiction. I am attracted by fantasy and the strange-seeming and find there some essence of experience. I feel an affinity with poets from a multicultural background, or those that have a multiracial identity such as Mimi Khalvati, Sujata Bhatt and Imtiaz Dharker...' (Astley, ed. *New Blood*, p.107). Much of Alvi's work engages with a surreal or fantastical world of fractured and partially recovered identity, working through sequences in her most recent poetry.

I Would Like to be a Dot in a Painting by Miró

I would like to be a dot in a painting by Miró.

Barely distinguishable from other dots,
it's true, but quite uniquely placed.
And from my dark centre

I'd survey the beauty of the linescape
and wonder – would it be worthwhile
to roll myself towards the lemon stripe,

Centrally poised, and push my curves
against its edge, to get myself
a little extra attention?

But it's fine where I am.
I'll never make out what's going on
around me, and that's the joy of it.

The fact that I'm not a perfect circle
makes me more interesting in this world.
People will stare forever –

Even the most unemotional get excited.
So here I am, on the edge of animation,
a dream, a dance, a fantastic construction,

A child's adventure.
And nothing in this tawny sky
can get too close, or move too far away.

[1993]

Throwing Out My Father's Dictionary

Words grow shoots in the bin
with the eggshells and rotting fruit.
It's years since the back fell off
to reveal paper edged with toffee-glue.
The preface is stained – a cloud rises
towards the use of the swung dash.

My father's signature is centre page,
arching letters underlined – I see him
rifling through his second language.

I retrieve it.
It smells of tarragon – my father's
dictionary, not quite finished with.

I have my own, weightier
with thousands of recent entries
arranged for me – like *chador*
and *sick building syndrome*
in the new wider pages.
I daren't inscribe my name.

[1993]

The Country at My Shoulder

There's a country at my shoulder,
growing larger – soon it will burst,
rivers will spill out, run down my chest.

My cousin Azam wants visitors to play
ludo with him all the time.
He learns English in a class of seventy.

And I must stand to attention
with the country at my shoulder.
There's an execution in the square –

The women's dupattas are wet with tears.
The offices have closed
for the white-hot afternoon.

But the women stone-breakers chip away
at boulders, dirt on their bright hems.
They await the men and the trucks.

I try to shake the dust from the country,
smooth it with my hands.
I watch Indian films –

Everyone is very unhappy,
or very happy,
dancing garlanded through parks.

I hear of bribery, family quarrels,
travellers' tales – the stars
are so low you think you can touch them.

Uncle Aqbar drives down the mountain
to arrange his daughter's marriage.
She's studying Christina Rossetti.

When the country bursts, we'll meet.
Uncle Kamil shot a tiger,
it hung over the wardrobe, its jaws

fixed in a roar – I wanted to hide
its head in a towel.
The country has become my body –

I can't break bits off.
The men go home in loose cotton clothes.
In the square there are those who beg –

and those who beg for mercy.
Azam passes the sweetshop,
names the sugar monuments Taj Mahal.

I water the country with English rain,
cover it with English words.
Soon it will burst, or fall like a meteor.

[1993]

321

JANE DRAYCOTT

(*b.* 1954)

Jane Draycott was born in London, and read English at Kings College, London, and Medieval Literature at the University of Bristol. She has worked as a teacher in London, Tanzania, Strasbourg and, most recently, Oxfordshire. Her books include two full-length collections, *Prince Rupert's Drop* (1999) and *The Night Tree* (2004). Draycott's often extended sentences allow for a multiplication of free-association as the reader is carried along by grammar and syntax, with meaning following in a sometimes ghostly aftermath. She writes: 'When I was in my early 20s I spent some time studying medieval dream poems, intrigued among other things by the unresolved nature of their visions, in which…the dreamer wakes abruptly in the face of something out of reach, ineffable, inexpressible. My interest in those dream worlds has never really left me…For longer than I can remember the work of Hopkins has sat like a talisman close to my ear, his furious effort of expression, the choreography of his rhythms and aural precision. Now the intensely attentive and sprung language of Alice Oswald fills me with the same admiration, partly perhaps because in it we hear a poetry like the earliest poetry, meant primarily for sounding rather than reading silently off the page.' (2005)

The Night Tree

Secondly there are the beams or sails
sometimes called petals or branches
which on account of their reaching out
through all the timetables of dark
we are forever working to maintain
and which passing vessels have likened
to the after-death appearances of saints
or the ashes of great seafarers set up
as a beacon at the gate of a new land
where like a mermaid a ship
would be surely certain to founder.

Next there is ourselves, each man
on his watch for the deception of fog
or shudder of the tower,
each keeping awake in his turn
for the sake of the light by his reading
of Plutarch's *Parallel Lives*, our one book
relayed on the stairs between watches,

or else in the pinning of moths flattened
like leaves on the lantern whose wings
like a searchlight come sweeping our walls
finding each of us out in our beds.

But first as I say there is the sea
which is a forest, our blades
cutting through like a photograph,
a sequence of light and dark pathways,
hourglasses, rain, where time travels slowly
as if at great height or in exile and men
report voices heard crying in darkness,
though for myself I think it is only the seals
calling to each other in their language
through all the leafiness of the night.

[2004]

Night driving

in unknown country, the burning car
on the slip road already in the rear-view,
Moscow, Hilversum, Allouis, Prague,
the back seat lit up like a torched city

then what sounds like a play about airmen
night training, an ad for a theme park,
an SOS shot in the dark for a woman
on holiday currently thinking she's free

and three fields away the headlong race
of a river running for years across Europe
without stopping or once looking back,
Home, Light, Third, home, light, home

and there again on the hour is the story
that won't bear repeating, returning again
like the name of the ill-fated village you'd swear
you passed on the dial several hours ago

with its riots and ribs of what looks like cloud
though it's hard to make out so we turn on
the local storm warning – *fast and feast, beauty*
and the beast, ahead, in the rear-view and burning.

[2004]

CAROL ANN DUFFY

(*b.* 1955)

Born in Glasgow, Duffy was brought up in Staffordshire and studied Philosophy
at the University of Liverpool. Active in the underground poetry scene in
Liverpool in the 1970s, her long friendship with the poet Adrian Henri intro-
duced her to surrealism and performance poetry. Her first collection, *Standing
Female Nude* (1985), was something of a landmark for poets in Britain, bringing
together an anti-establishment voice which was unafraid of exploring the
power of the colloquial and the cliché, with a compelling lyricism. Her use of
the dramatic monologue, while following in the wake of Liz Lochhead and
U.A. Fanthorpe, showed her ability to create identities through subtle shifts
of irony and register and did much to reconstitute the form as a currency in
contemporary writing. Her second collection *Selling Manhattan* was published
in 1987, and followed by *The Other Country* (1990) and *Mean Time* (1993). A
Selected Poems was published in 1994. Duffy's popularity and her reputation as
a poet who could speak to the wider general reading public reached its peak
with *The World's Wife* (1999), a series of dramatic monologues, spoken by women
characters from fairy tales and myths, which arose from her collaboration at
the National Theatre on Tim Supple's *Grimm Tales*. Throughout her work,
Duffy's lyrical poems show her wrestling with ideas about language and identity
which frequently stem from her interest in the philosophy of Wittgenstein.
Feminine Gospels (2002) continues in her exploration of female lives through the
dramatic monologue. The artistic importance of her former relationship with
poet, novelist and dramatist Jackie Kay is evidenced by the close interchange
of subject-matter in their work. Duffy has edited several anthologies and also
writes for children. *New Selected Poems 1984-2004* was published in 2004, and
her most recent volume of poems for adults is *Rapture* (2005).

Warming Her Pearls

Next to my own skin, her pearls. My mistress
bids me wear them, warm them, until evening
when I'll brush her hair. At six, I place them
round her cool, white throat. All day I think of her,

resting in the Yellow Room, contemplating silk
or taffeta, which gown tonight? She fans herself
whilst I work willingly, my slow heat entering
each pearl. Slack on my neck, her rope.

She's beautiful. I dream about her
in my attic bed; picture her dancing
with tall men, puzzled by my faint, persistent scent
beneath her French perfume, her milky stones.

I dust her shoulders with a rabbit's foot,
watch the soft blush seep through her skin
like an indolent sigh. In her looking-glass
my red lips part as though I want to speak.

Full moon. Her carriage brings her home. I see
her every movement in my head...Undressing,
taking off her jewels, her slim hand reaching
for the case, slipping naked into bed, the way

she always does...And I lie here awake,
knowing the pearls are cooling even now
in the room where my mistress sleeps. All night
I feel their absence and I burn.

[1987]

Plainsong

Stop. Along this path, in phrases of light,
trees sing their leaves. No Midas touch
has turned the wood to gold, late in the year
when you pass by, suddenly sad, straining
to remember something you're sure you knew.

Listening. The words you have for things die
in your heart, but grasses are plainsong,
patiently chanting the circles you cannot repeat
or understand. This is your homeland,
Lost One, Stranger who speaks with tears.

It is almost impossible to be here and yet
you kneel, no one's child, absolved by late sun

through the branches of a wood, distantly
the evening bell reminding you, *Home, Home,*
Home, and the stone in your palm telling the time.

[1987]

Small Female Skull

With some surprise, I balance my small female skull in my hands.
What is it like? An ocarina? Blow in its eye.
It cannot cry, holds my breath only as long as I exhale,
mildly alarmed now, into the hole where the nose was,
press my ear to its grin. A vanishing sigh.

For some time, I sit on the lavatory seat with my head
in my hands, appalled. It feels much lighter than I'd thought;
the weight of a deck of cards, a slim volume of verse,
but with something else, as though it could levitate. Disturbing.
So why do I kiss it on the brow, my warm lips to its papery bone,

and take it to the mirror to ask for a gottle of geer?
I rinse it under the tap, watch dust run away, like sand
from a swimming-cap, then dry it – firstborn – gently
with a towel. I see the scar where I fell for sheer love
down treacherous stairs, and read that shattering day like braille.

Love, I murmur to my skull, then, louder, other grand words,
shouting the hollow nouns in a white-tiled room.
Downstairs they will think I have lost my mind. No. I only weep
into these two holes here, or I'm grinning back at the joke, this is
a friend of mine. See, I hold her face in trembling, passionate hands.

[1993]

Havisham

Beloved sweetheart bastard. Not a day since then
I haven't wished him dead. Prayed for it
so hard I've dark green pebbles for eyes,
ropes on the back of my hands I could strangle with.

326

Spinster. I stink and remember. Whole days
in bed cawing Nooooo at the wall; the dress
yellowing, trembling if I open the wardrobe;
the slewed mirror, full-length, her, myself, who did this

to me? Puce curses that are sounds not words.
Some nights better, the lost body over me,
my fluent tongue in its mouth in its ear
then down till I suddenly bite awake. Love's

hate behind a white veil; a red balloon bursting
in my face. Bang. I stabbed at a wedding-cake.
Give me a male corpse for a long slow honeymoon.
Don't think it's only the heart that b-b-b-breaks.

[1993]

Prayer

Some days, although we cannot pray, a prayer
utters itself. So, a woman will lift
her head from the sieve of her hands and stare
at the minims sung by a tree, a sudden gift.

Some nights, although we are faithless, the truth
enters our hearts, that small familiar pain;
then a man will stand stock-still, hearing his youth
in the distant Latin chanting of a train.

Pray for us now. Grade I piano scales
console the lodger looking out across
a Midlands town. Then dusk, and someone calls
a child's name as though they named their loss.

Darkness outside. Inside, the radio's prayer –
Rockall. Malin. Dogger. Finisterre.

[1993]

Little Red-Cap

At childhood's end, the houses petered out
into playing fields, the factory, allotments
kept, like mistresses, by kneeling married men,
the silent railway line, the hermit's caravan,
till you came at last to the edge of the woods.
It was there that I first clapped eyes on the wolf.

He stood in a clearing, reading his verse out loud
in his wolfy drawl, a paperback in his hairy paw,
red wine staining his bearded jaw. What big ears
he had! What big eyes he had! What teeth!
In the interval, I made quite sure he spotted me,
sweet sixteen, never been, babe, waif, and bought me a drink,

my first. You might ask why. Here's why. Poetry.
The wolf, I knew, would lead me deep into the woods,
away from home, to a dark tangled thorny place
lit by the eyes of owls. I crawled in his wake,
my stockings ripped to shreds, scraps of red from my blazer
snagged on twig and branch, murder clues. I lost both shoes

but got there, wolf's lair, better beware. Lesson one that night,
breath of the wolf in my ear, was the love poem.
I clung till dawn to his thrashing fur, for
what little girl doesn't dearly love a wolf?
Then I slid from between his heavy matted paws
and went in search of a living bird – white dove –

which flew, straight, from my hands to his open mouth.
One bite, dead. How nice, breakfast in bed, he said,
licking his chops. As soon as he slept, I crept to the back
of the lair, where a whole wall was crimson, gold, aglow with books.
Words, words were truly alive on the tongue, in the head,
warm, beating, frantic, winged; music and blood.

But then I was young – and it took ten years
in the woods to tell that a mushroom
stoppers the mouth of a buried corpse, that birds
are the uttered thought of trees, that a greying wolf
howls the same old song at the moon, year in, year out,
season after season, same rhyme, same reason. I took an axe

to a willow to see how it wept. I took an axe to a salmon
to see how it leapt. I took an axe to the wolf
as he slept, one chop, scrotum to throat, and saw
the glistening, virgin white of my grandmother's bones.
I filled his old belly with stones. I stitched him up.
Out of the forest I come with my flowers, singing, all alone.

[1999]

PAULA MEEHAN
(*b.* 1955)

Born in Dublin, Paula Meehan studied at Trinity College Dublin and Eastern
Washington University in the USA. Her books include *Return and No Blame*
(1984), *The Man who was Marked by Winter* (1991), and *Pillow Talk* (1994),
Mysteries of the Home (1996) and *Dharmakaya* (2000). Adrienne Rich's blend
of the personal with the political has clearly been important to Meehan. But
Meehan often complicates autobiographical revelation by framing it through a
dialogue with a more objective voice, or by removing herself from presenting
that subjective experience as she looks at herself from afar. This leads to a
poetry which prizes emotional experience, but also reveals truth to be com-
plicated and multi-faceted. She has written several plays for children and
adults, including *Mrs Sweeney* (1999) and *Cell* (2000). Meehan is a member
of Aosdána and lives in Dublin.

My Love about his Business in the Barn

You're fiddling with something in the barn,
a makeshift yoke for beans to climb,
held together like much in our lives
with blue baling twine, scraps of chicken wire.

Such a useless handyman: our world could collapse,
frequently *has* with a huff and a puff.
You'd hoke a length of string from your back pocket,
humming a Woody Guthrie song, you'd bind

the lintel to stone, the slate to rafter,
'It'll do for the minute if the wind stays down.'
And so I've learned to live with dodgy matter:
shelves that tumble to the floor if you glance

at them sideways; walls that were not built
for leaning against; a great chasm in the kitchen
crossable only by a rope bridge; a blow hole
by our bed where the Atlantic spouts.

On stormy nights it drenches the walls, the ceiling.
Days you come home reeking of *Brut* and brimstone
I suspect you've been philandering underground
and not breaking your back beyond on the bog.

So is it any wonder when I see you
mooching in the barn this fine May morning,
a charm of finches lending local colour,
that I rush for my holy water, my rabbit's foot?

That I shut my eyes tight and wait
for the explosion, then the silence,
then the sweet aftershock when the earth skids
under me, when stars and deep space usurp my day?

[1991]

Autobiography

She stalks me through the yellow flags.
If I look over my shoulder I will catch her
striding proud, a spear in her hand.
I have such a desperate need of her –
though her courage springs
from innocence or ignorance. I could lie with her
in the shade of the poplars, curled
to a foetal dream on her lap, suck
from her milk of fire to enable me fly.
Her face is my own face unblemished;
her eyes seapools, reflecting lichen,
thundercloud; her pelt like watered silk
is golden. She guides me to healing herbs
at meadow edges. She does not speak
in any tongue I recognise.
She is mother to me, young
enough to be my daughter.

The other one waits in gloomy hedges.
She pounces at night. She knows I've no choice.
She says: 'I am your future.
Look on my neck, like a chicken's
too old for the pot; my skin moults
in papery flakes. Hear it rustle?
My eyes are the gaping wounds
of newly opened graves. Don't turn
your nose up at me, madam.
You may have need of me yet.
I am your ticket underground.' And yes
she has been suckled at my own breast.
I breathed deep of the stench of her self –
the stink of railway station urinals,
of closing-time vomit, of soup lines
and charity shops. She speaks
in a human voice and I understand.
I am mother to her, young
enough to be her daughter.

I stand in a hayfield – midday, midsummer,
my birthday. From one breast
flows the Milky Way, the starry path,
a sluggish trickle of pus from the other.
When I fly off I'll glance back
once, to see my husk sink into the grasses.
Cranesbill and loosestrife will shed
seeds over it like a blessing.

[1994]

RITA ANN HIGGINS

(*b*. 1955)

Rita Ann Higgins was born in Galway. One of 13 children, she left school at 14 and did not begin writing until her later 20s. Her books of poetry include *Goddess on the Mervue Bus* (1986), *Witch in the Bushes* (1988), *Philomena's Revenge* (1992), *Higher Purchase* (1996), *Sunny Side Plucked* (1996), *An Awful Racket* (2001) and *Throw in the Vowels: New and Selected Poems* (2005). Funny, taboo-breaking, and poignant her poems often seem like performance pieces which carry within them the voices of contemporary Ireland. Higgins often writes about women's position in relation to both church and family in poems which simultaneously resound with both anger and vulnerability. Also a dramatist, she is a member of Aosdána, and lives in Galway.

Middle-aged Irish Mothers

Germinating sopranos in conservative head squares
are the middle-aged Irish mothers in heavy plaid
coats, who loiter after Mass in churches,

    Lord make me an instrument of your peace;
    Where there is hatred, let me sow love;

to light candles for the Joes and Tommies of the drinking world,
the no-hopers, that they might pack it in,
if it's the will of God,

    Where there is injury, pardon;
    Where there is discord, union;

to pray for Susan's safe delivery, Bartley's gambling,
Mrs Murray's veins, that they would not bother her
so much, not forgetting Uncle Matt's shingles.

    Where there is doubt, faith;
    Where there is despair, hope;

Soon, not out of boredom, they will move diagonally
through their cruciform sanctuary to do the Stations
in echoing semi-song whispers,

    We adore thee O Christ we bless thee,
    because by thy cross thou hast redeemed the world;

sincere pleas to dear Jesus, that the eldest might
get off with a light sentence, pledges of no more smoking,
and guarantees of attendance at the nine Fridays,

    Where there is darkness, light;
    Where there is sadness, joy;

finally, for the Pope's intentions, Mr Glynn's brother-in-law,
the sweeps ticket that it might come up, but only if it's the will of God,
O Sacred Heart of Jesus, I place
all my trust and confidence in thee.

I like these middle-aged Irish mothers, in heavy plaid coats,
one of them birthed me on the eve of a saint's feast day,
with a little help from Jesus and his Sacred Heart.

[1986]

The Power of Prayer

I liked the way
my mother
got off her bike
to the side
while the bike
was still moving,
graceful as a bird.

We watched out for her
after Benediction.
It was a game –
who saw her head-scarf first,
I nearly always won.

The day the youngest
drank paraffin oil
we didn't know what to do.

All goofed round the gable end,
we watched, we waited,
head-scarf over the hill.

Knowing there was something wrong
she threw the bike down
and ran.

She cleared fences
with the ailing child,
Mrs Burke gave a spoon of jam,
the child was saved.
Marched indoors
we feared the worst,

our mother knew
what the problem was.

'Not enough prayers
are being said in this house.'

While the paraffin child
bounced in her cot
we prayed and prayed.

We did the Creed,
a blast of the Beatitudes
the black fast was mentioned,
the Confiteor was said
like it was never said before,
Marie Goretti was called
so was Martha,
we climaxed on the Magnificat.
After that it was all personal stuff.

I liked the way
my mother
got off her bike
to the side
while the bike
was still moving,
graceful as a bird.

For good neighbours with jam
for Pope's intentions
for God's holy will
for the something of saints
the forgiveness of sins
for the conversion of Russia
for Doctor Noel Browne
for the lads in the Congo
for everyone in Biafra
for Uncle Andy's crazy bowel
for ingrown toenails
and above all
for the grace of a happy death.

[1992]

SUJATA BHATT

(*b.* 1956)

Bhatt was born in Ahmedabad, India, grew up in Poona, and moved to the USA in 1968, and later to Germany, where she married the writer Michael Augustin; she lives in Bremen. Gujarati is her mother tongue. Her first collection, *Brunizem*, was published in 1988, for which she received the Commonwealth Poetry Prize (Asia) and the Alice Hunt Bartlett Award. Her later books are *Monkey Shadows* (1991), *The Stinking Rose* (1995), *Point No Point: Selected Poems* (1997), *Augatora* (2000) and *A Colour for Solitude* (2002). Many of Bhatt's poems incorporate Gujarati, which is translated within the poem, a strategy which while seeking to unify her two tongues, also interestingly destablises the authority of English within the poem. She has also translated Gujarati poetry into English for *In Their Own Voice: Penguin Anthology of Contemporary Indian Women Poets* (1993).

Muliebrity

I have thought so much about the girl
who gathered cow-dung in a wide, round basket
along the main road passing by our house
and the Radhavallabh temple in Maninagar.
I have thought so much about the way she
moved her hands and her waist
and the smell of cow-dung and road-dust and wet canna lilies,
the smell of monkey breath and freshly washed clothes
and the dust from crows' wings which smells different –
and again the smell of cow-dung as the girl scoops
it up, all these smells surrounding me separately
and simultaneously – I have thought so much
but have been unwilling to use her for a metaphor,
for a nice image – but most of all unwilling
to forget her or to explain to anyone the greatness
and the power glistening through her cheekbones
each time she found a particularly promising
mound of dung –

[1988]

Parvati

If this myth is alive
for me then why isn't it for you?
How does a myth stay alive?
How many people does one need in order
to keep a myth alive?

Do you know what it feels like
to pick green tea-leaves that grow
on the other side of the path across from the guava trees –
to pick green tea-leaves
moments before the water boils?

I don't know why I turn to Parvati, daughter
of the Himalayas – but I do.
'Parvati, oh Parvati
where is the mountain today, where did you
take it away?
Parvati
oh Parvati, hide the tea-leaves
while they're still growing –
don't let them come near Darjeeling.

Parvati
why did you let Twinings take everything?

Parvati
I must confess
I like Twinings the best.

Do you wash your hair everyday?
Do you have enough *shikakai*?'

In the first story she was
taking a bath, washing her hair,
becoming drowsy in the soft water,
she was slow, she dawdled in order to regain
all her energy
all her shakti-fragrant self
          for Shiva.

Those whose blood flows to the rhythm of om
whose souls resound om, om,
clear om, underwater om,
om spontaneously
without ever meaning to say it –
That om caught Parvati and kept her
alive, and keeps her always bathing
always braiding her hair.

I must have breathed om, however accidentally,
because Parvati stops me.
We argue. Why should I fight with her?
But I do.
Why can't she even protect the tea-leaves?

Heathen.
Pagan. Hindu.
What does it mean, what is a pagan?
Someone who worships fire?
Someone who asks Parvati to account for
the Industrial Revolution.

[1988]

Looking Through a French Photographer's Portrayal of Rajasthan with Extensive Use of Orange Filters

What has happened over here?
Has the day turned orange?
Or am I looking at these men
                    through flames?
Such loud crackling colours of wood,
as if fifty warriors were burning
                    on their funeral pyres,
as if fifty widows were running in
                    to join the saffron fire.

I am here   on one side
and the turbanned men are standing
                    on the other side.

They stand stiff
        jaws tight
unaccustomed to watching someone take aim
                        at their heads.
Somehow they don't notice the fire
    but look calmly beyond
            the flames
to the horizon.
And as I focus on their eyes
I too begin to see the cacti sprouting
                    in miles and miles of sand.
    As I follow their eyes
I find footprints of men and camels
        leading to the sky.

Next   the women
            tall and straight-backed
odhanis draped
        over their heads
the young girls
with large brass pitchers
balanced on their heads
are on their way home
                from the well.

Mirrors embroidered
    on peacock-green skirts
are swinging around their ankles.
Hurry, the women are moving briskly,
their faces are turned away
and the odhanis
    hide their profiles.
There is also yellow fog
    or is it smoke?
Orange mist hissing out of the bushes
    so I can not see the real sky.

Now here are some pictures
        of children playing.
A boy laughing through yellow fog,
tiger-coloured: his skin is gold,
                if gold could breathe.
His eyes, black
        lakes with moons inside.

The little girls of four and five
in their short dresses
squat so you see their white underwear.
By the time they are ten
their skirts are long enough
to hide their thighs.
Sometimes the men
cannot help smiling at the little ones
who walk up bold and curious, the children
who gaze long at the camera.

[1988]

JEAN 'BINTA' BREEZE

(*b.* 1956)

Born in Jamaica, Jean 'Binta' Breeze is a performer, dancer and choreographer. She studied at the Jamaican School of Drama and began to write and perform in Kingston and London in the 1970s. *Riddym Ravings* was published in 1988, followed by *Spring Cleaning* (1992), *On the Edge of an Island* (1997), *The Arrival of Brighteye and Other Poems* (2000) and *The Fifth Figure: A Poet's Tale* (2006). Her recordings include *Tracks* (with Dennis Bovell Dub Band, 1991) and *Riding on de Riddym: Selected Spoken Works* (1997). She is a poetry editor of *Critical Quarterly*, and divides her time between Leicester and the Caribbean.

In an interview with Julia Brosnan she explained: 'Dub poetry developed out of the system of making the B-side of a record an instrumental version of the A side. So when DJs started spinning their records at dances they ad-libbed their own words to the B-side. I think that's the true source of dub poetry – that it developed to accompany reggae music...I speak and think in Jamaican and English, with my poems it just depends...Every poem is different, they each decide their own music. Some go in jazz rhythms where something is improvised and not repeated, and some are in steady rhythms.' (mid 1990s)

The Wife of Bath Speaks in Brixton Market

My life is my own bible
wen it come to all de woes
in married life
fah since I reach twelve,
Tanks to Eternal Gawd,
is five husban I have
        (if dat is passible)

339

but all of dem was wort someting
in dem own way
doah dem say
dat troo Jesas only go to one weddin
in Canaan
we no suppose fi married
more dan once
but den again
dem say Im tell de Samaritan woman
by de well
dat doah she did have five husban
de laas one never count
      is wat Im mean by dat
      why jus de fif one lef out
      ow much she can have den
          four?
Im don't give no precise number
Well,
      people can argue it forever
      but me sure of one serious ting
      Im order we to sex an multiply
Im also say dat
      de man mus lef im madda an im fadda
      an cling to me
      but Im never say
      how many
      mi no hear no mention of bigamy
      or polygamy
      so why me or anyone
      should tink it is a crime
An wat about de wise king Soloman
look how much wife im tek, Lawd,
ah wish ah did have as much in bed as him!
God mus did give him some 'great' gif
No one alive did ever have such fun
But still
I will tank de Lawd
fah doah I have only five
I shall welcome de sixt one
wenever im choose to arrive
because I nat lacking up my foot at all
if one husban dead
anadda christian man will surely come

fah even de apostle say dat den mi free
to tek anadda man dat can please me
      betta to married dan to bun

Abraham, Joseph,
nuff adda holy man
did have nuff wife
Whey God forbid dat?
Yuh see no clear word?
Where Im ever order virginity?
      Dere is no such commandment!
is de apostle Paul come talk bout maidenhead
an him never qualify fi talk bout dat.
Im say a man may counsel a woman
but counselling is nat command
wat I do wid my body is my personal business
an if God did command virginity
nobady wouldn married
fah married woulda dead
an no more pickney wouldn born
so no new maidenhead.

How Paul him want to tek command
wen Jesas wouldn dweet
we all know pum pum is someting sweet
an nuff sword will falla it.
Whoever, jus like de apostle,
want to do widdouten sex
is free to choose dat,
but wid we, no badda vex
fah if my husban wear out an im dead
you free to marry me
dat is nat bigamy
an to enjoy good sex
is nat a frailty
nat unless yuh did decide, like Paul,
fi tek up chastity
because a man don't want pure gold pot
in im house
im want some mek wid good wood
as a spouse
an God did give we all a different gif
we choose wat we is suited for

341

everyone don't have to give up everyting fah Christ
Im neva aks we dat
dat is fah who want perfect peace
an you all know already
dat is nat me
I gwine mek de bes of all my years
fah dat is de joy an fruit of marriage
an why we have dese private parts so sweet
dem cyan jus mek so an don't put to use
except to piss
or tell man apart from woman
das wat you tink?
fram wat me feel already
dat could nat be so
a man mus give im wife er tings
Piss yes, an tell we apart
but wat pleasure dese instrument brings!

[2000]

Playing the Messiah

3 o'clock
and the rehearsal steams
we are in the theatre
house of God
the entrances are weaving
the exits can't be found first time

I am playing God
but cannot call on some experience
or memorable character
the power eludes me

God needs a place to sleep
a rucksack curled up in a corner

God needs a place to eat
only Burger King is open

but most of all
God needs a place to smoke

thunder and lightning
bolt from the chorus
the Shango litany is in full swing

I am dreaming
of tropical thunderstorms
something to break the clouds
bring chaos

this God I play is too measured
speaks in such cool tones

backstage is overpopulated
God can't find a resting place
the cue is late
the director calls repeat
of the first sequence
even God waits
when directors call

the chorus falters
starts again
I want to lift the roof
and open us to rain

outside
Shango appears
as called by the high priestess
from the stage
lightning in Leeds
thunder in Yorkshire
as Shango evens the score

my God smiles
in the face of Shango
I too am from him
I am rain
I cry round 3 o'clock each day

big sweeping tears
like Hallelujahs

[2000]

MAURA DOOLEY

(*b.* 1957)

Maura Dooley was born in Truro and grew up in Bristol. She was educated at the University of York, and gained a PGCE at Bristol. Her poetry books include *Explaining Magnetism* (1991), *Kissing a Bone* (1996) and *Sound Barrier: Poems 1982-2002* (2002). She edited *Making for Planet Alice: New Women Poets* (1997), *The Honey Gatherers: A Book of Love Poems* (2003) and *How Novelists Work* (2000), a book of essays by contemporary writers. She lives in London where she is a lecturer in Creative Writing at Goldsmiths College.

Interviewed by Lidia Vianu, Dooley explained: 'Growing up I read Philip Larkin, William Blake, W.B. Yeats, and Seamus Heaney most of all. Then the Metaphysicals, Miroslav Holub, Wallace Stevens, the New York School and Rimbaud. At school we read T.S. Eliot and D.H. Lawrence. All men, you'll notice. It's different now. We just did not have so many women in print then. But I'd say that music and song lyrics were at least as strong an influence at that time: Bob Dylan, Van Morrison, Elvis Costello, Joni Mitchell...then the end of a strong moment in the British folk scene, reggae and the beginnings of punk. I read Sylvia Plath when I was very young but didn't understand her till later. Then I read Paul Muldoon, Medbh McGuckian, early Derek Walcott, Michael Longley, Fleur Adcock, Gillian Clarke, Anne Sexton and at this time discovering some great work through translation: Marina Tsvetaeva, Czeslaw Milosz, Nina Cassian. In the late 80s I was stunned by C.K. Williams and Sharon Olds: lots of the Americans.' (2003)

Fundoscopy

> *I left the greatest masse of that unmeasurable mysterie as*
> *a heape too heavy for my undergoing; choosing rather to walk*
> *in a right line, than to run in a ring, whose mazefull*
> *compasse foretells much paine with little progress.*
> RICHARD BANNISTER 1622 (Treatise on the eye)

You send me your first book, a text
for students, where eyes swim out of their
ken and onto the page like planets.

What is this condition? What does it tell us?

This page suggests her left eye be examined closely
with your left eye, her right eye carefully with your
right. Rest your spare hand on her forehead, it says, but

how may this affect her vision? What are these lesions?

I read on without glasses, study the plates,
confirming what I have already guessed – the adult
retina is a transparent, inelastic, multilayered tissue:

what is the solution here? What is the likely diagnosis?

When you look at me like that I want
to answer all the questions, to push my hand
behind the crystalline lens, touch a nerve.

Is this an abnormality? What causes her visual problem?

It's like a moment in that film, perhaps,
when he thinks he sees her clearly through
the two-way mirror, but she can't see him at all.

[1991]

Explaining Magnetism

Isolated here in the South, fiddling with British Rail
network charts, inhabiting the Underground plan, I learn
again how West means left and East means right.
I used to know that North was always straight ahead,
every map showed that cardinal point, a long feathered
arrow, a capital N. Whichever way I walked the land
restored itself to my own order: true North.

A compass only confused, school got in the way,
pointing at things you couldn't see,
explaining magnetism. In order to find out
I just went straight ahead and up there,
out of sight, was never isolated but isolate.
Down here, we move as one and jump like hamsters,
onto the Circle line. The names don't help much,
recalling that dull board game and me,

broke again, moving a top hat listlessly,
back and forth, left to right, round and round.

[1991]

SARAH MAGUIRE

(*b*. 1957)

Born in London, Maguire trained as a gardener before reading English at the University of East Anglia. Her books include three collections, *Spilt Milk* (1991), *The Invisible Mender* (1997) and *The Florist's at Midnight* (2001), and two anthologies, *A Green Thought in a Green Shade* (2000) and *Flora Poetica* (2001). She is currently translating the Palestinian poets Mahmoud Darwish and Ghassan Zaqtan, and her selected poems, *Haleeb Muraq* (2003), was translated into Arabic by the Iraqi poet Saadi Youssef. She has worked as Poet in Residence at Chelsea Physic Garden and at Huntercombe Place Young Offenders' Institution, and is now Director of the Poetry Translation Centre at the School of Oriental & African Studies, London.

Writing in 1991, she says 'femininity [is] the theme I think is most important in my work. In a number of poems I've tried to ask, what does it mean to be "feminine", to be a woman? How then to make sense of the connections between what is most subjective and wider, more "political" issues…what I've tried to do…is push out of the lyric tradition, with its connotations of hermetic intimacy, into the broader contexts of the historical and social, without employing the exhortations of polemic, without losing sensuality or richness of language' (*Don't Ask Me What I Mean*, p.171). She names Sylvia Plath, Elizabeth Bishop and Adrienne Rich as three 20th-century poets who have influenced her.

Spilt Milk

Two soluble aspirins spore in this glass, their mycelia
fruiting the water, which I twist into milkiness.
The whole world seems to slide into the drain by my window.

It has rained and rained since you left, the streets black
and muscled with water. Out of pain and exhaustion you came
into my mouth, covering my tongue with your good and bitter milk.

Now I find you have cashed that cheque. I imagine you
slipping the paper under steel and glass. I sit here in a circle
of lamplight, studying women of nine hundred years past.

My hand moves into darkness as I write, *The adulterous woman
lost her nose and ears; the man was fined*. I drain the glass.
I still want to return to that hotel room by the station

to hear all night the goods trains coming and leaving.

[1991]

Liminal

The fold-out map of Europe in my Filofax
has marked your town: a smudge on the grey line
limiting the blush-pink of Poland from a dull,
Czechoslovakian beige. Old maps of Poland lurch about,
or disappear: the disruptions of Silesia (its strikes
and its pollutants) once named as German. From a window
you strain to catch the border: two states meeting
on a bridge furred with barbed wire and lights,
the decorations of security.

We're out of touch again. You're grappling with
The Origins of Geometry or Nietzsche's styles:
'Supposing truth to be a woman'.... You've got your
Spurs. And I'm way back, pondering the significance
of the blush in novels full of fainting women.
In Edgeworth's *Belinda* a Mrs Freke, fond of whole-boots
and breeches, 'an expert marksman', petrifies
a young girl on the point of a rocking-stone
for the amusement of soldiers.

[1991]

ELIZABETH GARRETT
(*b.* 1958)

Born in London, Garrett grew up in the Channel Islands. When she was 16
she returned to England to study music at the Wells Cathedral School. She
read English and French at the University of York, and wrote a D.Phil on
the Fool in modern English and French poetry at the University of Oxford.
Her first collection, *The Rule of Three*, was published in 1991, and followed
by *A Two-Part Invention* (1998). She explains how her musical training, 'an
unanalytical love of the sensual and musical properties of language developed
...into a need to explore and understand the way meaning is manipulated by
form. Poetry became the natural object – and eventually expression – of this
desire...Word-play is one of the antechambers of poetry...Poetry must haunt,
which is not a question of mere memorability, but something to do with the
undertow beneath the surface of word-sound and word-sense...If an image
strikes, it must also go on resounding' (Forbes, p.44). Garrett names Robert
Graves, John Berryman and John Donne as key influences on her work.

Lost Property

Kneel, and let us pray for the departed:
A sulphurous incense chokes the station vaults,
A pigeon coughs; the platform is deserted.
Guilty-eyed, while others slept in prayer
I scoured the hassock's cross-stitch for some fault
As though it were my soul; and found none there.

A labour of devotion: pious kisses
Smothering the cushion where my knees
Grew numb and bore the imprint of those stitches.
Burden of the Cross. A priest intones,
Feet shuffle for Communion to ease
The weight, and catch the last train home.

The rails are silent, empty as the aisle
When rush-hour's past. A platform sweeper brushes
Up confetti into piles.
It's growing dark. A thin girl stands and watches
As he sweeps the crumbs that drowsy birds
Have missed. I wake. And there are words
For this; but none so fittingly expressed
As by my own hand cupped around my breast.

[1991]

Double

Darling – I am not what I appear:
Single-hearted with my long brown hair
Plaited for safe-keeping.

Something I have undone –
A stray wisp, a random
Provocation – say, a grass clipping –

Has set my brown mane wild,
Casting oats in our careful field
While both our hands were sleeping.

This is no dream. Double I see
And am, courting duplicity
Like the suave surface of a stream

Flowing in two directions.
Am I the warped reflection,
The undertow, or the still scene

That witnesses its distortion,
Loving no less the portions
Of its selfhood that remain?

I am none and all.
The body in its close thrall,
The deceiving eye and mind.

I am my mother's daughter.
Cover my face with my hands,
My hands with water.

[1991]

MEG BATEMAN

(*b.* 1959)

Meg Bateman was born in Edinburgh. Brought up in an English-speaking
household, she studied at the University of Bristol before going on to study
Celtic at the University of Aberdeen where she wrote a PhD on medieval
Gaelic religious poetry. Having taught Gaelic at Edinburgh and Aberdeen,
she currently teaches at the Gaelic College, Sabhal Mòr Ostaig, on Skye, and
is a recent convert to Catholicism. Her first full-length collection of poems,
written in Gaelic and Irish, *Òrain Ghaoil/ Amhráin Ghrá*, was published by
Coiscéim, Dublin, in 1990. *Aotromachd agus Dàin Eile / Lightness and other
poems* (with facing English translations) was published by Polygon in 1997.

She writes (in 2002): 'My aesthetic in poetry has been shaped by what I
admire in Gaelic. Sorley MacLean excited me in the way he could accept
paradox even while leaving it unresolved. I also admired the supra-moral
frankness of some early Gaelic songs. I want to write poetry that is pared
down, with a minimum of adjectives or adverbs, so letting the nouns and verbs
take on a lapidary quality. Some people say my poetry is very personal but I
disagree. While I would shudder if someone read the raw feelings of my diary,
I never release a poem until I feel I have achieved a level of abstraction that
takes it beyond the embarrassingly confessional.' (*Dream State*, p.108)

Sìoladh na Gàidhlig

Thug thu tuigse dham inntinn
air sìoladh rud nach till a leithid,
air creachadh air a' chinne-daonna
nach gabh leasachadh...

Cailleach air bàsachadh aig baile,
ròpa d' acaire a' caitheamh;
nist tha mi a' faicinn nad shùilean
briseadh-cridhe na cùise.

[1997]

Dealbh Mo Mhàthar

Bha mo mhàthair ag innse dhomh
gun tig eilid gach feasgar
a-mach às a' choille dhan achadh fheòir –
an aon tè, 's dòcha,
a dh'àraich iad an-uiridh,
's i a' tilleadh a-nist le a h-àl.

Chan e gràs an fhèidh fhìnealta
a' gluasad thar na leargainn
a leanas rim inntinn, no fòs
an dà mheann, crùbte còmhla,
ach aodann mo mhàthar 's i a' bruidhinn,
is a guth, cho toilicht', cho blàth.

[1997]

The Decline of Gaelic

I had learnt from your words
of something unique dying out,
of humanity being robbed
without hope of reparation...

An old woman dies at home,
your mooring rope is fraying;
now I learn from your eyes
the heartbreak of the matter.

[1997]

Picture of My Mother

My mother was telling me
that a hind comes every evening
out of the wood into the hayfield –
the same one, probably,
they fed last year,
returning now with her young.

It isn't the grace of the doe
moving across the slope
that lingers in my mind, nor yet
the two fawns huddled together,
but my mother's face as she spoke,
and her voice, so excited, so warm.

[1997]

Taing dhut, a mhacain bhig

Taing dhut, a mhacain bhig,
airson gu bheil thu ann.
Bidh fiughair agam ri do ghlaodhaich
sa mhadainn; an dèidh m' obrach,
is ionann mise is nighean òg
a' dol an coinneimh a leannain.

Cha robh latha bho rugadh tu
nach d'fhuair sinn lorg air toileachas;
a dh'aindeoin bàs a' ghaoil a-staigh
is a' bhaile nach buin sinn dha a-muigh,
chuireadh an saoghal car eile
is do stòr a' sìordhol am meud.

[1997]

Thank you, my little son

Thank you, my little son,
for existing.
I long for your cries
in the morning; after work
I'm like a young girl
going to meet her sweetheart.

Not a day since you were born
have we not found happiness;
in spite of the death of love at home,
and a town we do not belong to beyond,
the world has kept turning,
increasing your store.

[1997]

GWYNETH LEWIS

(*b*. 1959)

Born in Cardiff, into a Welsh-speaking family, Lewis read English at Cambridge and spent six years in the States where she studied at Harvard and Columbia with Derek Walcott and Joseph Brodsky. She later wrote DPhil at Oxford on literary forgeries.

She has written three books in her first language, Welsh, *Sonedau Redsa* (1990), *Cyfrif Un ac Un yn Dri* (1996) and *Y Llofrudd Iaith* (1999). *Chaotic Angels: Poems in English* (2005) combines her three English-language collections. The first of these, *Parables & Faxes* (1995), won the Aldeburgh Poetry Festival Prize. *Zero Gravity* (1998) juxtaposes the launch of the space shuttle carrying her astronaut cousin with the illness and death of her sister-in-law. *Keeping Mum* (2003) is in part a translation of *Y Llofrudd Iaith*, and in its second half transforms into a completely new poem sequence about religious faith, as figured through the image of the angel. Lewis writes about the angel: 'To me they represent something very specific, always to do with communication. I started to understand what a modern angel might be when I learned that the technical term for an unidentified object on a radar screen is "an angel", that is a message which we can register, but not fully understand. Perhaps angels are a particularly sympathetic concept in the age of mass media, when we understand a lot about the process of communication. Annunciations, however, are always mysterious and the message perhaps only partly understood at the time. The angel brings in more than we can understand, with our lives as they are. If the angel's received, then the life has to change to accommodate the message. Angels aren't creatures with wings, wearing soft roses, but an act of communication where the weight of one world is brought down on another more superficial. These are always moments of difficulty and struggle.' (1995)

Having worked for many years as a television producer in Wales, Lewis has also written a chamber opera and an oratorio, and two autobiographical prose works, *Sunbathing in the Rain* (2002), which tells of her battle with depression and alcoholism, and *Two in a Boat* (2005), the story of her journey round the world with her husband, his illness and subsequent recovery. In 2005 Gwyneth Lewis was appointed the first National Poet of Wales.

from Welsh Espionage

V

Welsh was the mother tongue, English was his.
He taught her the body by fetishist quiz,
father and daughter on the bottom stair:
'Dy benelin yw *elbow*, dy wallt di yw *hair*,

353

chin yw dy ên di, *head* yw dy ben.'
She promptly forgot, made him do it again.
Then he folded her *dwrn* and, calling it fist,
held it to show her knuckles and wrist.

'Let's keep it from Mam, as a special surprise.
Lips are *gwefusau*, *llygaid* are eyes.'
Each part he touched in their secret game
thrilled as she whispered its English name.

The mother was livid when she was told.
'We agreed, no English till four years old!'
She listened upstairs, her head in a whirl.
Was it such a bad thing to be Daddy's girl?

1986 [1995]

from Parables & Faxes

VII *Oxford Booklicker* PARABLE

So the Lord said: 'Eat this scroll.'
I did and it was sweet and light and warm
and filled my belly. But I didn't speak
for all His urgings. Tolstoy's good
and Kafka nourishing. I lick

the fat from all the books I can
in the shops at lunchtime – Ovid, Byron, Keats....
The assistants know me, but they let me feast
on spaghetti sentences if I don't break the spines
of paperbacks and I replace them fast

so buyers never know their books
are licked of God. I am voracious
for the Word – a lexicon is wine
to me and wafer, so that home, at night,
I ruminate on all that's mine

inside these messages. I am the fruit
of God's expressiveness to man.
I grow on libraries, suck the grapes
of Os and uncials and still –
no prophecies. When I am ripe

I shall know and then you'll see the caravans,
processions, fleets, parades come from my mouth
as I spew up cities, colonies of words
and flocks of sentences with full-stop birds
and then, when I'm empty I shall open wide

and out will come fountains for the chosen few
to bathe in as time falls into brilliant pools,
translucent and ruined. Meantime I shall grow
stony with knowing, and my granite tongue
shall thirst (God's gargoyle!) for these blessings' blows.

[1995]

Ménage à Trois

I *Body*

I sent my body to Bollywood
to become a film star. She wore only beads
draped by the see-through Ganges.

A body unchaperoned by the soul
tends to try everything – some leading men
then, bored with that, occasional women.

She acquired a habit, some discreet tattoos,
married a gangster, went on the game,
had a nervous breakdown. The shame

nearly killed her. I paid the taxi
when she came back. Neighbours strained to see.
Home is the hardest place to be.

II *Soul*

She was known round here as the woman in white
– an agoraphobic – who ordered in
all her groceries. Considered anodyne

in social circles, this spinster soul
was slowly dying of irony
like a consumption. Her attic eye

was in need of a body to make its way
down to the street – an Antarctic waste
for her, a being who was so chaste

she was abstract, couldn't even blush,
much less know the comfort of sun on her bones,
the joy of a heart attack all of her own.

III *Third Party*

But the body's unfaithful and leaves the soul
for another lover. In dishabille
before the doctors, its geometry falls

for a death that wants it, sickness and all.
The grip is erotic – it takes you down
horizontal in your dressing gown,

takes speech, takes memories and then takes breath.
Only then can you feel the humming soul
abandon its story, its particular soil

to rise like a spaceship that has locked its doors
on wondrous technology, unearthly light
which we're forced to forget once it's out of sight.

[1998]

Her End

'The end was dreadful. Inside a dam burst
and blood was everywhere. Out of her mouth
came torrents of words, *da yw dant*
i atal tafod, gogoniannau'r Tad
in scarlet flowers – *yn Abercuawg*
yd ganant gogau – the blood was black,
full of filth, a well that amazed
with its vivid idioms – *bola'n holi ble mae 'ngheg?* –
and always fertile, *yes no pwdin llo,*
and psalms were gathering in her viscera
and gushing out of her, proverbs, coined words,
the names of plants, seven types of gnat,
dragonfly, rosemary, mountain ash,
then disgusting pus, and long-lost terms
like *gwelltor* and *rhychor*, her vomit a road
leading away from her, a force
leaving the fortress of her breath,
gwyr a aeth Gatráeth.
And after the crisis, nothing to be done
but watch her die, as saliva and sweat
of words poured out like ants – *padell pen-glin,*
Anghydffurfiaeth, clefyd y paill,
and, in spite of our efforts, in the grey of dawn
the haemorrhage ended, her lips were white,
the odd drop splashing. Then she was gone.'

(translated by Richard Poole with Gwyneth Lewis)

Da yw dant i atal tafod: A tooth is a good barrier for the tongue; *gogoniannau'r Tad*: the Father's glories; *yn abercuawg yd ganant gogau:* cuckoos sing in Abercuawg (from a 9th-century poem); *bola'n holi, ble mae 'ngheg*: my stomach asking where my mouth is; *yes no pwdin llo*: yes, no, calf's pudding (referring to the rich milk given by a cow who's just given birth); *gwelltor* and *rhychor*: the left- and right-hand oxen in a ploughing pair; *gwyr a aeth Gatráeth*: men went to Catraeth (from Aneirin's 6th-century poem, *Y Gododdin*); *padell pen-glin:* knee-cap; *Anghydffurfiaeth*: Nonconformity; *clefyd y paill:* hay fever.

[Welsh 1999 / English version 2004]

EVA SALZMAN

(*b.* 1960)

Born in Brooklyn, Eva Salzman moved to Britain in 1985. Her poetry books include *The English Earthquake* (1992), *Bargain with the Watchman* (1997) and *Double Crossing: New & Selected Poems* (2004). Michael Donaghy praised her work for its 'restless imagination, acute satiric intelligence and formal panache' commenting on her most recent work's 'slangy immediacy, song-led diction and splendid visual imagery'.

Interviewed by Lidia Vianu, she said: 'There's...this big protest among women writers that, hey, we write like writers, not like women, which is true enough, but I think some women writers are deliberately and strategically adopting a style (I never understood this cold-blooded quest for style...) which is masculine. They're reacting against the sort of male reviewer who may find us "enjoyable" or "promising", but saves his heavyweight adjectives of depth and profundity for the guys. Women who write about love and family are "domestic", while men are writing about the "big subjects" ' (2003). Elsewhere she has written of the importance of women poets to the development of her work: 'Emily Dickinson was the first woman poet to influence me...Sylvia Plath was nearly as great an influence. Her importance as a poet needs reiterating, partly so as to counter the tedious and persistent misapprehension that she's just a poet for angst-ridden teenagers. Almost equally irritating are those who label her a feminist poet, while it suits others to completely deny her feminist relevance, citing the fact that she was a woman and poet "of her time" – as if feminism hadn't been invented, and would have been a strange notion to an intellect like hers! She often gets represented as being on one "side" or another, which labelling limits how she is perceived as a writer – limits her scope and undervalues her gifts – which is ironic indeed. Although one hears in her the audacity and rage of the powerful yet impotent woman and poet, it's this aspect to her writing combined with an exquisite touch as regards language and image, and a facility with rhythm within the free-verse form, which all together makes her work great.' (2004)

Sexual Love

The motorboat's charge
trickles to shore, diminishing.
The bay tends back towards peace.

And that's why I like it;
though clamming by foot takes time,
a certain readjustment of the will.

At first, the mud's unwearable
for its soft give, the deepening
silent rip of ancient silk:

the way it clings around the ankles,
will never tear, or tears
repeatedly, the old healing.

[1997]

Conch

My grandmother doesn't hear me call; a white mist licks
her skull. She shuffles out to the jungle-yard
to pin a single greying cloth to the drying rack's
sun-dial spines, the dulling weather-vane
where the fading laundry's years have swung and aired.

The piece of washing turns its only two pages
back and forth, re-read by the wind, water veins
mapping the ground, while shadows throw vaguer
and vaguer epitaphs across the sheets snapping in the breeze.
The woman goes inside, and her door shuts again
into the memory I'll always hold of its splintered frieze.

But my real grandmother's sealed thousands of miles away
in her red-brick house deafened with treasure – bone-and-tulle
dancing skirts, dried quills, the family of bells
lined up in ever-decreasing size, their peals subsiding
to a white noise, her shell collection emptying the sea,
vowels bleached on another shore; and from the countless shelves
she's taken her umpteenth book to read in bed, yearning
for me, for the children, her ears burning.

[1997]

Physics

I'm skiving off again, this time pasting down old family photographs
in strict chronology, with tacky titles (the wasters' trick
I could call work, of ordering a mess in retrospect
to make it count) when I find my grandfather at thirty-six

and picture him, still earlier, clinging to his mother,
who, in turn, has him slung around her neck – a tin-type in a locket –
as they pass through Ellis Island where their bones are checked,
stale bread criminally stuffed in their unfashionable pockets.

There's bread here too. And his son, my father, has popped up
fully-formed in the Natural History Museum cafeteria
with its futuristic, stark formica, the cutlery magnetised
in wild patterns the waitress only dreams about, the interior

like a spaceship, and both looking used to travelling in time.
Though now, at ninety, his love of science is reduced to cranky bursts:
'Cripes, what's the point of everything?' he gruffly asks the air
as his rucked arm encompasses the dumbness of the universe

– words which tell me all I ever want to know about growing old.
So it's odd, this little astral-plane vignette; between the two
a möbius strip unfurls the constancy of the lunch ever to come,
the bread he always ate with every meal untouched, waiting like a clue

on the spartan counter – a planetary jumble of rolls
in a basket, and glimpsed behind the glass of undrunk water
a giant thumb; father and son half-turned in their chairs
expecting momentarily the prodigal daughter.

[1997]

Alex, Tiffany, Meg

rode fast convertibles, rose up like the Furies
blazing scarves and halters in a fire-trail.
The local boys, at first no more than curious,
went mad for the sting in their beautiful tails.

Such kindly girls; they deftly wound my hair
with strange accessories. Naked, like stone,
I bore the slender fingers and thundery stares
as they ripped and ripped away at my bikini-line.

Not ugly, nor evil, they were taken so seriously
their shadows slip beneath each lover, the Fates

re-grouping nightly, featured in the crumpled sheets
or the legacy of silk – my abandoned freight.
Pursued or in pursuit, I find your street
and fly into your bed. Calm this fury, please.

[1997]

JACKIE KAY

(*b*. 1961)

Born in Edinburgh, and brought up in Glasgow, Kay attended the Royal
Scottish Academy of Music and Drama before studying English at the University of Stirling. A novelist and dramatist, her first collection of poems, *The
Adoption Papers* (1991) drew on her own experiences as an adopted child of
Scottish/Nigerian descent who was brought up by white parents. This long
dramatic poem which intermingles the voices of birth mother and adoptive
mother and daughter perhaps owes something to Sylvia Plath's 'Three Women',
which, like *The Adoption Papers*, was later dramatised for radio. Kay's second
collection *Other Lovers* (1993) was followed by *Off Colour* (1998) and *Life Mask*
(2005). Her novel *Trumpet* (1998) explores the life of a jazz trumpeter, Joss
Moody, who lived her life disguised as a man. She has also published a collection of short stories, *Why Don't You Stop Talking* (2002), and a children's
novel, *Strawgirl* (2002).

Kay often uses the dramatic monologue to write in both male and female
voices as she explores gender, sexuality, and cultural difference. In an interview
with Laura Severin, she has talked about the importance of the poet Liz Lochhead to her work, as well as Tom Leonard, Audre Lorde, Nikki Giovanni and
Ntozake Shange. In the same interview she also spells out her connection to
a broader tradition of Scottish poetry, and jazz: 'I see myself as coming out
of two, quite distinct traditions. On the one hand, there's the tradition of
Scottish poetry itself – you know, Burns, Burns Suppers, and that kind of a
tradition in Scotland, where you would get to hear poetry being read and
performed out loud...I really do see myself as being part of a tradition that
wants to see the drama that is in poetry, through its poetic voices...On the
other hand, I also am very interested, and always have been, in music. I see
that my poetry is influenced by jazz and blues, as well as by Celtic folk songs
and music. Lots of the rhythms and the repetitions that are in my poetry are
closely related to music and come out of musical tradition. So, it's two, quite
distinct, but, to me, connected traditions.' (2001-02)

In *The Adoption Papers* sequence, the voices of the three speakers are distinguished typographically:

DAUGHTER: Palatino typeface
ADOPTIVE MOTHER: Gill typeface
BIRTH MOTHER: Bodoni typeface

from **The Adoption Papers**

Chapter 7: Black Bottom

Maybe that's why I don't like
all this talk about her being black,
I brought her up as my own
as I would any other child
colour matters to the nutters;
but she says my daughter says
it matters to her

I suppose there would have been things
I couldn't understand with any child,
we knew she was coloured.
They told us they had no babies at first
and I chanced it didn't matter what colour it was
and they said *oh well are you sure*
in that case we have a baby for you –
to think she wasn't even thought of as a baby,
my baby, my baby

I chase his *Sambo Sambo* all the way from the school gate.
A fistful of anorak – What did you call me? Say that again.
Sam-bo. He plays the word like a bouncing ball
but his eyes move fast as ping pong.
I shove him up against the wall,
say that again you wee shite. *Sambo, sambo,* he's crying now

I knee him in the balls. What was that?
My fist is steel; I punch and punch his gut.
Sorry I didn't you? His tears drip like wax.
Nothing he heaves *I didn't say nothing.*
I let him go. He is a rat running. He turns
and shouts *Dirty Darkie* I chase him again.
Blonde hairs in my hand. Excuse me!
This teacher from primary 7 stops us.
Names? I'll report you to the headmaster tomorrow.
But Miss. Save it for Mr Thompson she says

My teacher's face cracks into a thin smile
Her long nails scratch the note well well
I see you were fighting yesterday, again.
In a few years time you'll be a juvenile delinquent.
Do you know what that is? Look it up in the dictionary.
She spells each letter with slow pleasure.
Read it out to the class.
Thug. Vandal. Hooligan. Speak up. Have you lost your tongue?

To be honest I hardly ever think about it
except if something happens, you know
daft talk about darkies. Racialism.
Mothers ringing my bell with their kids
crying *You tell. You tell. You tell.*
– *No.* You tell your little girl to stop calling
my little girl names and I'll tell my little girl
to stop giving your little girl a doing.

We're practising for the school show
I'm trying to do the Cha Cha and the Black Bottom
but I can't get the steps right
my right foot's left and my left foot's right
my teacher shouts from the bottom
of the class Come on, show

us what you can do I thought
you people had it in your blood.
My skin is hot as burning coal
like that time she said Darkies are like coal
in front of the whole class – my blood
what does she mean? I thought

she'd stopped all that after the last time
my dad talked to her on parents' night
the other kids are all right till she starts;
my feet step out of time, my heart starts
to miss beats like when I can't sleep at night –
What Is In My Blood? The bell rings, it is time.

Sometimes it is hard to know what to say
that will comfort. Us two in the armchair;
me holding her breath, 'they're ignorant
let's have some tea and cake, forget them'.

Maybe it's really Bette Davis I want
to be the good twin or even better the bad
one or a nanny who drowns a baby in a bath.
I'm not sure maybe I'd prefer Katharine
Hepburn tossing my red hair, having a hot
temper. I says to my teacher Can't I be
Elizabeth Taylor, drunk and fat and she
just laughed, not much chance of that.
I went for an audition for *The Prime
of Miss Jean Brodie*. I didn't get a part
even thought I've been acting longer
than Beverley Innes. So I have. Honest.

Olubayo was the colour of peat
when we walked out heads turned
like horses, folk stood like trees
their eyes fixed on us – it made me
burn, that hot glare; my hand
would sweat down to his bone.
Finally, alone, we'd melt
nothing, nothing would matter

He never saw her. I looked for him in her;
for a second it was as if he was there
in that glass cot looking back through her.

On my bedroom wall is a big poster
of Angela Davis who is in prison
right now for nothing at all
except she wouldn't put up with stuff.
My mum says she is *only* 26
which seems really old to me
but my mum says it is young

just imagine, she says, being on
America's Ten Most Wanted People's List at 26!
I can't.
Angela Davis is the only female person
I've seen (except for a nurse on TV)
who looks like me. She had big hair like mine
that grows out instead of down.
My mum says it's called an *Afro*.
If I could be as brave as her when I get older
I'll be OK.
Last night I kissed her goodnight again
and wondered if she could feel the kisses
in prison all the way from Scotland.
Her skin is the same too you know.
I can see my skin is that colour
but most of the time I forget,
so sometimes when I look in the mirror
I give myself a bit of a shock
and say to myself *Do you really look like this?*
as if I'm somebody else. I wonder if she does that.

I don't believe she killed anybody.
It is all a load of phoney lies.
My dad says it's a set up.
I asked him if she'll get the electric chair
like them Roseberries he was telling me about.
No he says the world is on her side.
Well how come she's in there then I thinks.
I worry she's going to get the chair.
I worry she's worrying about the chair.
My dad says she'll be putting on a brave face.
He brought me a badge home which I wore
to school. It says FREE ANGELA DAVIS.
And all my pals says 'Who's she?'

[1991]

Close Shave

The only time I forget is down the pit
right down in the belly of it,
my lamp shining like a third eye,
my breath short and fast like my wife's
when she's knitting. Snip snap.
I've tried to tell her as many times
as I've been down this mine. I can't
bring myself to, she'd tell our girls
most probably. It doesn't bear thinking.

Last night he shaved me again.
Close. Such an act of trust.
And he cut my hair; the scissors snip
snipped all night as I lay beside Ella
(Good job she's not that interested)
I like watching him sweep it up.
He holds the brush like a dancing partner,
short steps, fox trot: 4/4 time.
I knew from the first time, he did too

Our eyes met when he came
to the bit above my lip. 6 years ago.
We've only slept the night together twice:
once when my wife's sister died,
once when the brother-in-law committed suicide.
She left our daughters behind that time.
My nerves made me come too quick
but I liked sleeping in his smooth arms
till dawn. He was gone

Before they woke, giggling round breakfast.
He says nobody else can cut my curls.
I laughed loud for the first time since
God knows when. You're too vain man.
We kissed, I like his beard on my skin,
how can you be a barber with a beard
I said to him; it's my daughters that worry me.
Course I can never tell the boys down the pit.
When I'm down here I work fast so it hurts.

[1991]

Dressing Up

(for Toby)

My family's all so squalid
I'm trying to put it behind
me – real typical working class
Scottish: Da beats Ma drinks it off.
I couldn't stomach it, banging

doors, turning ma music up top
blast. I told ma ma years ago. She'd
rather I murdered somebody than
that. She wasn't joking either.
Nobody gets hurt, it's not for

the image even I'm just dead
childish. Mascara I like, rouge,
putting it on after powder.
I love wearing lots of layers.
Ma ma always dresses boring

No frills. See at Christmas I had
on black stockings Santa would kill
for and even Quentin Crisp would
look drab beside my beautiful
feather boa – bright fucking red.

Ma ma didn't touch her turkey
Finally she said What did I do
I know what they call you, transvite.
You look a bloody mess you do.
She had a black eye, a navy dress.

[1991]

The Birth and Death of Bette Davis

On her way down
the birth canal
she shouted,
Fasten your seatbelts it's going to be a bumpy night.

She came out
smoking a cigarette saying,
I never ever want to do that again.
In the room was a pale nurse and a silver bowl.
Oh – and a momma.
In the bowl was the placenta, lush purple stuff.
Make this into puff pastry placenta pie
and feed it to my father,
she said, and then sucked for a moment on her mother.
One second was enough for her.
Goddamn, fetch me a gin,
she roared at the feeble midwife.
She flicked her cradle cap, tossed her single curl.

*

It was the one part
she never wanted:
one day she went out looking for her looks
and lost them.
Her skin was lined, bad dialogue on cellulite.
Her eyes were covered in film.
Her bow and arrow eyebrows were stuck in a tree.
In the room was a man
who never loved her, the bastard.
He told little lies under his coat.
She swore at him and fought the morphine
Her last line was her first.

She had the stars.

[1998]

KATHERINE PIERPOINT
(b. 1961)

Born in Northampton, Katherine Pierpoint has published one collection of poetry, *Truffle Beds* (1995), for which she received a Somerset Maugham Award. She was also named as the *Sunday Times* Young Writer of the Year in 1995. Her work carries the influence, both thematically and stylistically, of Marianne Moore, D.H. Lawrence and Ted Hughes. Pierpoint frequently writes about animals and the natural world, building up her poems with precise, sensuous and sometimes quirky detail. As she writes in 'Steeplejack', surely a tribute to Marianne Moore, 'the job starts with / the moment of looking'. Pierpoint's work reflects on the refracted sensations and ideas of these moments of perception, charting as she does an emotional geography in which a recording of landscapes and the natural world provide a context, and give access to, inner states of mind. With Kathleen Jamie and Alice Oswald, Pierpoint has been central in rekindling an interest in nature poetry which, while ultimately celebratory, nevertheless has a full awareness of the modern idiom and the postmodern fracturings of the contemporary world.

Going Swimmingly

The blue-rinsed pool is full of rhythmic, lone strokers.
It drew us in from the edges as though it were blotter-dry and we
      were rushing liquid.
Swimming, an occasional, unseen toe contact
Seems to come long after the other solemn face bobbed by;
The body lengthens, a pale streamer drifting out under a Chinese
      lantern.

Standing in the pool, blinking and pinching your nose, brings
A strange slewed perspective down to the wavering floor –
Firm, cream shoulders, telescoped to no trunk,
Standing on skewing, marbled shimmypuppet legs,
Fatdappled with fallen blue petals of curling light.

Swimming, everything is simplified.
The eye level so low, a baby's out along the drunken carpet.
A rhythmic peace, of rocking and being rocked,
Plaiting yourself into the water,
Ploughing an intricate, soft turtle-track along the undersurface,
Each stroke a silver link in the chain that melts behind you.

Sheer weight and size of water!
Remembering some geography and its clean, cross-section diagrams –
The sea is an upside-down mountain of water,
An upturned yogi
Alive with pulling, fluid muscles;
A pressing city of water; a universe;
The town pool is an inverted block of flats, something
Gathered and gently milling. Container for a small revolution.

Hands trying to pray. Legs slowly trying to fly.
Simple, straining juxtapositions –
Waterbuffalo! Hovercraft! Starfish!
The water on fire in volcanoes and set in earth in amber!

The swimmer broaches a strange but yielding density;
Leans quietly into a huge, enfolding flank.
Reaches over, forward and out; to re-test the limits,
Smooth the limbs,
Of a rediscovered lover.

[1995]

Cuckoo-spit

Cuckoo-spit on cowparsley.
The snowfroth parts under the finger, and inside
Sits the wicked-looking wet froglet of bilious bright green,
Quiet in his homespun castle,
Waiting.

The child screams, spins round, flip-wipes her hand
On thigh in one flamenco movement;
Then returns, and looks again.

[1995]

The Dreaming Bean

This is the germinal spot of gathering green.
A close-curled, blissful fist
Of dreaming bean, milk-wet opal in the pod.

Held in the damp, white hollow of down,
The touch of light sifts through slim walls of sap
Circling, drifting cool and fine, to a whispertip.

A juicebubble; single, wetblown membrane,
Sphere of spun water, held high to the sun
In convergent slipstreams of light and air.

Not yet a thing of earth, the bean lies curled and
Swelling into itself, welling like a favourite thought.
Its stem is a pointing finger, to focus colour, meaning and delight.

The stem refines, and then instils a greater world;
A gathering up and soundless pouring into a quiet green pool.
A flow of growing vision into the beholding eye.

The pod moves – small wimple, turning on the breeze –
And steadies again. The dreaming bean
Makes the slightest of slipping squeaks against the skin
Like a wet finger on the boat's white hull.

A drop of breathing seasound in the sappy shell,
Starting to dream of changing state,
Of firming the sap to smoothness,
Of forming two soft, mirrorlinked halves;
This bean, the young old milk-tooth of the earth.

[1995]

KATHLEEN JAMIE

(*b*. 1962)

Born in Renfrewshire, Kathleen Jamie's first collection *Black Spiders* (1982)
was published when she was just 20. Her poetry books include *A Flame in
Your Heart* (with Andrew Greig, 1986), *The Way We Live* (1987), *The Queen
of Sheba* (1994), *Jizzen* (1999), which takes its title from the Scottish word
for childbirth, *Mr and Mrs Scotland Are Dead: Poems 1980-1994* (2002), and
A Tree House (2004), which won the Forward Prize. She is also a prose writ-
er, with books including *The Golden Peak* (1993), a travelogue updated and
reissued as *Among Muslims: Meetings at the Frontiers of Pakistan* (2002), and
Findings (2005), a collection of essays.

Jamie writes in both Scots and English. She explains: 'In bursts of enthusiasm
I have tried to be a "woman writer" and a "Scottish Writer" but grew irritated
and feel confined.' Jamie has continued throughout her work to interrogate both
her femininity and her Scottishness. Such preoccupations are not evaded or
refused in her latest collection, but the volume sees her distilling her writing
into apparently simple but highly-energised lyrics as she repeatedly and variously
asks, 'How to live?' Here Jamie echoes the preoccupations of Heidegger in his
1951 essay on Hölderlin '...Poetically man dwells...', and she includes several
Scots versions of Hölderlin which are concerned with establishing 'hame' through
an exploration of the lush but increasingly fragile wonders of the natural world.

Mr and Mrs Scotland Are Dead

On the civic amenity landfill site,
the coup, the dump beyond the cemetery
and the 30-mile-an-hour sign, her stiff
old ladies' bags, open mouthed, spew
postcards sent from small Scots towns
in 1960: Peebles, Largs, the rock-gardens
of Carnoustie, tinted in the dirt.
Mr and Mrs Scotland, here is the hand you were dealt:
fair but cool, showery but nevertheless,
Jean asks kindly; the lovely scenery;
in careful school-room script –
The Beltane Queen was crowned today.
But Mr and Mrs Scotland are dead.

Couldn't he have burned them? Released
in a grey curl of smoke
this pattern for a cable knit? Or this:
tossed between a toppled fridge
and sweet-stinking anorak: *Dictionary for Mothers*
M:– Milk, *the woman who worries...*;
And here, Mr Scotland's John Bull Puncture Repair Kit;
those days when he knew intimately
the thin roads of his country, hedgerows
hanged with small black brambles' hearts;
and here, for God's sake, his last few joiners' tools,
SCOTLAND, SCOTLAND, stamped on their tired handles.

Do we take them? Before the bulldozer comes
to make more room, to shove aside
his shaving brush, her button tin.
Do we save this toolbox, these old-fashioned views
addressed, after all, to Mr and Mrs Scotland?
Should we reach and take them? And then?
Forget them, till that person enters
our silent house, begins to open
to the light our kitchen drawers,
and performs for us this perfunctory rite:
the sweeping up, the turning out.

[1994]

Rooms

Though I love this travelling life and yearn
like ships docked, I long
for rooms to open with my bare hands,
and there discover the wonderful, say
a ship's prow rearing, and a ladder
of rope thrown down.
Though young, I'm weary:
I'm all rooms at present, all doors
fastened against me;
but once admitted start craving
and swell for a fine, listing ocean-going prow
no man in creation can build me.

[1994]

Skeins o Geese

Skeins o geese write a word
across the sky. A word
struck lik a gong
afore I wis born.
The sky moves like cattle, lowin.

I'm as empty as stane, as fields
ploo'd but not sown, naked
an blin as a stane. Blin
tae the word, blin
tae a' soon but geese ca'ing.

Wire twists lik archaic script
roon a gate. The barbs
sign tae the wind as though
it was deef. The word whustles
ower high for ma senses. Awa.

No lik the past which lies
strewn aroun. Nor sudden death.

No like a lover we'll ken
an connect wi forever.
The hem of its goin drags across the sky.

Whit dae birds write on the dusk?
A word niver spoken or read.
The skeins turn hame,
on the wind's dumb moan, a soun,
maybe human, bereft.

[1994]

Crossing the Loch

Remember how we rowed toward the cottage
on the sickle-shaped bay,
that one night after the pub
loosed us through its swinging doors
and we pushed across the shingle
till water lipped the sides
as though the loch mouthed 'boat'?

I forget who rowed. Our jokes hushed.
The oars' splash, creak, and the spill
of the loch reached long into the night.
Out in the race I was scared:
the cold shawl of breeze
and hunched hills; what the water held
of deadheads, ticking nuclear hulls.

Who rowed, and who kept their peace?
Who hauled salt-air and stars
deep into their lungs, were not reassured;
and who first noticed the loch's
phosphorescence, so, like a twittering nest
washed from the rushes, an astonished
small boat of saints, we watched water shine
on our fingers and oars,
the magic dart of our bow wave?

It was surely foolhardy, such a broad loch a tide
but we live – and even have children
to women and men we had yet to meet
that night we set out, calling our own
the sky and salt-water, wounded hills
dark-starred by blaeberries, the glimmering anklets
we wore in the shallows
as we shipped oars and jumped,
to draw the boat safe, high at the cottage shore.

[1999]

St Bride's

(for Freya)

So this is women's work: folding
and unfolding, be it linen or a selkie-
skin tucked behind a rock. Consider

the hare in jizzen: her leverets' ears
flat as the mizzen of a ship
entering a bottle. A thread's trick;

adders uncoil into spring. Feathers
of sunlight, glanced from a butterknife
quiver on the ceiling,

and a last sharp twist for the shoulders
delivers my daughter, the placenta
following, like a fist of purple kelp.

[1999]

Meadowsweet

> *Tradition suggests that certain of the Gaelic*
> *women poets were buried face down.*

So they buried her, and turned home,
a drab psalm
hanging about them like haar,

not knowing the liquid
trickling from her lips
would seek its way down,

and that caught in her slowly
unravelling plait of grey hair
were summer seeds:

meadowsweet, bastard balm,
tokens of honesty, already
beginning their crawl

toward light, so showing her,
when the time came,
how to dig herself out –

to surface and greet them,
mouth young, and full again
of dirt, and spit, and poetry.

[1999]

Frogs

But for her green
palpitating throat, they lay
inert as a stone, the male
fastened like a package
to her back. They became,

as you looked, almost
beautiful, her back
mottled to leafy brown,
his marked with two stripes,
pale as over-wintered grass.

When he bucked, once,
neither so much as blinked;
their oval, gold-lined eyes
held to some bog-dull
imperative. The car

that would smear them
into one – belly
to belly, tongue thrust
utterly into soft brain –
approached and pressed on

Oh how we press on –
the car and passengers, the slow
creatures of this earth,
the woman by the verge
with her hands cupped.

[2004]

LAVINIA GREENLAW

(*b.* 1962)

Born in Essex, Lavinia Greenlaw read English at the University of Kingston
and later studied for a Masters in Art History at the Courtauld Institute. Her
work has shown a continuous and restless development since her first collection
Night Photograph (1993), which was concerned essentially with how we trust
ourselves and each other in a modern world. Her second collection, *A World
Where News Travelled Slowly*, was published in 1997 and her novel *Mary
George of Allnorthover* in 2001. In *Minsk* (2003) she delves into family history
and memories of her childhood in Essex. Characterised by an increasingly
dense use of language, Greenlaw still maintains the cool detached voice of her
earlier work.

Greenlaw has spoken of the importance of Elizabeth Bishop to her work:
'The excitement...of Bishop's poems, is in...the distance one can travel and
the doubletakes that make the journey so surprising. Above all, it has the dy-
namic perception Bishop so enjoyed in Hopkins, "the releasing, checking, timing
and repeating of the movement of the mind".' (*Strong Words*, p.276).

On Plath she explains in interview with Tim Kendall: 'Plath has been both
important and dangerous. She was one of the first poets I came across by my-
self, at about 16, and her rage, unease and charisma disturbed me. I thought
I would spill myself all over the page when I started to write, so someone
who did just that, however expertly, was to be avoided. Lowell was far more
attractive because his handling of autobiography is so scaldingly detached.
(Like many poets I love, he does something I could never do.) It has taken
me years to see through Plath's nakedness and into the heart of her work, to
admire the crackle of her voice. I read her more and more.' (1997)

Electricity

The night you called to tell me
that the unevenness between the days
is as simple as meeting or not meeting,
I was thinking about electricity –
how at no point on a circuit
can power diminish or accumulate,
how you also need a lack of balance
for energy to be released. *Trust it.*
Once, being held like that,
no edge, no end and no beginning,
I could not tell our actions apart:
if it was you who lifted my head to the light,
if it was I who said how much I wanted
to look at your face. *Your beautiful face.*

[1993]

Galileo's Wife

He can bring down stars.
They are paper in my hands
and the night is dark.

He knows why stone falls and smoke rises,
why the sand on the shore in the morning
is gone in the afternoon.

He gobbles larks' tongues from Tuscany
and honey from Crete. If only he could
measure me and find my secrets.

*

I have dropped pebbles into water
six hundred times this morning.
The average speed of descent

was three pulsebeats with a half-beat variable,
allowing for the different angle and force
with which each pebble hit the water.

378

Galileo wants me to explain my results.
He lectures on naval engineering
at the university tonight.

                    *

There has been a fire.
Our children were trapped in a tower.
He watched them fall, a feather, a stone,

and land together. He dictated notes
and ordered their bodies weighed before burial.
I sleep among their clothes.

I must leave Pisa.
He says I am to locate the edge of the world.
Galileo must complete the map.

He has a pair of velvet slippers.
It takes half an hour to lace my boots.
I like to keep my feet on the ground.

                    *

There is a cloud over Dalmatia.
It is the colour of my wedding dress.
Shadows burn stone.

The bears in Natolia
follow me to the marketplace
and carry food to the houses of the poor.

In Persia I walk east all day
across a desert. I look back at sunset.
The desert is a sea of orchids.

Tartaria is cold. Horses dance
on the path down the ravine. I fall
and the frozen air catches me.

In China I come to a walled city
where they know how to make a powder
that turns the sky to thunder and gold.

In the land of paper houses, a tidal wave
carries me up into the mountains.
I feed children with the fish in my pockets.

I fall asleep beside the ocean
and wake up in the New World
where my footsteps split yellow rock wide open.

A wind I refuse to name carries me home.
Galileo opens the door. I draw a circle
and he closes my eye with a single blow.

*

He says my boots have kept him awake
for the fifteen years I've been away.
He gives me pebbles and water.

Every night he is at the university
proving the existence of the edge of the world.
His students sleep and applaud.

I leave the truth among his papers
and thank the bears of Natolia
that I never taught him how to write.

[1993]

Love from a Foreign City

Dearest, the cockroaches are having babies.
One fell from the ceiling into my gin
with no ill effects. Mother has been.
I showed her the bitemarks on the cot
and she gave me the name of her rat-catcher.
He was so impressed by the hole in her u-bend,
he took it home for his personal museum.
I cannot sleep. They are digging up children
on Hackney Marshes. The papers say
when that girl tried to scream for help,
the man cut her tongue out. Not far from here.

There have been more firebombs,
but only at dawn and out in the suburbs.
And a mortar attack. We heard it from the flat,
a thud like someone dropping a table.
They say the pond life coming out of the taps
is completely harmless. A law has been passed
on dangerous dogs: muzzles, tattoos, castration.
When the labrador over the road jumped up
to say hello to Billie, he wet himself.
The shops in North End Road are all closing.
You can't get your shoes mended anywhere.
The one-way system keeps changing direction,
I get lost a hundred yards from home.
There are parts of the new *A to Z* marked simply
'under development'. Even street names
have been demolished. There is typhoid in Finchley.
Mother has brought me a lavender tree.

[1993]

A World Where News Travelled Slowly

It could take from Monday to Thursday
and three horses. The ink was unstable,
the characters cramped, the paper tore where it creased.
Stained with the leather and sweat of its journey,
the envelope absorbed each climatic shift,
as well as the salt and grease of the rider
who handed it over with a four-day chance
that by now things were different and while the head
had to listen, the heart could wait.

Semaphore was invented at a time of revolution;
the judgement of swing in a vertical arm.
News travelled letter by letter, along a chain of towers,
each built within telescopic distance of the next.
The clattering mechanics of the six-shutter telegraph
still took three men with all their variables
added to those of light and weather,
to read, record and pass the message on.

Now words are faster, smaller, harder
...*we're almost talking in one another's arms.*
Coded and squeezed, what chance has my voice
to reach your voice unaltered and to leave no trace?
Nets tighten across the sky and the sea bed.
When London made contact with New York,
there were such fireworks, City Hall caught light.
It could have burned to the ground.

[1997]

Clownfish

So bored we made a film of our lives
and played ourselves – botched reincarnations
of doctors, madmen, evangelists and spies.
The set was the holding tank, a room so void
that it gargled the dross bubbling up
from waist-high, silted, oracular speakers.
Adolescents drowning in our own soup,
we crooned their baggy truths...
Only we knew how to dance The Hoe,
how to unrhyme slang, the rules, the angle,
the camber in the mini-snooker's baize,
the warp and dimples of the ping-pong table,
the laws of croquet on a scuffed, erupting lawn.
We lived smack dab in the village eye,
bubbling up to mouth obscene charms
from the ousted admiral's port hole;
we ran nothing up his flag pole.
Low Celts with Viking horizons,
we torched the privet ship he'd clipped into shape
in a week. Our invasion was meant to repel.
My mother opened a fête, then lit a fuse:
Taxes for Peace, telegrams for Amnesty,
lifts for strangers, the communist vote.
She left *Protest and Survive* by the phone.
Neither ever occurred to us,
trailing one another's reputations
through the same barely resuscitated school

to return uprooted, re-accented but armed
with four bent pokers, four woodworks
in identical abstract free-form, to wait
for an end I imagined like the death of Hercules
my mouldering goldfish, who stuck it out
so long that when he went belly up,
some god draped a tea-towel over his bowl.

[2003]

JEAN SPRACKLAND

(*b.* 1962)

Born in Burton-on-Trent, Jean Sprackland studied Philosophy and English at
the University of Kent. She has lived in Southport, Merseyside, for 15 years
and recently worked as an education officer for the Poetry Society. She started
writing poetry at the age of 30 after going on an Arvon course at Lumb Bank,
tutored by Carol Ann Duffy. She writes: 'The first woman poet to have a
real, tangible influence on me was Carol Ann Duffy. I read *Standing Female
Nude* in 1991 and started experimenting with my own writing the following
year. It was a revelation to discover that a woman could write in such tough,
muscular language. I also began to understand for the first time the exciting
potential in taking on other voices. I particularly loved the fact that she
appropriated the voices of men when she felt like it – that seemed wonder-
fully audacious somehow' (Phillips, 2004). Her first collection, *Tattoos for
Mother's Day*, was published by the small Liverpool press, Spike, in 1997 and
shortlisted for a Forward Prize. Her second collection, *Hard Water* (2003),
was shortlisted for the Forward, Whitbread and T.S. Eliot poetry prizes.

The Ringlet

It begins like this:
a rumour tears through the class.
You search your memory and
a shiny brown ringlet of hair
like an impossibly perfect shell
spread on the shoulder of another girl
and how utterly you had to touch it.
The boys laugh, the girls scuttle and whisper.

Your last friend passes you a note in Chemistry:
I can't afford to be seen with you.
You write underneath: *I wish I was dead*
and you're surprised at the truth of it.
She holds the paper to the bunsen burner
till you smell scorched fingernails.

This is how you learn it all wrong, how
you take on the lie. They start to scare you,
the motorbike girls who meet in the woods,
cropped and booted. You'll never be in their gang.
Women are not to be together
and you should not have touched the ringlet.
You watch the boys in the yard,
kicking, spitting, scuffling in the dust.
There must be something you haven't understood.

[1997]

Translating Birdsong

The whole mix of different sounds is a symphony of the unknown.
GEOFF SAMPLE, Garden Bird Songs and Calls

I'm drawn to the happiness of birds.
They never lack confidence
or find themselves silenced by a crowd.
Whatever the voice of a particular species
it uses it reliably. I'm sure there is no
elective mute in the world of birds.

Curlew, probing the mud for food,
pausing to make *three slow*
deep whistling notes, accelerating into
a long liquid bubbling or rippling trill,
speak up, explain yourself! But
I'm the inarticulate one, shaking the minidisk,
snapping the pencil lead, thoughts
stubbing against that sound.
Alarm call, breeding, yes yes.
But what are birds saying?

Our best shot is metaphor and mimicry.
Little bit of bread and no cheese.
When our own tongues fail us,
we call on those of our tools and machines.
The Great Tit: *'teacher-teacher'*,
metallic, a saw being sharpened.
Or the Grasshopper Warbler:
a high-pitched, mechanical churring,
the winding of a fishing reel.

Eavesdropping by some frozen field
or sullen river, I imagine birds
are keeping their counsel, guarding the secrets
of their endangered languages,
not to be annexed or colonised...

No, that's not it.
Surely they know I'm on their side.
The bird and me: two prisoners
tapping on the pipes.
Longing to connect, but getting only
the syntax, never the meaning,
nothing at all of that.

[2003]

VONA GROARKE

(*b.* 1964)

Vona Groarke was born in Edgeworthstown, Co. Longford, and grew up on
a farm near Athlone. Her books include *Shale* (1994), *Other People's Houses*
(1999), *Flight* (2002), which was shortlisted for the Forward Prize in 2002,
and won the Michael Hartnett Poetry Award in 2003, and *Juniper Street* (2006).
She has won several other awards and held residencies in Ireland and the US.
Groarke writes: 'When I write, it's like running my hand over a length of
cloth, picking out patterns, testing the give, rubbing the fabric between thumb
and forefinger to feel out the texture and the flaws. The words present them-
selves. I take odd bits and bobs of language and try to sew them up. I pin
together snippets of history, memory, snatches of borrowed narratives, imag-
ined events or outcomes, assumed lives and stolen words. I want to see if the
stitches show.' (2005)

Imperial Measure

*We have plenty of the best food, all the meals being as good as if
served in a hotel. The dining-room here is very comfortable.*

P.H. PEARSE, the GPO, Easter 1916, in a letter to his mother

The kitchens of the Metropole and Imperial hotels yielded
       up to the Irish Republic
their armoury of fillet, brisket, flank. Though destined for
       more palatable tongues,
it was pressed to service in an Irish stew and served on fine
       bone china
with bread that turned to powder in their mouths. Brioche,
       artichokes, tomatoes
tasted for the first time: staunch and sweet on Monday, but
       by Thursday,
they had overstretched to spill their livid plenitude on the
       fires of Sackville Street.

A cow and her two calves were commandeered. One calf was
       killed,
its harnessed blood clotting the morning like news that
       wasn't welcome
when, eventually, it came. The women managed the blood
       into black puddings
washed down with milk from the cow in the yard who smelt
       smoke on the wind
and fire on the skin of her calf. Whose fear they took for loss
       and fretted with her
until daylight crept between crossfire and the sights of
       Marrowbone Lane.

Brownies, Simnel cake, biscuits slumped under royal icing.
       Éclairs with their cream
already turned. Crackers, tonnes of them: the floor of
       Jacobs' studded with crumbs,
so every footfall was a recoil from a gunshot across town, and the
       flakes
a constant needling in mouths already seared by the one drink
       – a gross
or two of cooking chocolate, stewed and taken without
       sweetener or milk.
Its skin was riven every time the ladle dipped but, just as
       quickly, it seized up again.

Nellie Gifford magicked oatmeal and a half-crowned loaf to
     make porridge
in a grate in the College of Surgeons where drawings of field
     surgery
had spilled from Ypres to drench in wounds the whitewashed
     walls
of the lecture hall. When the porridge gave out, there was
     rice:
a biscuit-tin of it for fourteen men, a ladleful each that
     scarcely knocked
the corners off their undiminished appetites; their vast,
     undaunted thirst.

The sacks of flour ballasting the garrison gave up their
     downy protest under fire.
It might have been a fall of Easter snow sent to muffle the
     rifles or to deaden the aim.
Every blow was a flurry that thickened the air of Boland's
     Mill, so breath
was ghosted by its own white consequence. The men's
     clothes were talced with it,
as though they were newborns, palmed and swathed, their
     foreheads kissed,
their grip unclenched, their fists and arms first blessed and,
     then, made much of.

The cellars of the Four Courts were intact at the surrender,
     but the hock
had been agitated, the Riesling set astir. For years, the wines
     were sullied
with a leaden aftertaste, although the champagne had as full a
     throat as ever,
and the spirits kept their heady confidence, for all the stock-
     piled bottles
had chimed with every hit, and the calculating scales above it
     all
had had the measure of nothing, or nothing if not smoke, and
     then wildfire.

[2002]

To Smithereens

You'll need a tiller's hand to steer this through
the backward drift that brings you to, as always,
one fine day. August 1979. A sunlit Spiddal beach.

Children ruffle the shoreline. Their nets are full
of a marvellous haul of foam and iridescent sand
and water that laughs at them as it wriggles free.

They hardly care: they are busy spilling buckets
of gold all over the afternoon. But further back,
something spreads over the beach like scarlet dye

on the white-hot voice of the radio. The mams
and aunts pinned onto Foxford rugs put down
their scandalous magazines and vast, plaid flasks

as a swell from over the rocks showers them
with words like *rowboat, fishing, smithereens.*
You hear it too, the news that falls in slanted beats

like metal shavings sprayed from a single,
incandescent point to dispel themselves
as the future tense of what they fall upon.

Let's say you are lifted clear of the high-tide line
into another order of silence. Exchange the year.
The cinema's almost empty. She has taken you

to *Gandhi* at the Ritz. You are only a modernist
western wall away from the Shannon and the slipknot
of darkness the river ties and unties in the scenes.

Her breath is caught up in it: she's nodding off.
Her head falls back on the crimson plush and then
her carriage bears her on and on, shunting towards

the very point where all the journeys terminate
with the slump and flutter of an outboard engine
reddening the water with its freight. It's here

that every single thing casts itself off, or is brightly cast,
into a flyblown, speckled plural that scatters tracks
in the heat and dust of the locked projection-room.

The railway bridge one up from ours shakes out
each of its iron rails in readiness, and she is woken
by words that spill over the confluence of the Ganges

and the Shannon at our backs. *To smithereens?*
she says. *I'm pretty sure it's Indian. It means
to open (like an Albertine), to flower.*

[2006]

KATE CLANCHY

(*b.* 1965)

Born in Glasgow and educated in Edinburgh and Oxford, Kate Clanchy is
one of the best known of the younger generation of women poets writing in
Britain today. Her work is frequently elegiac, reminiscent in its evocations of
childhood of the lyrical work of Elizabeth Jennings and Carol Ann Duffy. Her
books include *Slattern* (1995), which won a Forward prize, *Samarkand* (1999),
and *Newborn* (2004), her extended sequence about her relationship with her
first child, as well as an anthology of poems about birth and motherhood, *All
the Poems You Need to Say Hello* (2004).

She writes: 'I couldn't fit my life into the life of the women writers I
admired...I was offered, instead, and have led, the life that women writers
have always dreamed of. I have earned my own money, found my room of
my own, controlled my fertility, chosen my friends...I have lived like a man
...but mostly I was still struggling with the wish, not to write, but to be the
object of someone else's writing – to be a martyr, a victim, a muse an object of
desire.' Citing the importance of Duffy, whose work she says 'transformed'
her writing, she continues 'here was a woman writing about desire, anger, loss,
and not in disguise, through the mirrors and refractions that I had been taught
to look for, but directly, in full colour, with music, with smells' (*Don't Ask
Me What I Mean*, pp.31-32).

Slattern

I leave myself about, slatternly,
bits of me, and times I liked:
I let them go on lying where
they fall, crumple, if they will.

I know fine how to make them walk
and breathe again. Sometimes at night,
or on the train, I dream I'm dancing
or lying in someone's arms who says
he loved my eyes in French, and again
and again I am walking up your road,
that first time, bidden and wanted,
the blossom on the trees, light,
light and buoyant. *Pull yourself
together*, they say, quite rightly,
but she is stubborn, that girl,
that hopeful one, still walking.

[1995]

Love

I hadn't met his kind before.
His misericord face – really
like a joke on his father – blurred
as if from years of polish;
his hands like curled dry leaves;

the profligate heat he gave
out, gave out, his shallow,
careful breaths: I thought
his filaments would blow,
I thought he was an emperor,

dying on silk cushions.
I didn't know how to keep
him wrapped, I didn't know
how to give him suck, I had
no idea about him. At night

I tried to remember the feel
of his head on my neck, the skull
small as a cat's, the soft spot
hot as a smelted coin,
and the hair, the down, fine

as the innermost, vellum layer
of some rare snowcreature's
aureole of fur, if you could meet
such a beast, if you could
get so near. I started there.

[2004]

Miscarriage, Midwinter

For weeks we've been promising
snow. You have in mind
thick flakes and a thick white sky;
you are longing to roll up
a snowman, to give him a hat
and a pebbly smile. We have ice
and I've shown you, under
the lid of the rainwater barrel, a single
spine forming, crystals pricked
to the delicate shape of a fir, but
what can I say to these hard
desolate flakes, dusting our path
like an industrial disaster?
It's dark, but I'm trying to scrape
some together, to mould just
the head of the world's smallest
snowman, but it's too cold and
it powders like ash in my hand.

[2004]

ALICE OSWALD

(b. 1966)

Trained as a classicist, and later working as a gardener, Oswald is one of the
most distinctive poets of her generation. Her books include three poetry titles,
The Thing in the Gap-Stone Stile (1996), her long dramatised poem *Dart* (2002),
which won the T.S. Eliot Prize, and *Woods etc* (2005), and the anthology, *The*

Thunder Mutters: 101 Poems for the Planet (2005). She lives with her husband, the dramatist Peter Oswald, and their three children in Devon.

Alice Oswald writes: 'Poems, like dreams, have a visible subject and an invisible one. The invisible one is the one you can't choose, the one that writes itself. Not a message that comes at the end of the poem, more like a pathological condition that deforms every word – a resonance, a manner of speaking, a nervous tic, a pressure. And this invisible subject only shows up when you're speaking the language that you speak when no one is there to correct or applaud you. Remembering that language is the whole skill of writing well' (*Get Writing*, 2004).

Wedding

From time to time our love is like a sail
and when the sail begins to alternate
from tack to tack, it's like a swallowtail
and when the swallow flies it's like a coat;
and if the coat is yours, it has a tear
like a wide mouth and when the mouth begins
to draw the wind, it's like a trumpeter
and when the trumpet blows, it blows like millions
and this, my love, when millions come and go
beyond the need of us, is like a trick;
and when the trick begins, it's like a toe
tiptoeing on a rope, which is like luck;
and when the luck begins, it's like a wedding,
which is like love, which is like everything.

[1996]

Owl Village

There is a place between an owl
and a tall crowd of equal lines,
a wood of wishbone trees.

Half air, half village,
it murmurs, like the mind upon the brain

and people with carrier bags
walking symmetrically between their hands,
they live like that in a poise of pressures.

The neighbours regard each oddity until it goes

*

At eight o'clock, I opened the window to the woods
and an owl about the size of a vicar
tumbled across in a boned gown

and then a fleet of owls, throwing the hoot between them,
owls with two faces singing Ave and Ouch Ave and Ouch...

*

and you and I – comprehension burst its container
twice, in that the ear
extends through us beyond the ear –

we grew aware of the villagers
in bird clothes afloat among the trees
singing Libera me Domine Deo

and the disseverence of ourselves,
as if we stood, one dead, the other alone.

[1996]

The Melon Grower

She concerned him,
but the connection had come loose.
They made shift with tiffs and silence.

He sowed a melon seed.
He whistled in the greenhouse.
She threw a slipper at him

393

and something jostled in the loam
as if himself had been layed blind.
She misperceived him. It rained.

The melon got eight leaves, it lolled.
She banged the plates.
He considered his fretful webby hands.

'If I can sex' he said 'the flowers,
very gently I'll touch their parts
with a pollen brush made of rabbit hairs.'

The carpels swelled. He had to prop them on pots.
She wanted the house repainting.
He was out the back watering.

He went to church, he sang 'O Lord how long shall the wicked...?'
He prayed, with his thumbs on his eyes.
His head, like a melon, pressured his fingers.

The shoots lengthened
and summer mornings came with giant shadows
and arcs as in the interim of a resurrection.

She stayed in bed, she was coughing.
He led the side-shoots along the wires.
She threw the entire tea-trolley downstairs.

And when the milk was off
and when his car had two flat tyres
and when his daughter left saying she'd had enough,

he was up a ladder hanging soft nets from the beam
to stop the fruit so labouring the stem.
The four globes grew big at ease

and a melony smell filled the whole place
and he caught her once, confused in the greenhouse,
looking for binder-twine. Or so she says.

[1996]

Excursion to the Planet Mercury

certain evenings a little before the golden
foam of the horizon has properly hardened
you can see a tiny iron island
very close indeed to the sun.

all craters and mirrors, the uncanny country
of the planet Mercury – a mystery
without I without air,
without you without sound.

in that violently magic little place
the sky is racing along
like a blue wrapper flapped and let go
from a car window.

now hot now cold
the ground moves fast,
a few stones frisk about
looking for a foothold

but it shales it slides
the whole concept is only
loosely fastened
to a few weak tweaks of gravity.

o the weather is dreadful there:
thousand-year showers of dust
all dandruff and discarded shells
of creatures too swift to exist:

paupers beggars toughs
boys in dresses
who come alive and crumble
at the mercy of metamorphosis.

no nothing accumulates there
not even mist
nothing but glimmering beginnings
making ready to manifest.

as for the catastrophe
of nights on mercury,
hiding in a rock-smashed hollow
at about two hundred degrees below zero

the feather-footed winds
take off their guises there,
they go in gym shoes
thieving and lifting

and their amazed expressions
have been soundproofed, nevertheless
they go on howling
for gladness sheer gladness

[2005]

GRETA STODDART

(*b*. 1966)

Born in Henley-on-Thames, Greta Stoddart grew up in Belgium and Oxford
and studied in Paris and Manchester. She is a freelance writer and lives in
London. Her first collection, *At Home in the Dark* (2001), won the Geoffrey
Faber Memorial Prize. Stoddart's work is characterised by a constant alert-
ness to the external world but also to shifts in mood which alter her percep-
tion of it. Seeing and not seeing are a constant theme throughout her work
and her often elegiac poems generate moments of self-reflection which seem
always to surprise not only the reader but the poet. On the question of gender
and poetry she writes: ' "Literature is literature no matter who produces it"
said Elizabeth Bishop. She's right of course. The least important factor of a
poem is the person who wrote it...As we enter the 21st century women poets
can hopefully, finally, become poets.' (2005)

The Night We Stole a Full-Length Mirror

I'd have walked straight past if you hadn't said
Look at the moon and held my head in your hands
and turned it slowly round to face a skip,
its broken skyline of one-legged chair,
ripped out floor, till I saw it moving
– so slow, so bright – across the silver glass.

We stood there for ages, a bit drunk,
staring at the moon hanging there
as if it were for sale and we an old couple
weighing it up but knowing in our hearts
it is beyond us – A cat jumps out
and before we know it we're stealing back to my flat,
the great thing like a masterpiece in our hands,
its surface anxious with knees and knuckles,
the clenched line of your jaw and your lips
kissing the glass over and over with curses.
You lean it so it catches the bed and me,
I nudge it with my toe so it won't hold my head.
Switching off the light my skin turns blue
and when you come in on the scene and we see
ourselves like this we start to move like real
professionals and my head, disowned and free,
watches what our bodies are doing and somewhere
the thought *I can't believe we weren't made for this*
and I can't stop looking even though the ache
in my throat is growing and soon there will be tears
and I can hear you looking and I know what you're
looking at and it doesn't matter but it isn't me.
You left me behind in a bar in Copenhagen St.
the one with the small red lamps and my face hung
a hundred identical times along the stained wall
invoking like some old speaking doll
the dissatisfaction I come back and back to
and there's this really pretty Chinese waitress
you're trying not to look at while I'm talking to you.
Then you get up and I'm left alone so I lift my head to look
at the man who's been staring at me since I walked in.
He's huge and lonely and lifts his glass and nods
and all the women along the wall break into smiles.
Then you're back and whispering *your breasts your breasts*
and your hands are scrambling up the wet stone
of my back and I imagine the lonely man is there
behind the silver screen sipping his drink,
his eyes thick and moist behind the glass;
I know he's waiting to catch my eye but I won't
be seen to know I'm being watched. Not
till it's over and we collapse, all of a sudden
and awkward, and the room becomes itself again,
filling the mirror with its things, our two faces

staring in, calm and dull and self-absorbed.
Then we look at each other and are surprised
as if we weren't expecting to find the other
here and the smile is quick, like a nod slipped in
between two conspirators returned to the world
of daylight, birdsong, the good tug of guilt
before we tilt the mirror up-, sky-, heaven-ward.

[2001]

The Blindfold

Once in a room in Blackpool we had to make do
with the grubby band that held aside the curtain.
I perched on the edge of the bed while he
tied the knot once then (ouch) twice
sending me in that pretend dark back
to knicker-wetting games of Blind Man's Buff,
arms flailing down a hall of coats,
seeking ever greater dark in cellars,
deep in wardrobes, cornered in the arms of –

In that brief blindness you are bereft
but alert to the senses left to you
like the game-show hopeful conjuring out of his dark
a sofa, fridge, a week in the sun, or the night nurse
at noon, the nose-job patient counting the days
– all that dreaming under wraps! Even the hostage
inhaling oil-smeared cloth maps the cadence
of road and the condemned in his limbo
interprets every sound through the gauze of memory.

But who wouldn't seize the chance left
open by someone's careless hand as I did
that last dirty weekend when I lied to his
how many fingers? but did at least close my eyes
to lend a kind of authenticity to my guess.
And though I usually craved the not knowing
where or how his touch would next alight
now I could peek, like a thief through a letterbox, at him
still faithful to the rules of a game we'd made up

398

that I'd just dropped and it struck me then that in all
our time together, my tally of infidelities,
this was the closest I'd come to betrayal;
and when my keeper reached forward I flinched
knowing my time had come to confess, naked
as the day, babbling, and dazzled by the light.

[2001]

JULIA COPUS

(*b*. 1969)

Born in London, Julia Copus read Latin at the University of Durham. She has
published two collections, *The Shuttered Eye* (1995) and *In Defence of Adultery*
(2003). She writes: 'The first poetry book I fell in love with was Sylvia Plath's
Collected Poems. I'd never come across poems like these before – urgent, insis-
tent, genuine, rhythmically supple – poems it was hard to be away from for
long. I've read other books since which have influenced me – probably far more
usefully – but none that has provoked quite the same sort of exhilaration. Dis-
covering those first poems is an unrepeatable experience, I think – like falling
in love for the first time. It wakes something up inside you which until then
you didn't realise had fallen asleep.' (Phillips, 2004). Fairytale and myth are
juxtaposed with personal history of family breakdown in her poetry. In her
most recent work she turns to science as a medium to continue her explorations
of love, relationships and the family: in 'Forgiveness' she uses a term from
physics which denotes 'impact resistance, fracture toughness, fatigue-crack
growth, etc'. She has also written a BBC radio play *Eenie meenie macka racka*.

Love Like Water

Tumbling from some far-flung cloud
into your bathroom alone, to sleeve
a toe, five toes, a metatarsal arch,
it does its best to feign indifference
to the body, but will go on creeping
up to the neck till it's reading the skin
like braille, though you're certain it sees
under the surface of things and knows
the routes your nerves take as they branch
from the mind, which lately has been curling

in on itself like the spine of a dog
as it circles a patch of ground to sleep.
Now through the dappled window,
propped open slightly for the heat,
a light rain is composing
the lake it falls into, the way a lover's hand
composes the body it touches – Love,
like water! How it gives and gives,
wearing the deepest of grooves in our sides
and filling them up again, ever so gently
wounding us, making us whole.

[2003]

Topsell's Beasts

Who can say for certain that such creatures
don't exist – sea-wolves and unicorns,
and lamias with their *exemptile eyes*
which they can lever out and lay aside
for rest after a kill? Why can't we believe,
as people like us used to believe,
that lemmings graze in clouds,
that apes are terrified of snails,
that elephants grow meek and timid when they see
a lovely girl, that mice may be spontaneously
ingendered in the earth, weasels give birth
through tunnels in their ears, or reindeer
when they walk make noises like
the sound of cracking nuts? So much
of what we know we take on trust.
Trust, then, that though you find me 'hard to handle',
on long late days full to the lintel
with love like this, I may be calm and gentle –
pliant, even, like the camelopardal
with his fifteen-foot long neck diversely coloured
and *so easie to be handled that a child
may lead him with a line of cord, homeward.*

[2003]

Forgiveness

Even the most delicate
cut-crystal champagne flutes
can mop up 90 decibels
with very little visible
effect (their placid throats
remain intact), but if a note's
played steadily, and at the proper
frequency, sooner or later
they will shatter. Those with a lower
lead content last longer.
And so with us: some of us buckle
under the smallest
slight, while others acquire
a lustre, like the sheer
gleam of a pearl,
as if something that's valuable
and rare is grown from the gritty
onslaughts they endure.
Perhaps it's just
that what they ask of us
is more realistic – maybe this
alone has made their hearts
more pliable than ours,
more elastic.

[2003]

COLETTE BRYCE
(*b.* 1970)

Born in Derry, Colette Bryce moved to Britain in 1988 to study English Literature at university. After working as a teacher and bookseller, she is now a freelance writer, and was Fellow in Creative Writing at the University of Dundee in 2002-05 and North East Literary Fellow at Newcastle and Durham Universities in 2005-07. She has published two collections, *The Heel of Bernadette* (2000), which won the Aldeburgh Festival Poetry Prize and the Eithne Strong Award for Irish writers, and *The Full Indian Rope Trick* (2004), which was shortlisted for the T.S. Eliot Prize.

Bryce frequently writes lyrics of love and faith. She inhabits an often surreal world where the body is fragile, often threatening to break, dissolve or disappear, and where a doubt in the existence of the self is countermanded by a desire for the spiritual. On the subject of all-women anthologies she writes: 'Do we still need anthologies of women poets, and were they ever a good thing? I'm thinking of Elizabeth Bishop's famous refusal to lend her work to them. That an anthology of men poets would be seen as absurd is sometimes offered as an argument, but of course the history of poetry in English is comprised of anthologies featuring only the work of male poets. I was taught from such an anthology at an all-girls school...In the early 90s, when I was trying to find my way as a young writer, I could not imagine fitting into a Northern Irish tradition that was almost exclusively male. Finding women poets as points of reference was essential for me: the American poets Elizabeth Bishop, Muriel Rukeyser, Sylvia Plath, Audre Lorde and Sharon Olds; European poets in translation, Akhmatova, Tsvetayeva, Szymborska; and younger contemporary English and Scottish poets who were then beginning to make their mark. Poetry publishing in Britain and Ireland has evolved to include the voices of women and this must be irreversible. But while publishing has opened up, criticism has not, and the work of some of our best women poets continues to be neglected or ignored in the current critical climate. This does not inspire faith that the work of women poets is entering the canon.' (2005)

The Deposition

Look how the faithful struggle with the body,
fumble for a pulse, all fingers and thumbs:
the cue balls of the eyes roll upward
in the skull; the skin glistens and stinks.
They are straightening the clothing
out of some sense of decency. Two of them
shoulder it, awkward, to the stairs,
a cruciform; the head lolling, jaw
faltering open on its hinge.
The feet trail, leave behind a slipper.
Staggering under its startling weight
of inanimate meat and bone under gravity,
they make it to the doorway, bed, deposit me,
leave me alone. They are true believers.
I am their mother. They trust me to rise
and find my way back, lie down in the body,
wake to inhabit another of my lives.

[2004]

The Full Indian Rope Trick

There was no secret
murmured down through a long line
of elect: no dark fakir, no flutter
of notes from a pipe,
no proof, no footage of it –
but I did it,

Guildhall Square, noon,
in front of everyone.
There were walls, bells, passers-by;
a rope, thrown, caught by the sky
and me, young, up and away,
goodbye.

Goodbye, goodbye.
Thin air. First try.
A crowd hushed, squinting eyes
at a full sun. There
on the stones
the slack weight of a rope

coiled in a crate, a braid
eighteen summers long
and me
I'm long gone,
my one-off trick
unique, unequalled since.

And what would I tell them
given the chance?
It was painful; it took years.
I'm my own witness,
guardian of the fact
that I'm still here.

[2004]

The Word

He arrived, confused, in groups at the harbours,
walking unsteadily over the gangways;
turned up at airports, lost in the corridors,
shunted and shoved from Control to Security;
fell, blinking and bent, a live cargo
spilled from the darks of our lorries,
dirty-looking, disarranged, full of lies, lies,
full of wild stories – threats and guns and foreign wars;
or He simply appeared, as out of the ground,
as man, woman, infant, child, darkening doorways,
tugging at sleeves with *Lady, Mister, please, please*

There were incidents; He would ask for it –
His broken English, guttural; swaying
His way through rush-hour trains, touching people,
causing trouble; peddling guilt in the market place,
His thousand hands demanding change, flocking
in rags to the steps of the church, milking
the faithful, blocking the porch, He was chased –
but arrived in greater numbers, needs misspelt
on scraps of paper, hungry, pushy, shifty, gypsy,
not comprehending *No* for an answer. What could we do?
We turned to the Word; called to our journalists, they heard

and hammered a word through the palms of His hands: SCAM.
They battered a word through the bones of His feet: CHEAT.
Blood from a bogus crown trickled down,
ran into His eyes and His mouth and His throat,
OUT: He gagged, but wouldn't leave.
We rounded Him up with riot police,
drove Him in vanloads out of our streets,
away from our cities, into the tomb
and left Him there, a job well done.
We are safer now, for much has changed,
now the Word is the law is a huge, immovable stone,

should He rise again.

[2004]

404

SINÉAD MORRISSEY

(*b*. 1972)

Born in Portadown, Co Armagh, Morrissey read German and English at Trinity College Dublin and lived in Japan and New Zealand before returning home to Belfast in 1999. In 1990 she was the youngest recipient of the Patrick Kavanagh award, and in 2005 was joint winner with Kerry Hardie of the Michael Hartnett Poetry Award. Her books include *There was a Fire in Vancouver* (1996), *Between Here and There* (2002), which was shortlisted for the T.S. Eliot Prize, and *The State of the Prisons* (2005). She writes: 'Society in Northern Ireland is rigidly divided between the Nationalist and Loyalist communities. Coming from a Communist household, militantly atheist, was just one factor that contributed to a sense of dislocation, of belonging to neither community. Both my brother and I were given Irish names, attended Protestant schools, lived in Catholic areas, knew neither the Hail Mary nor the words of "The Sash", were terrified by agonised Catholic statues and felt totally excluded from the 12th July celebrations...To be nothing – neither Catholic nor Protestant – was too removed from the dominant frame of reference to be believed...Dislocation is only one side of the coin, and my unorthodox Northern Ireland childhood also left me with a sense of enormous freedom. When my parents got divorced and our house in Belfast was sold, I moved to Germany for a year to try and control the ensuing sense of disorientation...I became fascinated by the fragile reality of places and the role that memory plays in building homes.' (2002)

& Forgive Us Our Trespasses

Of which the first is love. The sad, unrepeatable fact
that the loves we shouldn't foster burrow faster and linger longer
than sanctioned kinds can. Loves that thrive on absence, on lack
of return, or worse, on harm, are unkillable, Father.
They do not die in us. And you know how we've tried.
Loves nursed, inexplicably, on thoughts of sex,
a return to touched places, a backwards glance, a sigh –
they come back like the tide. They are with us at the terminus
when cancer catches us. They have never been away.
Forgive us the people we love – their dragnet influence.
Those disallowed to us, those who frighten us, those who stay
on uninvited in our lives and every night revisit us.
Accept from us the inappropriate
by which our dreams and daily scenes stay separate.

[2002]

Clocks

The sadness of their house is hard to defeat. There are at least
      three clocks per room.
There are two people with nothing to do but to be in each room
      and be separate.
The person each room was decorated by was seconded to a plot in
      a cemetery
that is walked to every day, and tended like a bedroom sanctuary.
      No notice given.
The clocks do all the talking. He visits the grave in the middle of
      a three-hour loop
and knows the year of completion of every castle in Ireland. His route
is always the same: the round tower via the aqueduct via the
      cemetery via the ramparts
via the Battle of Antrim during the Rising of the United Irishmen
      in 1798,
the slaughter of which is more present if he's deep in the morning
of his April wedding breakfast or locked into the moment they
      fitted the oxygen mask
and she rolled her bruised eyes back. She is unable to find the stop
      for the bus to Belfast
and stays indoors. The nets turn the daylight white and empty.
She has worn the married life of her sister so tightly
over her own, the noise of the clocks makes her feel almost without skin.
Sometimes she sits in her sister's chair, and feels guilty.
She has *Countdown* for company and a selective memory –
the argument at the funeral with her niece over jewellery and, years ago,
the conspiracy to keep her single, its success. Time settles over
      each afternoon
like an enormous wing, when the flurry of lunchtime has left them
and the plates have already been set for tea. He reads extensively–
from *Hitler and Stalin, Parallel Lives*, to *Why Ireland Starved* –
but has taken to giving books away recently to anyone who calls.
Winter or summer, evenings end early: they retire to their separate
      rooms
at least two hours before sleep. It falls like an act of mercy
when the twenty-two clocks chime eight o'clock in almost perfect
      unison.

[2005]

Genetics

My father's in my fingers, but my mother's in my palms.
I lift them up and look at them with pleasure –
I know my parents made me by my hands.

They may have been repelled to separate lands,
to separate hemispheres, may sleep with other lovers,
but in me they touch where fingers link to palms.

With nothing left of their togetherness but friends
who quarry for their image by a river,
at least I know their marriage by my hands.

I shape a chapel where a steeple stands.
And when I turn it over,
my father's by my fingers, my mother's by my palms

demure before a priest reciting psalms.
My body is their marriage register.
I re-enact their wedding with my hands.

So take me with you, take up the skin's demands
for mirroring in bodies of the future.
I'll bequeath my fingers, if you bequeath your palms.
We know our parents make us by our hands.

[2005]

CAITRÍONA O'REILLY
(b. 1973)

Caitríona O'Reilly was born in Dublin and brought up in Wicklow. She was educated at Trinity College Dublin, where she completed a PhD on American poetry in 2001. She is a freelance writer and critic who has held several residencies. Her books include *The Nowhere Birds* (2001), which won the Rooney Prize for Irish Literature, and *The Sea Cabinet* (2006). She writes: 'My doctoral work focused on an examination of the links between consciousness and imagined space in the work of Emily Dickinson, H.D., and Sylvia Plath. In the physical and psychological landscapes imagined by these writers I traced the development of a specifically modernist consciousness: from Dickinson's exhilarating and limitless internal spaces, through H.D.'s nurturing maternal utopias, to Plath's imprisoning and deadening structures. This central theme allowed me to examine the conflicts between personal and artistic freedom and the social and biological conformism as evidenced in the work of these three poets, and to describe the profound effect such conflicts had on their writing.' (2005)

A Lecture Upon the Bat

of the species *Pipistrellus pipistrellus*.
Matchstick-sized, from the stumps of their tails
to the tips of their noses. On reversible toes,
dangling from gables like folded umbrellas.

Some of them live for thirty years
and die dangling. They hang on
like the leaves they pretended to be,
then like dying leaves turn dry.

*Suspicions amongst thoughts are like bats
amongst birds*, Francis Bacon writes,
they fly ever by twilight. But commonsense,
not sixth sense, makes them forage at night.

For the art of bat-pressing is not dead.
Inside numberless books, like tiny black flowers,
lie flattened bats. Even Shakespeare
was a keen bat-fowler, or so it's said.

In medieval beast books
extract of bat was a much-prized
depilator. *Reremice be blind as moles,
and lick powder and suck*

*oil out of lamps, and be most cold
of kind, therefore the blood
of a reremouse, nointed upon the legs,
suffereth not the hair to grow again.*

And how toothsome is fruit-bat soup
when boiled in the pot for an hour!
Small wonder then that the Mandarin
for both 'happiness' and 'bat' is 'fu'.

Bats have had a bad press.
Yet they snaffle bugs by the thousand
and carefully clean their babies' faces.
Their lives are quieter than this

bat lore would have us believe.
Bats overhead on frangible wings,
piping ultrasonic vespers. Bats
utterly wrapped up in themselves.

[2001]

A Brief History of Light

And the light shineth in darkness;
and the darkness comprehended it not.

The dazzle of ocean was their first infatuation,
its starry net, and the fish that mirrored it.
They knew enough to know it was not theirs.
Over the hill a dozen furnaces glowed,
the gold gleamed that was smelted in secret,
and the trapped white light shone bitterly
at the heart of the hardest stone on earth.
But they knew enough to know it was not theirs.
Then their hoards of light grew minor,
since none could view the sun straightly,
and jealousy burned their lives to the core.
So they made a god of it, shedding glory,
shedding his light on all their arguments.
Did they know enough to know it was not theirs?
The god in his wisdom preceded them westwards,
and the forests, in whose pillared interiors
black shapes dwelled, were banished for good.
They promised an end to the primitive darkness:
soon there was nothing that was not known.
They thought: *Our light is made, not merely reflected –*
even the forked lightning we have braided!

And they banished the god from the light of their minds.
But they mistook the light for their knowledge of the light,
till light, and only light, was everywhere.
And they vanished in this, their last illumination,
Knowing barely enough to know it was not theirs.

[2001]

Envoi

And although it will be
the same story –
the going out

under dark stars
that seem to pin
your skull to the sky

you will do it:
bending your ear
to their furious desires.

'We realised some time
ago that restlessness
was not to be assuaged' –

so it will challenge
your store of images,
those cheques you draw

against yourself.
Who can say
if a loved face will lie

at the end of it?
Death, desirelessness:
such kinless things.

2005

ACKNOWLEDGEMENTS

1. PUBLICATION ACKNOWLEDGEMENTS

The poems in this anthology are reprinted from the following books, all by permission of the publishers listed unless stated otherwise. Thanks are due to all the copyright holders cited below for their kind permission:

Fleur Adcock: *Poems 1960-2000* (Bloodaxe Books, 2000).

Gillian Allnutt: 'Bringing the Geranium in for Winter' from *Blackthorn* (Bloodaxe Books, 1994), 'Sarah's Laughter' from *Lintel* (Bloodaxe Books, 2001).

Moniza Alvi: *The Country at My Shoulder* (1993), reprinted in *Carrying My Wife* (Bloodaxe Books, 2000).

Elizabeth Bartlett: *Two Women Dancing: New & Selected Poems*, ed. Carol Rumens (Bloodaxe Books, 1995).

Meg Bateman: *Aotromachd agus Dàin Eile / Lightness and other poems* (Polygon, 1997), by permission of Birlinn Ltd.

Patricia Beer: *Collected Poems* (Carcanet Press, 1988).

Frances Bellerby: *Selected Poems*, ed. Anne Stevenson (Enitharmon Press, 1986), by permission of the publisher and the Estate of Frances Bellerby.

Sujata Bhatt: *Brunizem* (1988), reprinted in *Point No Point: Selected Poems* (Carcanet, 1997).

Eavan Boland: *Collected Poems* (Carcanet Press, 1995).

Jean 'Binta' Breeze: *The Arrival of Brighteye and other poems* (Bloodaxe Books, 2000).

Gwendolyn Brooks: *Selected Poems* (HarperCollins, 1963/1999), by permission of Brooks Permissions.

Colette Bryce: *The Full Indian Rope Trick* (Picador, 2004), by permission of Macmillan Publishers Ltd.

Anne Carson: *The Beauty of the Husband* (Jonathan Cape, 2001), by permission of the Random House Group Ltd.

Amy Clampitt: *The Collected Poems of Amy Clampitt* (Faber & Faber, 1998).

Kate Clanchy: 'Slattern' from *Slattern* (Chatto & Windus, 1995; Picador, 2001), 'Love', 'Miscarriage, Midwinter' from *Newborn* (Picador, 2004), by permission of Macmillan Publishers Ltd.

Gillian Clarke: 'Border', 'Marged', from *Collected Poems* (Carcanet Press, 1997); 'The Field-Mouse', 'Women's Work', 'Translation' from *Five Fields* (Carcanet Press, 1998).

Wendy Cope: *Making Cocoa for Kingsley Amis* (Faber & Faber, 1986).

Julia Copus: *In Defence of Adultery* (Bloodaxe Books, 2003).

Frances Cornford: *Collected Poems* (London: Cresset Press, 1954), reprinted in *Selected Poems*, ed. Jane Dowson (Enitharmon Press, 1996), by permission of The Trustees of Mrs Frances Crofts Cornford Deceased Will Trust.

Elizabeth Daryush: *Collected Poems* (Carcanet Press, 1976).

Imtiaz Dharker: *Purdah* (1989), reprinted in *Postcards from god* (Bloodaxe Books, 1997).

Maura Dooley: *Sound Barrier: Poems 1982-2002* (Bloodaxe Books, 2002).

Hilda Doolittle (H.D.): *Collected Poems 1912-1944* (Carcanet Press, 1997); extract from *Tribute to the Angels* from *Trilogy* (Carcanet Press, 1973).

Jane Draycott: *The Night Tree* (Oxford Poets/Carcanet Press, 2004).

Freda Downie: *Collected Poems*, ed. George Szirtes (Bloodaxe Books, 1995).

Carol Ann Duffy: 'Warming Her Pearls and 'Plainsong' from *Selling Manhattan* (Anvil Press, 1987), 'Small Female Skull', 'Havisham' and 'Prayer' from *Mean Time* (Anvil Press, 1993), by permission of Anvil Press Poetry Ltd. 'Little Red-Cap' from *The World's Wife* (Picador, 1999), by permission of Macmillan Publishers Ltd.

Helen Dunmore: *Out of the Blue: Poems 1975-2001* (Bloodaxe Books, 2001).

Jane Duran: *Breathe Now, Breathe* (Enitharmon Press, 1995).

Menna Elfyn: 'Cell Angel' from *Cell Angel* (Bloodaxe Books, 1996), 'Cusan Hances'/ 'Handkerchief Kiss' from *Cusan Dyn Dall/Blind Man's Kiss* (Bloodaxe Books, 2001).

Ruth Fainlight: *Burning Wire* (Bloodaxe Books, 2002).

U.A. Fanthorpe: *Collected Poems 1978-2003* (Peterloo Poets, 2005).

Vicki Feaver: 'The River God', 'Women's Blood', 'Judith' from *The Handless Maiden* (Jonathan Cape, 1994), by permission of Random House Group Ltd; 'Glow Worm' and 'Hemingway's Hat' from *The Book of Blood* (Jonathan Cape, 2006) by permission of the author.

Elaine Feinstein: *Collected Poems and Translations* (Carcanet Press, 2002).

Veronica Forrest-Thomson: *Collected Poems and Translations*, ed. A. Barnett (Lewes, E. Sussex, Allardyce, Barnett, 1990). Copyright © Veronica Forrest-Thomson, Jonathan Culler & the Estate of Veronica Forrest-Thomson 1967, 1971, 1974, 1976, 1990. Copyright © Allardyce, Barnett, Publishers 1990. Reprinted by permission of Allardyce, Barnett, publishers.

Elizabeth Garrett: *The Rule of Three* (Bloodaxe Books, 1991).

Louise Glück: 'Poem' from *The House on Marshland* (1975), 'Lullaby' from *Ararat* (1990), reprinted in *The First Five Books of Poems* (Carcanet Press, 1997); 'Matins', 'Matins', 'Trillium' and 'The Red Poppy from *The Wild Iris* (Carcanet Press, 1992).

Jorie Graham: 'The Geese' and 'San Sepuchro' from *The Dream of the Unified Field: Selected Poems 1974-1994* (Carcanet Press, 1996), and 'The Guardian Angel of Self-Knowledge' from *The Errancy* (Carcanet Press, 1997).

Lavinia Greenlaw: 'Electricity', 'Galileo's Wife', 'Love from a Foreign City', from *Night Photograph* (1993), 'A World Where News Travelled Slowly' from *A World Where News Travelled Slowly* (1997), 'Clownfish' from *Minsk* (2003), all from Faber & Faber.

Vona Groarke: 'Imperial Measure' from *Flight* (Gallery Press, 2002), 'To Smithereens' from *Juniper Street* (Gallery Press, 2006).

Kerry Hardie: 'Stranger' and 'Things That Are Lost' from *Cry for the Hot Belly* (Gallery Press, 2000); 'Sheep Fair Day' from *The Sky Didn't Fall* (Gallery Press, 2003).

Rita Ann Higgins: *Throw in the Vowels: New & Selected Poems* (Bloodaxe Books, 2005).

Selima Hill: All poems from *Trembling Hearts in the Bodies of Dogs: New & Selected Poems* (Bloodaxe Books, 1994), except 'Prawns de Jo' from *Bunny* (Bloodaxe Books, 2001).

Frances Horovitz: *Collected Poems*, edited by Roger Garfitt (Bloodaxe Books, 1985).

Kathleen Jamie: 'Mr and Mrs Scotland Are Dead', 'Rooms', 'Skeins o Geese' from *Mr and Mrs Scotland Are Dead: Poems 1980-1994* (Bloodaxe Books, 2002); 'Crossing the Loch', 'St Bride's' and 'Meadowsweet' from *Jizzen* (Picador, 1999), 'Frogs' from *The Tree House* (Picador, 2004), by permission of Macmillan Publishers Ltd.

Elizabeth Jennings: *New Collected Poems* (Carcanet, 2002), by permission of David Higham Associates Ltd.

Jenny Joseph: 'Warning' and 'The Inland Sea' from *Selected Poems* (Bloodaxe Books, 1992), 'Ant nest' from *Extended Similes* (Bloodaxe Books, 1997), by permission of the author and Johnson & Alcock Ltd.

Jackie Kay: All poems frooum *The Adoption Papers* (Bloodaxe Books, 1991), except 'The Birth and Death of Bette Davis' from *Off Colour* (Bloodaxe Books, 1998).

Mimi Khalvati: *In White Ink* (Carcanet Press, 1991), reprinted from *Selected Poems* (Carcanet Press, 2000).

Denise Levertov: *New Selected Poems*, ed. Paul A. Lacey (Bloodaxe Books, 2003).

Gwyneth Lewis: 'Welsh Espionage' (V) and 'The Oxford Booklicker' from *Parables & Faxes* (1995), 'Menage à Trois' from *Zero Gravity* (1998), 'Her End' from *Keeping Mum* (2004), all from Bloodaxe Books.

Liz Lochhead: *Dreaming Frankenstein & Collected Poems* (Polygon, 1982), by permission of Birlinn Ltd.

Audre Lorde: *The Black Unicorn* (W.W. Norton & Company, 1978), by permission of Charlotte Sheedy Literary Agency.

Mina Loy: *The Lost Lunar Baedeker*, ed. Roger L. Conover (Carcanet Press, 1997), by permission of the publisher and the Estate of Mina Loy.

Medbh McGuckian: 'Slips' from *The Flower Master* (1982; rev. ed., 1993), 'Vanessa's

Bower', 'From the Dressing-room' and 'Aviary' from *Venus and the Rain* (1984; rev. ed., 1994), 'Coleridge' and 'The Dream Language of Fergus' from *On Ballycastle Beach* (1988; rev. ed., 1995), all published by the Gallery Press.

Mairi MacInnes: *Elsewhere & Back: New & Selected Poems* (Bloodaxe Books, 1993), by permission of the author [or The Pebble: Old and New Poems (W.W. Norton & Company, 2000 - SFA to confirm]

Sarah Maguire: *Spilt Milk* (Secker & Warburg, 1991), by permission of the author.

Una Marson: *The Moth and the Star* (Una Marson, Jamaica, 1937), copyright holder not traced.

Paula Meehan: 'My Love about his Business in the Barn' from *The Man who was Marked by Winter* (Gallery Press, 1991), 'Autobiography' from *Pillow Talk* (Gallery Press, 1994)

Charlotte Mew: out of copyright.

Edna St Vincent Millay: 'Wild Swans' and 'The Buck in the Snow from *Selected Poems* (Carcanet Press, 1992) 'When I too long have looked upon your face' from *Collected Poems*, ed. Norma Millay (HarperPerennial, NY, 1981).

Elma Mitchell: *People Etcetera: Poems New & Selected* (Peterloo Poets, 1987): copyright © Harry Chambers, by permission of the publisher.

Naomi Mitchison: 'Dick and Colin at the Salmon Nets' from *The Delicate Tree* (Jonathan Cape, 1933), 'The House of the Hare' from *The Cleaning of the Knife and Other Poems* (Canongate, 1978), by permission of Lois Godfrey.

Marianne Moore: *The Poems of Marianne Moore*, ed. Grace Schulman (Faber & Faber, 2003).

Sinéad Morrissey: '& Forgive Us Our Trespasses' from *Between Here and There* (Carcanet Press, 2002); 'Clocks' and Genetics' from *The State of the Prisons* (Carcanet, 2005).

Grace Nichols: All poems from *The Fat Black Woman's Poems* (Virago Press, 1984), except 'Out of Africa' from *Lazy Thoughts of a Lazy Woman* (Virago Press, 1989), reproduced by permission of Curtis Brown Ltd, London on behalf of Grace Nichols.

Eiléan Ní Chuilleanáin: 'The House Remembered' from *The Second Voyage* (Gallery Press, 1986); 'The Real Thing' and 'The Secret' from *The Brazen Serpent* (Gallery Press, 1994).

Nuala Ní Dhomhnaill: 'An Crann' / 'As for the Quince' and 'Ceist na Teangan' / 'The Language Issue' from *Pharaoh's Daughter* (Gallery Press, 1990); 'Dípfríos' / 'Deep-Freeze' from *The Astrakhan Cloak*, tr. Paul Muldoon (Gallery Press, 1992); poems © Nuala Ní Dhomhnaill, translations © Paul Muldoon.

Sharon Olds: 'Ecstasy', 'I Go Back to May 1937', 'The Lifting' from *Strike Sparks: Selected Poems 1980-2002* (Alfred A. Knopf, Inc, 2004; Jonathan Cape, 2005); 'It' from *The Gold Cell* (Alfred A. Knopf, Inc, 1987); 'His Smell' from *The Father* (Jonathan Cape, 1992), by permission of the Random House Group Ltd and Alfred A. Knopf, division of Random House.

Caitríona O'Reilly: 'A Lecture upon the Bat' and 'A Brief History of Light' from *The Nowhere Birds* (Bloodaxe Books, 2001); 'Envoi' from *The Sea Cabinet* (Bloodaxe Books, 2006).

Alice Oswald: All poems from *The Thing in the Gap-Stone Stile* (Oxford University Press, 1996), except 'Excursion to the Planet Mercury' from *Woods etc* (Faber & Faber, 2005), by permission of Peters, Fraser & Dunlop.

Ruth Padel: *Rembrandt Would Have Loved You* (Chatto & Windus, 1988), by permission of the Random House Group Ltd.

Pascale Petit: *The Zoo Father* (Seren Books, 2001).

Katherine Pierpoint: *Truffle Beds* (Faber & Faber, 1995).

Ruth Pitter: *Collected Poems* (Enitharmon Press, 1990), by permission of the publisher and the Ruth Pitter Estate.

Sylvia Plath: *Collected Poems*, ed. Ted Hughes (Faber & Faber, 1981).

Kathleen Raine: *The Collected Poems of Kathleen Raine* (Golgonooza Press, 2000), by permission of The Estate of Kathleen Raine.

Sylvia **Townsend Warner**: *Collected Poems* (Carcanet Press, 1992), by permission of the copyright holder, Susannah Pinney.

Susan Wicks: *Night Toad: New & Selected Poems* (Bloodaxe Books, 2003).

Anna Wickham: *Anna Wickham: Selected Poems* (Chatto & Windus, 1971) by kind permission of George W. Hepburn, Margaret & James Hepburn.

Sheila Wingfield: *Collected Poems 1938-1983* (Enitharmon Press, 1983).

Every effort has been made to trace copyright holders of the poems published in this book. The editor and publisher apologise if any material has been included without permission or without the appropriate acknowledgement, and would be glad to be told of anyone who has not been consulted.

2. EDITOR'S ACKNOWLEDGEMENTS

I would like to thank the School of English at the University of Liverpool for its generosity in relation to my research and maternity leave, and for their financial assistance in the final stages of completing this book.

Heartfelt thanks also for help to Julia Bird, Colette Bryce, Alan Clark, Alison Donnell, Jane Draycott, Jane Duran, Vicki Feaver, Jenny Joseph, John Lucas, Chris McCabe, Colin Morgan, Janet Phillips, Chris Prince, Caitríona O'Reilly, John Redmond, Carole Satyamurti, Pauline Stainer, Greta Stoddart. Thanks, too, to Judith Palmer and Maurice Riordan for their interest and conversations at an early stage; especially to Hester Jones, Alison Mark and Jill Rudd for their invaluable cheer and always thoughtful suggestions. Very special thanks and love to David and Angela Rees-Jones, and Glad and Terry Murphy whose help with childcare made all the difference. Most of all a huge debt to Michael Murphy without whose patience, help and sense of humour, this book would not have been finished.

3. WORKS CONSULTED

(Some of these works are referred to in the Introduction or in the notes on poets with abbreviated titles.)

Barbara Adams: *The Enemy Self: Poetry and Criticism of Laura Riding* (Challenging to Literary Canon) (University of Rochester Press, 1990).

Fleur Adcock (ed): *Twentieth Century Women's Poetry* (Faber & Faber, 1987).

Neil Astley (ed): *New Blood* (Bloodaxe Books, 1999).

Jack Barbera and William McBrien (eds): *Me Again: The Uncollected Writings of Stevie Smith* (Virago Press, 1981).

Elizabeth Bishop: *The Collected Prose* (Chatto and Windus, 1994).

Laurel Blossom: 'Sharon Olds', *Poets & Writers Magazine* (September/October 1993), 30-32.

Gwendolyn Brooks: *Selected Poems*, with a note by Hal Hager (Harper and Row, 1963).

Clare Brown and Don Paterson (eds): *Don't Ask Me What I Mean: Poets in their Own Words* (Picador, 2003).

Sharon Bryan (ed): *Where We Stand: Women Poets on Literary Tradition* (W.W. Norton, 1994).

Jeni Couzyn (ed): *The Bloodaxe Book of Contemporary Women Poets: Eleven British Women Writers* (Bloodaxe Books, 1985).

Roger L. Conover (ed): *Mina Loy: The Lost Lunar Baedeker: Poems* (Carcanet, 1997).

Tony Curtis (ed): *How Poets Work* (Seren Books, 1996).

Elizabeth Daryush: *Selected Poems* (Carcanet, 1972).

Joanne Feit Diehl: *Elizabeth Bishop and Marianne Moore: The Psychoanalysis of Creativity* (Princeton University Press, 1993).

Freda Downie: *Collected Poems*, edited by George Szirtes (Bloodaxe Books, 1995)

Jane Dowson (ed): *Women's Poetry of the 1930s: A Critical Anthology* (Routledge, 1996).

Jane Dowson & Alice Entwistle: *A History of Twentieth-Century Women's Poetry* (Cambridge University Press, 2005).

Peter Forbes (ed): *Poetry Review* (New Generation Poets Special Issue), 84 no.1 (Spring 1994).

Janice Moore Fuller: 'Music, Translation and Poetry: An Interview with Menna Elfyn', in *Asheville Poetry Review*, 9 no.2 (2002).

Thomas Gardner: *Regions of Unlikeness: Explaining Contemporary Poetry* (University of Nebraska Press, 1999).

Victoria Glendinning: *Edith Sitwell: A Unicorn Among Lions* (Weidenfeld & Nicolson, 1981).

Louise Glück: *The First Five Books of Poems* (Carcanet, 1997).

Richard Greene (ed): *Selected Letters of Edith Sitwell* (Virago Press, rev. ed. 1998).

Kerry Hardie: 'On writing *A Winter Marriage*' (2003): see www.twbookmark.com.

Claire Harman (ed): Sylvia Townsend Warner: *Collected Poems* (Carcanet, 1982).

W.N. Herbert and Matthew Hollis (eds): *Strong Words: Modern Poets on Modern Poetry* (Bloodaxe Books, 2000)

Tim Kendall (ed): *Thumbscrew*, 8 (Summer 1997).

Bonnie Kime Scott (ed): *The Gender of Modernism: A Critical Anthology* (Indiana University Press, 1990).

John Lucas: *Starting to Explain: Essays on Twentieth-Century British and Irish Poetry* (Trent Editions, 2003).

Mairi MacInnes: 'Why Poetry' (first published in *The New Yorker*, 1996), in *The Ghostwriter* (Bloodaxe Books, 1999).

Alison Mark: *Veronica Forrest-Thomson and Language Poetry* (Northcote House, 2001).

Nuala Ní Dhomhnaill: 'Why I Chose to Write in Irish: The Corpse That Sits Up and Talks Back', *New York Times*, 8 January 1995: see www.soc.culture.celtic.middlebury.edu.

Sharon Olds: interview, *see* www.english.uiuc.edu/maps/poets/m_r/olds/excerpt.htm.

Donny O'Rourke (ed): *Dream State: The New Scottish Poets* (Canongate, 1994), second edition, 2002.

Alice Oswald: BBC *Get Writing* website: www.bbc.co.uk/dna.getwriting.module18.

Alicia Suskin Ostriker: *Stealing the Language: The Emergence of Women's Poetry in America* (Women's Press, 1987); *see* p.215 for the discussion of 'revisionary mythmaking' quoted in the Introduction.

John Pearson: *Façades: Edith, Osbert and Sacheverell Sitwell* (Macmillan, 1978).

Janet Phillips: interviews with women poets on International Women's Day (8 March 2004) at www.poetrysociety.org.uk/news/news.htm.

Kathleen Raine: *Defending Ancient Springs* (Golgonooza Press, 1985).

Anne Ridler: *A Taste for the Truth: An Interview with Carole Satyamurti* (Enitharmon, 2001).

Carole Satyamurti: ' "First Time Ever": Writing the Poem in Potential Space' in *Psychoanalytic Studies*, 3 nos 3⁄4 (2001), 295-306.

Laura Severin: an interview with Jackie Kay, in *Free Verse: A Journal of Contemporary Poetry and Poetics* (electronic journal), issue 2 (Spring 2002): http://english.chass.ncsu.edu/freeverse.

Laura Severin: *Poetry Off the Page: Twentieth-Century British Women Poets in Performance* (Ashgate, 2004).

Anne Sexton: *The Complete Poems*, with a foreword by Maxine Kumin (Houghton Mifflin, 1981).

R.D. Smith (ed): *The Writings of Anna Wickham: Freewoman and Poet* (Virago Press, 1984).

Jean Sprackland: interview with Mimi Khalvati, Autumn 2001, at www.poetryclass.net.

Anthea Trodd: *Women's Writing in English 1900-1945* (Longman, 1998).

Lidia Vianu: *Desperado* interviews with British poets, *see:* http://lidiavianu.scriptmania.com.